What people a

# The Druid Garden

Luke Eastwood's book *The Druid Garden* is an authoritative and comprehensive approach to the subject. The book begins with the big picture, an exploration of the history of gardens, before focusing the reader on the many different layers of soil that make up the ground beneath our feet. Practicalities of gardening, such as planting, creating ponds, even keeping fowls and bees, are combined with spiritual elements; the section about how to connect with the plants in your garden is particularly insightful. Eastwood goes on to provide information on a range of trees, shrubs and herbs found in Celtic culture, exploring the practicalities of how to grow them but also considering historical uses and folklore. There is even a rotation plan for your garden crops and ethical ways of dealing with pests. This is an invaluable resource for both the novice and more experienced gardener alike.

**Andrew Anderson**, author of *The Ritual of Writing* and *Pagan Portals: Artio and Artaois*

It is rare to find a gardening book that provides extensive practical information while clearly honouring the sacred. In *The Druid Garden*, Luke Eastwood manages to do exactly that. Using easily accessible language, he provides us with a comprehensive guide to gardening imbued with innate spirituality and environmentalism. A master gardener and Druid, Luke blends ancient wisdom with hands-on experience and shows how this knowledge can be used by modern day gardeners for the benefit of the Earth and all creation. Suitable for beginners as well as experienced gardeners, this book is packed with valuable information and is a precious gift for our world in these times.

**Carole Guyett**, author of *Sacred Plant Initiations*

*The Druid Garden* is a fascinating journey into the heart of human interaction with the natural world. It deftly weaves together history, practice, and spirituality into a cohesive whole. An essential aid both for those seeking practical advice for growing a garden and those seeking a more harmonious approach to the world around them.

**Morgan Daimler**, author of *A New Dictionary of Fairies* and *Where the Hawthorn Grows*

Combining history, philosophy, folklore, science and sustainability, this book shows you how to bring Druidic principles into your garden. For me, this is a perfect demonstration of how to be a modern Druid.

**Nimue Brown**, author of P*agan Planet & Druidry And The Future*

## By the same author

Where the Hazel Falls (Editor)

The Druid's Primer

The Journey

Through the Cracks in The Concrete the Wilderness Grows

Kerry Folk Tales

How to Save the Planet

Articles: www.lukeeastwood.com

# The Druid Garden

## Gardening for a Better Future, Inspired by The Ancients

# The Druid Garden

Gardening for a Better Future,
Inspired by The Ancients

## Luke Eastwood

Illustrated by Elena Danaan

Introduction by Ellen Evert Hopman

**MOON
BOOKS**

Winchester, UK
Washington, USA

JOHN HUNT PUBLISHING

First published by Moon Books, 2021
Moon Books is an imprint of John Hunt Publishing Ltd., No. 3 East Street, Alresford
Hampshire SO24 9EE, UK
office@jhpbooks.net
www.johnhuntpublishing.com
www.moon-books.net

For distributor details and how to order please visit the 'Ordering' section on our website.

Text copyright: Luke Eastwood 2020

ISBN: 978 1 78904 607 6
978 1 78904 608 3 (ebook)
Library of Congress Control Number: 00000000

UK: Printed and bound by CPI Group (UK) Ltd, Croydon, CR0 4YY
Printed in North America by CPI GPS partners

We operate a distinctive and ethical publishing philosophy in
all areas of our business, from our global network of authors to
production and worldwide distribution.

# Contents

This book is dedicated to the late Eve Kaye and Anthony Kaye, who were instrumental in the early development of the Biodynamic movement in Ireland, to my former horticulture teacher Carl Dacus and the late John Wyse-Jackson, who was a true gentleman and a great supporter of my work.

*"We have a mighty task before us. The earth needs our assistance."*
Laurens van der Post

"That is a well at which are the hazels and inspirations of wisdom, that is, the hazels of the science of poetry, and in the same hour their fruit and their blossom and their foliage break forth, and these fall on the well in the same shower, which raises on the water a royal surge of purple. Then the salmon chew the fruit, and the juice of the nuts is apparent on their purple beffies. And 'Seven Streams of Wisdom' spring forth and turn there again."

From Whitely Stokes' translation of the Connla legend, Revue Celtique, xv. 457 (1894)

# Acknowledgements

My thanks to all those who have led to this book happening – my parents for giving me an interest in nature, Carl Dacus my old teacher at Dublin School of Horticulture, Elaine and Richard Warren (of Springmount Garden Centre, Co. Wexford) for giving me my first job in horticulture and to all those from whom I have learned. I'd also like to thank Mattheus Wagter (former Chairman of BDAAI) for his advice and knowledge. Thanks to the late Eve Kaye for the work, the tea and the chats.

Thanks to Barbara Lee, Cait Branigan, the late Oliva Robertson, Philip Carr-Gomm, Deirdre Wadding, Vinnie Woods, Anna Coote, Eimear Burke, Paul Corcoran, John Michael Greer, Caitlín Matthews, the late Howard Campbell, FOI, PFI, PLR, Cyril Harrington and Penny Billington for supporting my Druid work and writing, now or in the past. Thank you to Bev and Del Richardson especially, Alex Duffy, Davyd & Emma Farrell and John Wyse-Jackson for their kindness to me. Thank you to my partner Elena, Amy and all of my friends and family for their support, especially Sarah & Gary (at last). Thanks to all the writers whose work has inspired and informed me, in particular Niall Mac Coitir, Elen Sentier and Ellen Evert Hopman, who was kind enough to write the introduction. Thank you to John Knox for the editing, Christine Best and Eimear Burke for offering their help with the herbs. Huge thanks to Kevin Camus for the Breton names and to Fionna Ware and Duncan Brown (Editor *Prosiect Llên Natur* for *Cymdeithas Edward Llwyd*) for help with Welsh names. Many thanks to my Editor, Trevor Greenfield. for all his hard work and to Nimue Brown, for her magical online abilities. A special thank you to Elena Danaan for the illustrations and for information on the *Jardin De Simples*.

# The Druid Garden - Introduction

I am writing this introduction during the peak of the Corona virus pandemic here in the United States. This disease, both frightening and dire, is just one more challenge facing humanity at a time of mounting catastrophes. Last year there were devastating wild fires in Australia, where an estimated one billion animals (and at least thirty-four humans) perished. Similar conflagrations occurred in Siberia, California, the Arctic, and even in the Amazonian rain forest. At the same time there were unprecedented floods and hurricanes world-wide.

As the world's glaciers are quietly melting, the snows of Kilimanjaro, the Himalayas and other mountainous areas are steadily disappearing. There are wars and massive refugee migrations and the mass extinction of insects, birds and animals.

At this moment I am in forced isolation at home, trying not to become infected and helping to flatten the curve of disease so hospitals do not become overwhelmed. I haven't shopped in weeks. This has given me time to stop, take stock of the perils before us, and open my heart to the suffering. As usual, I turn to nature and to the small strips of garden around the house, to bring me peace.

I am a Druid. In ancient times, and still today, trained Druids are expected to be "experts" at something. Luke Eastwood has shown through these pages that he is a Master Gardener. We require our gardens more than ever in this time of chaos and disruption. We need new "Victory Gardens" for food, medicine, and for solace. We must create them to replace our bee-barren deserts called "lawns" so that threatened insects, birds and other species can thrive. We require them as a quiet, sane antidote to the fast-paced, reckless mass consumerism that has hypnotized our modern culture.

This book will teach you where to begin, from the soil up. You will learn simple composting techniques and how to make your own fertilizer. You will be taught how to plan a garden – either a simple plot of companion vegetables, or a Druidic sacred space. You will be inspired to create natural barriers such as stone walls or fences made from tree branches. You will be shown how to propagate edible plants to bring you health and to help you commune with the natural world.

You may be inspired through these pages to create a pond to help amphibians and other threatened species find a home. You will be encouraged to replace your unproductive and wasteful lawn with a wild meadow, raise poultry with respect, and grow flowers for bees and other pollinators.

Sacred Land offerings and Land Blessings are included in this volume; by uttering these your mystical bond with the plant and soil kingdoms will be strengthened. There are elaborate instructions for which trees to plant, and how to nurture their growth. There are tips for the cultivation of shrubs, herbs and grasses. The lore and sacred history of these is provided, to further deepen your understanding.

Whether you decide to create a Druidic circle of sacred trees, a garden labyrinth, or a medieval garden devoted to the Four Elements (Earth, Air, Fire and Water), you will find instructions here.

It is time for a book like this. We humans desperately need to stop, slow down, and reflect on how we can be partners with the natural world, by doing the sacred work of gardening, in our own back yards. There is a current world-wide movement of children who are crying for their future and for a solution to global warming and climate change. Perhaps the Earth has heard them and has given us the gift of a virus that has made us finally stop and listen. The skies are clearing as industry grinds to a halt. Maybe we can see more clearly now that it is

3

time for humanity to radically change course. This book will aid in that effort.

    Ellen Evert Hopman

    Written at the April Full Moon, 2020

Ellen Evert Hopman M.Ed. is Archdruid of Tribe of the Oak (*Tuatha na Dara*) and lives in an oak forest in New England. She is the author of "Secret Medicines from Your Garden", "A Druid's Herbal of Sacred Tree Medicine", "Tree Medicine Tree Magic", "Scottish Herbs and Fairy Lore", "Secret Medicines of Your Kitchen", "A Legacy of Druids", and other volumes. www. elleneverthopman.com

# Chapter 1

# Why a Druid Garden?

The very idea of a Druid's garden may seem rather bizarre when one considers that the concept of gardening, as we now know it, probably did not exist in the time of the earliest Druids and even in Roman times, it was likely an alien concept to the 'uncivilised' peoples of western Europe.

That is not to suggest that the Druids, or Celtic people generally, had no knowledge of agriculture, or the nurture and use of the plant kingdom, which is far from the case. Evidence suggests that the ancient Celts had great knowledge of the natural world, perhaps as much as, or more than, other contemporary civilisations such as the Greeks and Romans. However, their understanding, values and application of their knowledge appears to be very different from the Greco-Roman values that have greatly influenced and moulded the attitudes and practices of modern western civilisation regarding nature.

It is well known that the Romans were excellent architects and great farmers and as they spread further into western Europe, they introduced their highly organised, urbanised system of living into areas that had largely been wild or semi-wild. The western Celts had no cities close to the scale or complexity of Rome, formal roads were relatively uncommon, with generally small communities, often semi-nomadic, eking out an existence in lands that were largely wooded, with little cultivation.

Of course, this way of life was gradually undermined and virtually eradicated from Europe as Roman and post-Roman civilisation spread. In some remote corners, such as Ireland and parts of Scandinavia, the influence of the Christian church, and the post-Roman civilisation it brought with it, was slow to take hold. This enabled the older culture, its practices, beliefs and knowledge, to survive longer than elsewhere and, amazingly, to partially remain into the modern era, through both surviving documentation and folk customs.

It is perhaps rather ironic that as the Celtic culture was dying in Scotland and Ireland, due to foreign (colonial) influence, the beginnings of the Druid revival in Britain occurred in the mid seventeenth century, with the work of eccentric historian/ archaeologist John Aubrey. Although the first revival Druid order is credited as 1717 (to Irishman John Toland), interest in Druidism and ancient sites in England grew in the latter half of the previous century, just as the remnants of Gaelic culture largely disappeared.

At that time, revival Druids turned their attention very much towards the Druidry of the Greek and Roman era in western Europe and the Bardism of Wales. It was not until much later that the folk practices and Gaelic literature of Ireland and Scotland were examined, revealing a connection with the ancient history and culture that had surprisingly managed to survive largely intact into the renaissance period.

One must wonder why such a revival occurred, firstly in Britain, and subsequently in other countries. There appears to be no connection at all between the rapid decline of Celtic culture and the Druid revival, however at that particular time the industrial revolution was just beginning to come into existence.

Most of Britain and Ireland had been heavily wooded prior to the Norman invasions of England, Wales, Scotland and Ireland, which took place over approximately a hundred-year period. Over time, due to feudalism, expanding population, reduction in common land, sheep farming and increased demand for wood, much of England and Wales lost its woodland cover. After the Elizabethan conquest of Ireland, the still largely wooded country was systematically stripped of its forests, to provide wood for barrel making, shipping and charcoal for the production of iron, as part of the Elizabethans' need to recoup the huge expenses that had almost bankrupted England during the conquest. In Scotland, union with England resulted from Scotland's abysmal costly and failed attempt at colonialism in Panama, Central America. This union led to land clearances in rural Scotland, with sheep replacing crofters, which not only destroyed Gaelic communities but denuded the country of most of its trees. It also led to a huge number of deaths and to a mass exodus to the New World, vastly reducing the Scottish population in the islands and highlands in particular.

As the denuding of the British Isles took place it was not just farmland that replaced the forests, industrial zones began to appear, as mining for metals and subsequently coal began in earnest. This was the first stirrings of the gradual move from a relatively slow agrarian lifestyle towards an increasingly urban, industrial and rapid moving lifestyle. Even at its early stages, the scars on the landscape, noise, mess, pollution, migration, growing slums etc. became apparent to observers. I suspect that this transformation of lifestyle and landscape, that began most enthusiastically in England, had a deep psychological effect on many of the people of the time. I do not believe that the rise of interest in the Druids, their beliefs and practices, coinciding with the rise of industrialisation is a mere coincidence.

Just as we are now aware of the great losses to the environment, I am sure that it must have been even more shocking to see the rapid changes at that time, given that life had changed extremely slowly, prior to the introduction of the technology that created the industrial revolution. It must have been hugely distressing to see huge areas of forest chopped down, massive pits dug for extraction of iron ore and coal. As mechanisation increased in areas such as textiles and agriculture, population shifts began towards towns where employment could be found, but where people often lived in worse squalor than in rural areas.

Most poor people were unable to resist the relentless drive of progress, regardless of their feelings on the subject. Apart from the rise and failure of the Luddite movement, the voice of the poor, who had little or no choice, has largely been silent. It is those of the educated and wealthy, that opposed 'progress', who were at liberty to bemoan the demise of the natural world and the transformation of human society. It is such people that comprised the early Druid revival, the poor were generally too busy trying to survive to concern themselves with such indulgences.

As the industrial age progressed, so too did the Druid revival, with a massive upsurge of interest in all things Celtic during the Victorian era – not just in England, but throughout the British Isles.

It is as if the rapid changes in the landscape and in the structure of human society resonated deeply within the human psyche, leading to a reaction against the unchecked transformation of life on this planet - the human connection with nature weakening as technological progress increases. Interestingly, as we entered the 20$^{th}$ century, people such as pioneering psychologist Carl Jung and anthroposophist philosopher Rudolf Steiner were instrumental in highlighting the growing schism between the human and the natural world, and the need to reconnect with nature. The relevance of what they had to say is perhaps even more relevant today than it was at the time, as if they foresaw the great challenges that humanity now faces. Neither Jung or Steiner were Druids, but their understanding of nature and the place that humanity should take within it has much in common with modern Druidry.

The Druid movement, while still obscure, continued to grow quietly as the 20$^{th}$ century progressed, as the human population and both industrial and military technology continued expanding at an ever-increasing rate.

It had been realised by the turn of the 20$^{th}$ century that nitrogen played a vital part in plant growth and experiments in nitrogen fixation (from the air) led to German scientist Fritz Haber developing a process to create ammonia, which was the basis for nitrate fertilizers. However, the Haber process was initially used mostly to make explosives for use in World War one (WWI) and far more extensively with other processes, by the participants of World War two (WWII), particularly in America.

During and particularly after WWII the manufacture and use of nitrogen based artificial fertilizers increased dramatically, with its use continuing to rise world-wide into our current century, despite the well-known negative effects on the environment.

Again, during WWI, the use of chemical agents as weapons (poison) against troops was first implemented by the French. However, there are accounts of using crude smoke weapons by the ancient Chinese, Romans and Greeks, but WWI was the beginning of chemical weapon use; although in fact it had been seriously considered earlier - during the Crimean and American Civil wars.

After WWI, research into chemical weapons continued unabated, with rapid advances in synthetic chemistry, although this was kept secret. A by-product of this lethal industry was the creation of pesticides, such as organophosphates and the organochlorine DDT, before and during WWII. Most of these chemicals were originally developed with the intention of using them in warfare. It was in the post-war years that many of the compounds developed in the war effort were repurposed as herbicides and insecticides.

In the post war period, restrictions on esoteric knowledge and what was generally referred to as 'witchcraft' were lifted, enabling a rebirth of Paganism and interest in the magical arts, that had hitherto been necessarily underground. Interest in esoteric matters and religions from around the globe blossomed in western society, particularly during the massive social unloosening of the 1960s. At the same time, the beginnings of the environmental movement took hold, gathering pace, in no small part, due to the work of Rachel Carson and publication of her seminal book 'Silent Spring' in 1962.

Although she was largely ridiculed at first, her work was instrumental in the eventual outcry against toxic pesticides such as DDT and its eventual withdrawal, due its catastrophic effects on the environment, including humans.

The sudden boom in interest in conservation and protecting the environment coincided exactly with both the hippie culture and the resurgence of interest in the esoteric arts, including Druidism. Although the hippie movement was a passing phenomenon, both the Druid and environmental movement have continued to grow and become more mainstream. Although environmentalism is generally secular, the Neo-

Pagan and particularly the Druid movement has embraced environmentalism as part of its core values, as awareness of humanity's total dependence on a healthy ecosystem has grown.

While the environmental movement has gathered strength, so too has industrialisation and social change brought on by globalisation. With that too has come the acknowledgement that climate change is at least in part due to human influence on the planet and its ecosystem. Despite the fact that the human population has risen from about 1.5 billion in 1900 to over 7.8 billion now, government, academic and business organisations tried to dismiss the obvious truth that we have reshaped the world to our needs and heavily impacted on all other life here.

Now that it is largely accepted that humans have had, and continue to have, a huge impact on the life of this planet, we as a species are still not able to agree on how to solve this problem, now and in the future, despite huge political efforts to address the situation.

While we wait for politicians to legislate to deal with the difficulties ahead of us, the problems such as deforestation, desertification and loss of biodiversity continue to plague us and, in many cases, this worsens as time passes. Rather than just accusing the politicians of 'fiddling while Rome burns', which changes nothing, perhaps we all need to do more ourselves to improve the situation for both ourselves and future generations.

Part of taking an active role in bringing positive changes to a very environmentally pressured world is re-engaging or engaging far more with the natural world, in our everyday lives and this is where the Druid garden comes in.

Although we know little about what the ancient Druids did in terms of gardening, we can extrapolate their holistic world view in the context of modern Druidry. In effect, the whole world becomes a garden that needs to be tended and protected, when viewed from a modern Druidic standpoint. Of course, one does not need to be a Druid to be interested in gardens, protecting the environment and saving the planet from cataclysmic destruction. However, Druidism does offer a distinctive spiritual viewpoint and knowledge that can be incorporated into the practical actions we take. No less, Neo-Druidry often incorporates and adopts methods and practices from other cultures and spirituality where it seems appropriate to integrate them.

One does not need to be a Druid or an environmentalist to see that humanity now faces unique challenges to stop and reverse the destructive trend of the last few centuries, that has brought us to a now recognised crisis point. The actions that human beings take during the remainder of this century, and perhaps even the next few decades, appear to be crucial to the future of all life on this planet, not just human life. If indeed, as many scientists have concluded, we are now living in the Anthropocene era, we cannot just rely on nature to fix itself. We have to discover and implement creative ways to heal the damage that we have done and ensure that our future existence has minimal negative effects and far greater positive effects on the geological and biological systems that we interact with.

Obviously, technological innovation can be greatly helpful in bringing about positive results, but I do not believe this alone will save us from destroying our species and many others along with it. I sincerely believe that we have as much to learn from the past in terms of harmonious and non-destructive living as we do from the future. Many techniques and methods that have been considered obsolete, traditional or alternative are being found to be highly effective and far less destructive than much of the industrial and technological methods, that often create as many problems as they solve.

There has to be a place in our future for the spiritual as well as the technological, for the ancient as well as the modern – after all we are not just logical beings, we have physical, emotional and spiritual aspects to our existence that increasingly need to be factored into life, if we are to succeed in avoiding a dystopian future.

A holistic, integrated approach to our own immediate environment is a good starting point and this is where this book humbly intends to act as a launch pad for ideas that may be helpful in transforming our own lives and our relationship with the world of nature. Unfortunately, our understanding of the Druids' approach to agriculture, gardening and general living is quite limited, so in neo-Druidism we are forced to 'fill in the blanks' as best we can. Hence, much of what I have to offer here is not Druidic in the traditional sense, although I consider it suitable to integrate with a Druid's point of view.

I hope that this work proves to be useful to those who would describe themselves as on a Druid path, but I also hope that those who are simply interested in gardening or helping the environment will find it equally interesting and helpful too, regardless of whatever spiritual beliefs they may or may not have.

## Chapter 2

# Gardening Through the Ages

*"Those who cannot remember the past are condemned to repeat it."*
George Santayana (1863 - 1952)

In the beginning there was no such thing as gardening. We are all familiar with the story of the Garden of Eden, but this is most probably a metaphor for the primordial state of the world when humans lived much like other animals. In our primitive state humans were hunter-gatherers, our ability (or perhaps desire) to manipulate the environment was very limited – we caught or hunted animals and gathered grains, berries and plant foliage or roots.

It is guessed that after the ice-age ended, perhaps around 10,000 BCE, man began to discover cultivation, i.e. the beginnings of farming. Estimates for when this started vary enormously and are impossible to prove or disprove and the same applies to the level of human population at that time – often considered to be about five million people. If one considers that the human population was very small at this time then it is likely that in most areas of the habitable world there was an abundance of all life – huge quantities of both animals and plants that precluded the necessity for cultivation or animal husbandry.

Whether it was due to expansion in population, accidentally acquired knowledge or the desire for an easier existence, humans did begin rudimentary cultivation and domestication of some animals. It is possible that this began in one place or in many different locations around the planet. With civilisation evolving at very different rates around the world, it is likely that small communities began agriculture while most others continued as hunter-gatherers. Even today, small societies of hunter-gatherers still exist in parts of Africa, Australia and Asia.

Historians often disagree about when agriculture began although recent archaeological finds might offer some clues. The prehistoric stone temples of Göbekli Tepe, constructed at least as early as 9000 BCE, are an immense undertaking which could not have been undertaken without massive organisation, including the means to feed a large workforce.

It has been suggested that the huge amounts of butchered and cooked animal remains are those of wild animals that had been hunted nearby. However, given that hundreds of people would have been required to construct the 20 circles so far found (only 5-10% of the site excavated) a small army of hunter-gatherers would be needed to feed the workers. Although there is no evidence of permanent settlements, farming or agriculture at the site at the time, evidence of corralled animals and domesticated wheat has been found only miles away, from approximately 500 years later.

The feat of feeding such a huge workforce, purely from hunting and gathering, appears so huge that it seems hard to imagine how it could have been achieved. Perhaps rudimentary growing and keeping of animals had already started near enough for these people to be kept fed? Perhaps, these workers were kept fed by early forest gardeners who brought herds of animals, bread and vegetables to the site?

Without far more exploration of the region, no-one can be sure of how these people managed to survive during the construction period and this may still remain unknown, even after full excavation. The fact that a man-made stone structure with complex carvings existed at least as early as 9000 BCE came as a shock to world, demonstrating how much we do not know about the origins of civilised human behaviour.

Whatever the exact starting point may be, the earliest form of gardening is regarded as forest gardening, thought to have developed within the tropics in forest/jungle land, near rivers or in wet regions such as deltas or monsoon foothills. In such places cultivation of plants would have been relatively easy – valuable trees, bushes, vegetables, herbs and even medicinal plants would have been encouraged and protected whilst those that were not useful would have been removed. A series of layers (generally seven) is created using as much diversity as possible, which has many benefits.

At its beginnings, forest gardening would have made perfect sense, given that the human population was very small and most of the land mass had become covered in trees in the period after the ice age ended (the interglacial that we are still in). This method of gardening is highly productive, sustainable over long periods of time and very ecologically sound. Approximately 12 thousand years later, despite the massive changes in terrain, forest gardening still exists in Africa and Asia and has inspired pioneers within the modern Permaculture movement, such as Robert Hart and Geoff Lawton.

As human populations grew and people became more widespread there was an expansion into other areas, where forest gardening was more difficult or unsuitable. Around 9000 BCE is the earliest known evidence of enclosure of land, presumably for the keeping of animals and for the production of crops to eat. This was the beginnings of farming as we know it, highly practical and with little or no aesthetic purpose – anything grown that was not for food was almost certainly for medicinal or other practical purposes.

It is generally thought that domestication of plants and animals began in Mesopotamia and spread to near-by regions, archaeological evidence certainly indicates the domestication of cattle, goats and pigs in that area and also cereals and pulses in very ancient times by Neolithic people. There is also strong evidence of early agriculture in China and Thailand, with it also spreading into Europe, the Americas and southern Asia by around 5000 BCE.

By this time the human population was beginning to expand relatively quickly, which most probably meant that a hunter-gatherer lifestyle was becoming unsustainable in many areas, hence an increasing dependence on agriculture was necessary to sustain and increase human communities. Having discovered what plants were edible and pleasant to eat, it was possible to collect seed and clear land specifically for growing of crops. It was also discovered that plants could be cultivated and bred to produce more useful or better strains than their wild antecedents. The same was applied to wild animals that could be selected for desirable properties, such as docility or high milk volumes, and bred to produce domestic livestock.

In order to facilitate these new methods of providing food, it was necessary to both clear land and enclose it – to prevent animals from escaping or being attacked/stolen and also to protect crops from being damaged or eaten. Rudimentary fields would have sprung up around cave dwellings and later on around homes made of branches and reeds or mud bricks. However, there was probably also a large level of reliance on nomadic herding and hunting.

The invention of the plough made cultivating the ground and sowing crops easier, leading to the possibility of larger communities – towns and eventually cities. Ploughs were originally designed for hand use, but by the emergence of civilisations in Mesopotamia (Sumer), Egypt and India the use of animals such as oxen had made this far more efficient. As city states developed into empires, farming had necessarily become advanced in order to be able to support large urban populations.

The Sumerian civilisation (in modern day Iraq) made extensive use of irrigation in what was not a vastly different climate from today. Summers were hot and winters much wetter and cooler, with floodwater inundations allowing the widespread use of irrigation channels to provide water for agriculture. It has been suggested that the first ornamental gardens came into existence in Mesopotamia, but there is no surviving evidence to prove that this is the case. Tablets have been found that describe the use of herbs for medicinal purpose, so from that we might conclude that herb gardens were grown for medicinal and culinary use.

Archaeological evidence of horticulture in Sumer and Egypt can be found from the fourth millennium BCE, with references in mythology and tomb inscriptions of planting of large trees to provide shade, presumably for both people and smaller plants, with later tomb examples detailing gardens of the deceased.

In Egypt, trees were planted in the cities as sacred groves, around tombs and within domestic gardens, with fruit trees such as date palm, fig, or nut bearing trees being most popular.

From military campaigns, trees and plants were brought back from abroad and introduced, such as the pomegranate tree. Images carved for Tuthmosis II in a Karnak temple clearly show plants (from Mesopotamia) being accepted as tribute in the form of fruit trees from conquered territories.

Dating from around 2000 BCE, a wooden model was found in the tomb of an Egyptian official, which clearly represents a domestic garden, with trees and a rectangular pool. Around 2000 species of flowering and aromatic plants, in desiccated form, as well as depictions have been found in excavations of Egyptian tombs.

The Egyptians believed that the gods were pleased by gardens, hence most temples were surrounded by, or close to, gardens which had a religious value, often featuring trees associated with the gods of the Egyptian pantheon.

As well as food, the Egyptians grew many flowering plants, particularly fragrant ones, that were used in religious ceremonies, as were the perfumes and oils made from their flowers or foliage. Examples of perfumes and fragrant oils have frequently been found within tombs, that were presumably used in funeral rites and interred along with other grave goods.

Like the Sumerians, the Egyptians were fond of brewing beer (from cereals) but they also grew grape vines from which they made wine and they also grew olive trees, mostly for the production of oil.

Even in its infancy, agriculture ran into problems – continual planting, harvesting and replanting of fields led to eventual depletion of soil; with the lack of fertility forcing communities to move to new areas – often 'slashing and burning' to clear new areas as still occurs today.

In areas where irrigation was common, growing of crops was sustainable for much longer periods of time, although even this could become impractical in time. Mesopotamia is the classic example of the failure of irrigation – over a very long time period mineral salt levels built up in the soil due to evaporated irrigation water and the drawing up of salts from lower levels in the soil. In effect, the very thing that made the land fertile, irrigation, eventually led to the soil salination becoming so high that it was toxic to plants. It is thought that by around 2000 BCE the land around the Tigris and Euphrates rivers had become unusable for agriculture, thus being the main factor in the demise and collapse of the Sumerian empire. Even today, irrigation can be problematic, with salinity build-up being a major concern, as well as the increasing scarcity of fresh water in many areas of the world.

In Egypt, the Nile river has been the major source of water for agriculture and horticulture since the earliest human settlements. Irrigation is still used today in much the same way as it was in ancient times, however the annual inundations have been regulated since the 1970s. This has prevented unpredictable floodwaters but is also thought to have prevented the depositing of nutrient rich silt onto the land during flooding, and also prevented the washing away of much of the salinity that builds up in the soil due to irrigation. Huge subsurface drainage projects have been undertaken to help deal with the salinity problem and artificial fertilizers are now extensively used to make up for the lack of nutrient deposits. The lack of sediment deposits is also thought to have contributed greatly to coastal erosion.

Gardening is regarded as having spread to Europe via Greece and Rome via the older civilisations of Egyptian or Mesopotamian cultures. However, gardening also developed in other cultures such as India and China. The Hindu *Rigveda* (approx. 1500 BCE) describes cultivation and growing techniques although many experts believe that agriculture in the region may have begun as early as 9000 BCE.

As early as 2500 BCE, sugar cane was cultivated in India, later to be discovered in around 500 BCE by the Persians and later the Greeks. Although the Indians developed the process of crystallizing sugar around 500 BCE it remained a luxury commodity, produced almost exclusively in India until the 18th century. It was imperial colonisation which brought broad agricultural and social changes, due to plantations, as the Western demand for sugar increased.

In ancient China, around 3000 BCE, there were already written manuals describing medicinal use of herbs, which also appeared in Mesopotamia at a similar date. About 300 years later, hemp and rhubarb were cultivated in China. Records exist of imperial parks and gardens going back to around 1600 BCE in the Shang dynasty – for hunting, pleasure and food production, although this may well have begun much earlier. As with India, agriculture is thought to have begun much earlier in China, and China was in fact home to many innovations that were largely unknown in other countries until much later. Cast iron ploughs were known to be in use after the invention of the blast furnace in 475 BCE. Around 200 BCE seed drills were being manufactured to greatly increase the efficiency of seed sowing, that had previously been done through hand scattering. Evidence of wheelbarrows exists in murals from around 100 CE, although this innovation may well have been invented much earlier.

In the Americas potatoes are thought to have been domesticated from perhaps 8000 BCE, in the Andes, by ancestors of the Incas, but confirmed evidence only exists from around 2500 BCE. Maize, squash and beans had all been domesticated in this region by 4000 BCE. Over three thousand potato varieties exist in the South Americas, spreading throughout the continent, although only a handful of varieties were introduced to the rest of the world by the Spanish, from the mid-16th century onwards – leading to vulnerability to disease in many modern potatoes, due to lack of genetic diversity.

As agricultural techniques gradually improved and development of better varieties of crops by crossbreeding occurred, the provision of sustainable food supplies for large populations became easier, although still subject to the ravages of natural disasters. Greater food security and stable civilisations made the cultivation of gardens for aesthetic reasons possible, although this was confined to royalty in antiquity and gradually became more common among nobility and wealthy members of society, as time passed.

As already mentioned, ornamental gardens existed in Mesopotamia, Egypt, China and other parts of Asia. In Europe it appears that gardening remained somewhat more utilitarian until later on. If we consider the writing of Homer on the garden of Alcinous which, although impressive, was given over to production of fruit, grapevines and vegetables. Perhaps later Persian influence may have led to the development of ornamental gardening in Greece and subsequently in Rome.

It was the Persians that created perhaps the most famous garden in history – the hanging gardens of Babylon, one of the seven wonders of the ancient world. Reputedly constructed by King Nebuchadnezzar II, for his wife Amytis, sometime after 605 BCE. It was described as a series of tiered gardens with walls of brick, within the confines of the royal palace/citadel, that was irrigated from the nearby Euphrates river. However, no archaeological evidence has been found at the site of Babylon and there are no extant records of it from the time - its earliest descriptions are from about 300 years later. Some consider these gardens to be purely mythological but it has also been suggested that they have become confused with the earlier gardens at Nineveh, built by Assyrian King Sennacherib, some hundred years earlier. Bas relief pictures of the gardens and aqueducts have been found at the city (modern day Mosul in Iraq) and Sennacherib's own writings describe his achievements in creating canals with sluice gates, aqueducts and water screws to bring water to his gardens.

Darius I (born 550 BCE) is reputed to have had a 'paradise garden' – a typically Persian walled garden that was usually rectangular and often contained water features, as well as cultivated trees and plants. His invasions of Eastern Europe and Greece may have been the beginnings of cultural exchanges that increased greatly after the takeover of the Persian Empire by Alexander the Great, after 334 BCE.

Alexander's conquests not only introduced Greek culture into Persia and beyond but led to Persian influence in Greece and its western possessions, leading to an increased interest in ornamental gardening, as opposed to horticulture for purely practical purposes. Greek philosophers such as Aristotle possessed impressive gardens, which was inherited by Theophrastus (who also wrote about plants). Epicurus also owned a garden where it is believed he taught his students. Ptolemaic ideas from Alexandria, in Hellenic Egypt, and those of Roman Lucullus, who conquered the Pontic kingdom, had great influence on the development of gardening in the Roman world. Lucullus, returning to Rome in 66 BCE with immense plundered wealth, spent much of it on civic projects including extensive gardens in Rome constructed in the Persian style.

By the beginning of the common era, the world population had grown to an estimated 170 million people. Rome had transformed from a rural agricultural society into a city state kingdom, a republic and finally an empire that reached from western Asia and north Africa into the western edges of Europe. The large estates in Italy that supplied the Roman cities were commonly managed by overseers (hired by absentee owners) who farmed the land with the use of slave labour from wars and dependent tenants. Rome also relied greatly on imported foods such as olive oil from Spain and grains from Egypt. By the time of the collapse of the Roman empire, serfdom was well established within Roman agriculture and this system was introduced throughout its conquered territories.

In much of north Africa, the Middle East and Asia, agriculture and gardening was long established, however much of Europe (outside Roman territory) remained as relatively simple tribal kingdoms with unsophisticated agriculture. Gradual interaction with or conquest by the Roman republic and later empire led to the introduction of Roman ideas. Small communities that often lived in tiny fortified villages with the lands around for farming and hunting were gradually transformed by building of roads, clearance of forest and construction of towns in the Roman style. Romans taking possession of formerly wild territories built extensive villas and farmed the land in a network of fields around, in much the same way as was done in what is now Italy.

The Romans adapted earlier Persian rectangular gardens, adding semi-circular and geometric alcoves, columns, fountains both in public and private settings, and often within the courtyards of their villas. Romans are generally credited with the invention of topiary (training and shaping of perennials) as well as the spread of many species of plants across Europe – roses, leeks, turnips and various fruits.

Roman civilisation not only had a huge cultural effect on the human population, especially of Europe, but massively transformed the landscape of conquered territories. A huge empire required massive income from war loot, taxation and from trade, and the Romans were more than happy to exploit largely untapped resources in their dominions. Over time this led to extensive deforestation, construction of large urban centres with roads connecting them and division of land into estates for large scale farming. Throughout the Roman provinces slave labour and peasant tenants were utilized, which formed the basis of the later feudal system. By the time of the collapse of the Roman empire, in the early 5th century CE, serfdom was well established in Europe.

Following the introduction of Christianity into the Roman empire, by Constantine, censorship of non-Christian literature and knowledge gradually increased from the mid-4th century onwards. This not only affected religious texts but all knowledge connected with generally polytheistic religions and philosophy throughout the empire. Huge quantities of books were burned by clergy and their followers for the most tenuous of connection to Paganism, leading to a catastrophic loss of classical culture and knowledge, long before the collapse of the Roman empire.

While all aspects of horticulture continued to prosper outside of Roman control, in places such as Persia, Arabia, China and Japan, it dramatically declined in Europe following the chaos of Rome's decline; although in the eastern Roman empire (Byzantium) classical culture (including horticultural knowledge) remained to some extent. In the mid-6th century coffee was domesticated in Arabia and a system of flower arranging was developed in Japan. Meanwhile, the Roman Church kept alive much of the horticultural knowledge of the Romans with its network of enclosed monasteries and convents being able to grow food, flowers, medicinal herbs and produce alcoholic beverages such as beer and wines.

In the extreme edges of Europe (Ireland, Scotland and Scandinavia) the Romans had little or no influence and people probably used long established techniques that may have begun developing in the late Neolithic period. Certainly, archaeological evidence of agriculture in the British Isles exists from around 5000 BCE but knowledge of the non-Roman practices, well into the medieval period, is hard to find.

In Scandinavia, the farming practice *Landnám*, based on separate winter and summer (shieling) methods and locations, is thought to have originated during the Roman empire period in Sweden and Norway. It is documented to have been introduced into Iceland and Greenland from the 9th century but being inappropriate for the volcanic soils there, led to widespread erosion and environmental degradation. This method of farming revolved around animal husbandry with livestock for milking and eating kept on high ground, from spring to autumn in or around forest areas, some distance from residential farmsteads that were on lower ground. These lower grazing areas were left fallow until the winter when those animals that were not slaughtered were brought down to the settlements. This system was introduced across much of northern Europe by Viking conquests from the 8th century onwards.

In Ireland, the Druids were the learned elite of society until the gradual conversion to Christianity initiated by St. Patrick. Druidic knowledge extended far beyond religious functions, including the arts, history, administration of justice, healing and astronomy, and had also presumably included horticulture. While it is often regarded that Celtic learning was purely oral in nature, it is documented that compendiums of knowledge were commissioned by high kings long before Patrick arrived. In the early 5th century Patrick ordered the destruction of all works of the Druids, being considered Satanic – a clear indication that a body of literature did exist. Presumably what has survived of ancient knowledge (reproduced by monks) was sanitised to be acceptable to the Church, or survived through oral transmission until more tolerant times. As a result, like the Druidic culture of Britain and Gaul, only fragments remain of how they lived and their botanical and horticultural knowledge.

While post-Roman Europe suffered centuries of turmoil, horticultural traditions were kept alive in Moorish Spain (from 711 CE) and in the Eastern Roman Empire of Byzantium. In Spain, the Moors extended and improved irrigation systems created by the Romans and also introduced new crops such as citrus fruits, peaches, figs, apricots, sugar cane, spinach, artichokes, cotton and rice. Vineyards were cultivated despite the Muslim prohibition of alcohol, presumably just for the fruit. Crocuses were grown specifically for the production of saffron, from the stigma and styles collected from the flowers. Mulberry bushes were planted in order to enable the cultivation of silkworms for the production of silk, another valuable commodity which had originated in China in the 4th millennium BCE.

In Japan, developing out of sacred rock arrangements around 5th century CE, gardens developed gradually as both spiritual and ornamental places, utilizing natural stone arrangement as a central feature. Garden design began to be documented from around the 10th century CE, with the form continuing to develop into the modern period.

In (formerly Byzantine) Egypt, the Arabs expanded the irrigation systems that were already highly developed, enabling wheat and other crops to be exported. In the Byzantine empire silkworms were also introduced for cultivation and Persian and Roman horticultural ideas still flourished until the empire's gradual decline.

In most of Europe the horticultural innovations of Roman and earlier cultures were kept alive by monasticism. Although responsible for the destruction of perhaps ninety percent of all classical writings, the Church through its monasteries, preserved much of what we have of classical literature as well as classical knowledge of gardening, herbal medicine and botany during the 'dark ages' of feudal Europe.

In Byzantium the monastic tradition, although differing from that in most of Europe, was also widespread and was significant in the flourishing and retention of horticultural knowledge. Monks grew food in and surrounding the monasteries. Although archaeological evidence is scarce, monastic foundation documents and accounts of Byzantine saints describe gardening practices of the period.

Through most of Europe gardening was kept alive by monasticism, in the early medieval period, although based on practicality rather than aesthetic considerations, this was generally consisting of kitchen and medicinal gardens, orchards, vineyards, cloister garths (grassed quadrangle) and pasture for animals. Some cloister gardens would have been more complex, as places of rest and meditation, perhaps including a fountain or fish pond. At around the same time, development of the manorial system from the Roman model continued to flourish, with a feudal lord employing the forced labour of peasants of one or more villages within the confines of the estate. A typical estate could be as much as 800 hectares, operated in much the same way as monastic estates, although primarily for the benefit of the lord instead of a religious community.

Often manors were entirely self-sufficient, providing not only food, vegetables and meat but also fish, honey from bees, bread (from their own mill and bakery), wool, leather and dairy products (from livestock), oils and alcoholic beverages. What originally began as a two-field system (one fallow) evolved to the Roman model three-field system, described as 'food, feed and fallow' until eventual enclosure of open fields and gradual adoption of a four-field system, from the early 16th century onwards.

Up until the beginning of the Renaissance in 14th century Italy, Europe could be said to have stagnated culturally. Pace of change was indeed slow and new ideas were not forthcoming or readily accepted, to a large extent. This was changed by the unsuccessful crusades against the Islamic world, plagues (the mid-14th century black death particularly) and the gradual decline of Byzantium. The printing press, developed by Guttenberg, also had a tremendous impact on the dissemination of ideas across Europe. Although widely credited with the invention, moveable type had in fact been invented in China (using clay blocks) around 1041 CE, four hundred years earlier.

A flood of scholars from Asia Minor (Byzantium) and interaction with the Arabs, who had retained translations of classical literature, initiated a revival of interest in the classical culture of ancient Greece and Rome. This took hold primarily in Florence, spreading quickly to the powerful Venetian state and eventually Rome and the Papal states.

Rediscovered works of Pliny (younger and elder), Varro and Ovid inspired a renewed interest in both gardens and architecture, leading to a move away from the enclosed (walled), purely functional, monastic style gardens into a more open and more aesthetically pleasing form. Alberti, writing in the 15th century, on architecture, advocated the creation of gardens for viewing from the house and that these gardens should be designed with a pleasurable experience in mind. Obviously, such indulgence was only available to those of significant wealth, but none-the-less his ideas were highly influential and spread, along with the renaissance generally, to France and throughout Europe eventually.

The renaissance in Italy created an interest in botany and plants generally, outside the confines of the monastery, where interest was mostly medicinal. The university of Padua spearheaded this renewal with the first chair of botany and renewed study of medicinal plants. In 1543 Padua created the first botanical gardens, bringing in plants from all over Europe, nations that traded with the Venetian state and eventually all over the world. Initially focusing on medicinal plants, it imported exotic species, which it was necessary to protect from theft by building a circular wall around the gardens.

The Padua gardens set a trend that spread throughout Italy and France and gradually to most countries in Europe. Likewise, the general interest in gardens flourished throughout Europe, particularly among royalty and aristocracy as a demonstration of their magnificence and power - to their rivals and to the public.

Renaissance gardening, as well as showcasing the wealth and sophistication of the owner, demonstrated man's mastery over nature – with formal styles of gardening developed in Persia and Rome taken to new heights. The Italian gardens inspired the French renaissance gardens, which were even more opulent than their predecessors. They featured elaborate water works and fountains, container plants, formal topiary and hedging as well as complex paths, stairs and ramps interconnecting the various sections. Designed to illustrate measure and proportion as well as the cultivated tastes of the owners, they also often featured architectural elements and statuary reminiscent of ancient Rome.

The renaissance garden in turn influenced the increasingly elaborate and complete French formal garden, typified by Versailles of King Louis 14th. Such gardens were usually flat, geometrically and symmetrically arranged. They were more integrated with the grand house or castles they surrounded and different sections connected or flowed into each other better. This represented the peak of artificiality and the desire of man to manipulate the natural environment, primarily for pleasure. Incredibly expensive to create and maintain, their popularity declined by the end of the 18th century as the less formal English landscape garden and Chinese styles began to become popular.

Colonisation of Ireland, by the English, had resulted in the decimation of Irish forests, primarily for making charcoal (for iron), barrel making and ship building. With as little as one percent of its once immense tree coverage left, it was in the estates of the wealthy colonists that this trend was reversed. Having the land, cheap indigenous labour and the wealth to do so, the Anglo-Irish created impressive gardens and parklands, clearly influenced by renaissance and English gardens and importing large numbers of foreign species. Even today in Ireland, much of the broadleaf woodland and substantial gardens dates from the Elizabethan period onwards, created by the colonial aristocracy.

Not long after the deforestation of Ireland, by the British, much the same occurred in Britain itself with the onset of the industrial revolution and the land clearances in Scotland. With increases in population, clearance of forests increased for use in farming and for charcoal used in iron production and other industry. By the end of the Stuart period there was so little timber available that it was imported from New England and Europe. The economic and population growth of the industrial revolution continued to worsen the problem with the decline in forest habitats, continuing until after World War I. A similar situation existed in most of Europe and in the USA, due to industrialisation and increased demand for farmland.

With the wild natural forests disappearing at an alarming rate, wealthy private individuals began planting and developing the picturesque garden style, particularly in England, inspired by the romantic movement. Although still contrived, it attempted to emulate the natural landscape rather than the overly manicured baroque style. For those with sufficient wealth to do so, it was possible to create idyllic landscapes, often featuring lakes, follies (such as fake ruins) as well as a wide selection of native and imported trees and shrubs.

Meanwhile, with increasing urbanisation and growing impoverished populations, most people were too busy trying to survive to take an interest in gardening. If they did possess any land at all it was almost definitely given over to the growing of food and the keeping of any animals. As common land continued to shrink, as well as forest, it became increasingly difficult for ordinary individuals to maintain pigs or other livestock, unless they owned sufficient land themselves.

With increased urbanisation and a noticeable decline in the rural environment it became evident that there was a need for public parks and gardens. Throughout Europe, parks and gardens began to develop in urban settings through the 18th century, initially only for those who could afford them. However, as urban centres continued to grow around the world, the creation of generally free public parks by governments increased, as a much-needed resource for a world human population that had passed one billion by 1800.

With ever-increasing international trade and travel, plant and animal species continued to be transported around the world, often unintentionally, leading to problems of both disease and invasive species. Well-known examples of such are rhododendron plants in Europe and rabbits in Australia. By the end of the 20th century, with gardening becoming a common hobby in much of the world, huge numbers of non-native species have been transferred all over the globe. Some of these plants have propagated themselves so successfully that they have become highly problematic invasive species, along with the accompanying pests and diseases that have been spread by plant exports.

From the mid-18th century, primarily from the work of Johann Friedrich Mayer, gypsum began to be used as a fertilizer but with little understanding of how it benefitted plants. Manure had long been used in agriculture and in the 19th century Guano (desiccated bird and bat faeces) became widely traded, copied from longstanding agricultural practices observed in South America, by Europeans. It was collected in the Americas, Caribbean and Africa, mostly for export to USA and Europe until saltpeter and the beginnings of nitrogen-based fertilizers led to its decline in the later half the of the 1800s.

As understanding of plant biology and chemistry increased, artificial fertilizers became more popular in gardens and in agriculture particularly, with industrial processes making it cheaper as the technology progressed. In the early 1800s, pioneering fertilizer companies were established in England, with European and North American competitors emerging shortly after. By the 1870s, the international industrial fertilizer trade was well established, competing with the Guano market. During World War I, nitrate production for fertilizers shifted dramatically to its use in making explosives. With a British blockade, saltpeter exports to Germany were curtailed, forcing them to successfully develop synthetic nitrates. Post war, these techniques were used in production of nitrogen-based fertilizers, with innovations of ammonium-based compounds from the 1920s onwards.

Beginning in the 1930s, the so called "Green Revolution" began to take place, primarily affecting agriculture but also eventually transforming public and domestic gardening practices to a huge extent. From a labour-intensive process, involving also animals and large quantities of organic manure and naturally derived fertilizers, traditionally produced seed and long-established watering methods, horticulture was transformed in a few decades. Use of new crossbreeding techniques to produce desired hybridized plants, increased reliance on artificial fertilizers and pesticides, advanced irrigation and mechanisation and consolidation into larger scale farms, all served to both increase efficiency and transform the basic look and methods of horticultural practice, that had previously evolved slowly.

By the 1960s these technological innovations had led to massive growth in the agro-chemical industry and combustion-engine machinery, primarily in USA and Europe, with the new technological philosophy being exported around the globe in developing countries as the century progressed.

This was not without its doubters and significant setbacks (such as the DDT pesticide scandal) and the establishment of growing alternative 'organic' movement in horticulture. Never-the-less, the situation today is that most of the developed and developing world, both agriculturally and domestically employs modern techniques, largely to the exclusion of time honoured and proven natural methods. At this point in time horticultural commerce spans the globe with a decreasing number of companies controlling the markets for agrochemicals, technical equipment, plant and seed production and ever-increasing and worrying innovation now at a genetic level (GMOs). For all its benefits, the negative effects of this highly technological approach are now becoming increasingly evident - degradation of land due to deforestation, over-grazing and over-farming, huge run-off of soil and nutrients into rivers and seas.

Wildlife has been hugely affected too, with increasingly large-scale farming there are whole areas of monocultures, giving a barren environment for animal life and little or no plant diversity permitted. The same can be seen on a smaller scale in towns and cities where verges and borders, as well as gardens consist almost entirely of grass, sometimes with not a single plant, shrub or tree to be found. While governments and organisations may be aware that such a situation is unhealthy, little has changed in practical terms in many countries, despite increased efforts to educate people about the need for bio-diversity.

What appeared to be a significant benefit to humanity has turned out, over time, to be far more of a problem than could be imagined, due to a non-holistic and extremely narrow view of our actions and its effects on the whole environment. However, it has not been all bad, at the same time as the 'green revolution' began to take hold, it gave birth to a counter movement that rejected the whole ethos of technological horticulture, long before it was proven to be flawed. Organic farming was a term first used by Walter James in 1940, who viewed the farm as an organism that functions best with an ecological, holistic approach. The beginnings of this movement go further back, before the term 'organic' was used, with the response to the shift towards artificial fertilizers in the early 1900s, primarily in Germany.

The first organised response came from occultist philosopher Rudolf Steiner, formulating theories and practices known as Anthroposophic Agriculture, which he presented in the form of lectures from 1924 onwards, initially farmers from six countries attended but interest soon spread, although on a small scale, throughout Europe. This system, later called Biodynamics, which is basically organic agriculture, also incorporates spiritual and astrological elements within its methods. Although Steiner's ideas are somewhat unconventional, described as pseudo-science by mainstream horticulture and agriculture, they have proven to be at least as effective as conventional organic methods. Tests carried out in Germany show that it gives better soil health efficiency than conventional farming. Although still not widely accepted, Biodynamics is now practiced in over 50 countries around the world and continues to grow as an alternative to intensive conventional methods.

Permaculture, like Biodynamics, is closely related to the Organic Movement, although it is a system based on observation of natural ecosystems and forest farming, still found in some cultures. The term is a contraction of the words permanent and agriculture, coined during 1978 in Australia by Bill Mollison and Holmgren, with the release of the book Permaculture One. Although incorporating earlier ideas of no-dig gardening, forest farming (mostly from Australia and Japan) it was developed as a complete system of agriculture. It was intended as an alternative to conventional growing which they saw as damaging soil and water, over-using resources, causing topsoil and biodiversity loss and relying on artificial inputs such as fertilizer.

The core principles are 'care for the earth'; 'care for the people' and 'settling limits to population and consumption'. The system works by integrating different layers of growth – trees, shrubs, herbaceous plants, etc, an eighth layer (fungi) also often incorporated. The garden is generally divided into several zones surrounding the home, worked with varying intensity, some of which are allowed to grow wild. If a garden is created using the 12 design principles described in the permaculture design course it should be provide a sustainable eco-system that is self-contained and provide an abundance of food and wood products without the need for external input.

Permaculture, while still a very small movement, has moved far beyond Australia, being taken up around the world with the encouragement of the founders to the Permaculture Design Course, for their students to spread and teach the system as a sustainable system of growing. Since the 1980s Permaculture has expanded in scope beyond just agriculture to incorporate an integrated and alternative mode of living that encompasses ecological housing, economics and social aspects. As such, Permaculture is now a complete way of life, rather than just a system of agriculture and the term is now more accurately described as Permanent Culture, reflecting its wider mandate as a complete sustainable way of life. Having spread across Asia, Europe and the Americas since the 1970s, the movement continues to grow and becomes increasingly relevant as the problems of conventional farming are becoming continually more evident over time.

While Biodynamics and Permaculture remain a minority interest in both agriculture and gardening, interest in Organic growing (particularly food) has increased significantly in the period after World War II. This growth was greatly accelerated by the awareness (1960s onwards) of the adverse effects of pesticides and artificial fertilizers on the wider environment, soil heath, watercourses and ultimately the world's oceans. By the 1990s, after pressure for regulation and standards, certification was introduced in Europe and North America. Since then the interest in Organic methods and the market for Organic products has rapidly increased, despite the far higher prices associated with Organic products. Today Organic products extend far beyond food – healthcare, beauty, household and textile products can all be bought as certified Organic.

While Organic food has not been conclusively scientifically proven to be more nutritious than conventional food, studies have indicated that the level of pesticide by-products is much lower (e.g. 1/6) in Organic produce. Also, Organic food has no or negligible GMO content, which given the doubtful safety of this technology, means it is improbable that it would suffer from any undesirable effects that GM food may have.

So, over time, one can see a gradual transition from basic techniques in the growing of food to an increasingly technical and mechanised method of both agriculture and recreational/ amenity gardening. In most of the world, in any areas that might be called developed, the evidence of this change is highly apparent and has become increasingly widespread and noticeable from the second half of the last century.

We now live in a world where, for the first time, more than half of people live in urban environments, 80% of the world's tree cover is gone and wild spaces are increasingly lost to agriculture. In urban areas biodiversity is in crisis, as apart from public parks, most cities and towns have little or no green spaces. People are busy and have little time or energy to spend on keeping gardens, never mind growing their own food, and so most gardens are monocultures of grass with few or no ornamental plants. In some cases, even the lawn has been removed in 'architectural gardens' where concrete, stone, gravels and metals replace the soil with more easily maintained structures and plants become a novelty feature in an otherwise sterile environment.

In my travels around various cities - London, New York, Los Angeles, Chihuahua, New Delhi, Paris, Berlin and many others I could not fail to notice the general absence of the natural world, with what few plants and trees there are struggling out of confined spaces, in a stifled and polluted atmosphere. Of course, efforts are being made to 'green' cities and reclaim some of the wasted space, but with ever-increasing demand for housing and office space, such efforts are dwarfed by the constant need for expansion.

Even in rural areas, small towns and villages are becoming increasingly urbanised and agriculture is gradually being upscaled, with small farms being consolidated into larger and usually more industrialised operations. The gardens and grounds of business premises I see are most often almost entirely closely cut grass, surrounded by fences or walls, with hedges and hedgerows losing out to the easy maintenance of an artificial barrier.

Most gardens are bereft of biodiversity, with few or no trees and what shrubs and plants that are to be found are most often entirely foreign to the landscape and of limited benefit to wildlife. Especially lacking from most gardens are not just plants in general, but native species that are generally most beneficial to wildlife such as birds, insects and small mammals, that struggle to survive in countryside that has been increasingly stripped of their refuges.

What has now become 'normal' to most people is in truth far from normal, if considering the vast history of human civilisation. Human societies have degraded or even collapsed localised environments in the past, but only recently has it taken on such a grand scale and become the dominant way, so successfully that, now nature is effectively 'on the run' from us. Our obsession with a tidy and ordered world, where everything is under control is undermining the very building blocks of life, forcing wild and vibrant nature into a smaller and smaller corner of our planet.

This all sounds rather grim and pessimistic; however, it is not all bad news – there is still hope for change and the means to bring it about. Part of the tragic demise of the natural world around us has been a backlash against the destruction and destructive modes of living. This movement is growing, not just in the area of Organic farming but as a general awareness of a need to change, which has launched guerrilla gardening, increased community initiatives both in rural and urban areas and growing concern for our forests and remaining wild spaces. It has also launched a social and political response such as Friends of The Earth, Greenpeace, and more recently, Extinction Rebellion.

While there is increased pressure for governments to take action to change how society treats the environment, with changes in education offering hope for a major transformation in attitudes towards nature; it is at a basic personal level that we can make the most difference. Whether living on a massive farm or in a tiny urban apartment, we can all participate in gardening in a healthy and positive way, that will help to make a difference - this is what this book is all about.

Illustration by Philip Armstrong ©Historic Environment division of
the Dept for Communities NI

Illustration by Philip Armstrong ©Belfast Hills Partnership

At the core of making a difference is understanding – by understanding what we have been doing wrong we can set about doing things the right way. We need a way that is in balance with the natural world and which is nurturing for life and the earth, rather than destructive.

Humans did not set out to damage and degrade the planet, that has arisen as a side effect of our innovation and success as a species. However, now that history is proving that our disconnection from the natural processes of life is damaging everything, including ourselves, we still have the opportunity to turn things around by working with nature instead of against her.

# Chapter 3

# The Sacred Soil

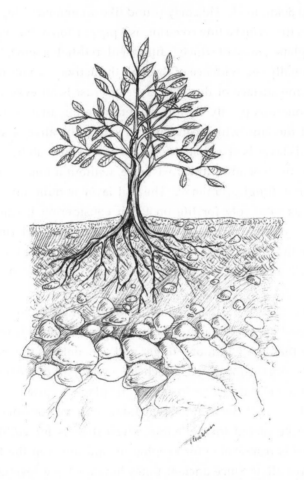

*"No creature, not even swine, befouls its nest with such abandon as does homo sapiens... Today soils are tired, overworked, depleted, sick, poisoned by synthetic chemicals... Malnutrition begins with the soil. Buoyant human health depends on wholesome food, and this can only come from fertile and productive soils."*
Christopher Bird & Peter Tompkins, *Secrets of the Soil*

The surface of the Earth is covered by a thin layer of rock which we call the crust. Earth's crust varies greatly from only a few kilometers in some places under the sea but on land averages around 30km thick. This may sound like an immense depth, but in truth this is just a tiny covering as a proportion of the diameter of the planet, most of which is filled with red-hot magma, that we occasionally see evidence of through the activity of volcanoes.

On the surface of this thin layer of crust is an even thinner layer, microscopically thin in planetary terms, that is the only part of the land which can truly be said to be alive or contain life. This layer is of course the soil, in or on which all living land organisms depend for their existence, without it there would be no plants, fungi or animals. The soil layer is quite miraculous given its vital role for life on Earth considering it can be as shallow as a few inches up to a few feet thick. Considering how minute this life-giving layer of the Earth is, it is quite incredible that such a multitude of species is able to exist and be sustained by it.

What is even more incredible is that the Earth's soil is itself composed of several layers, the uppermost of which is often no deeper than the width of a finger and yet contains the majority of living organisms in soil, which are a vital part of the health of everything else that lives in and on the planet's surface.

Perhaps it is no wonder that humans have considered the land to be sacred for millennia, given that its incredibly thin expanse is responsible for keeping us and much of the Earth's creatures alive. Since ancient times humans have revered both the Sun and the Earth as divine entities which furnish us with the means to live. The simplest of cultures could see that it is the Sun that warms the Earth daily and causes plant life to grow on its surface. It was also clear that humans and animals depended totally upon the Earth, for a place to live, plants and their fruit or seeds to eat and other animals to eat that survive on a plant diet.

Over time a simple reverence for the Sun and the Earth

developed into religious beliefs and ceremony and ritual surrounding our dependence. This often takes the form of supplication as sacrifice or offerings, usually based around the observable cycles of the Earth moving around the Sun, which we call the seasons. Sun and Earth may have originally been worshipped or revered themselves, as is still the case among some indigenous cultures, but in many instances our ancestors anthropomorphized the Sun and Earth (and also the Moon), giving them a human or semi-human form.

Long before the development of agriculture the divine was represented by the feminine form with exaggerated sexual features (e.g. the Willendorf Venus), presumably a goddess symbolising the Earth and the fertility that comes from it. In a hunter gatherer society humans were still aware that the food they needed came directly from the land or from the animals that lived off the land. Also, the fresh water that humans and animals need flows on and through the land, unlike the vast seas and oceans that are undrinkable.

At Catal-Hoyuk, in Turkey, perhaps the oldest known city, the mother goddess was still very much in evidence as humans began transitioning to a less nomadic and more agriculturally based civilisation, this is also very much the case with ancient Malta and early Egypt.

In later times, with the development of agriculture, deities came to be defined in broader terms, including crops, the harvest and general fertility. A multitude of Earth gods existed, many of which are still known, such as Ki from Sumer, Prithvi in India, Gaia from Greece, an unusual male Earth god Geb, as well as the later goddess Isis (both from Egypt) and Danu/Anu found in Ireland.

Over time as a more patriarchal and agrarian world developed, the importance of the Earth goddesses, and female deities generally, began to decline as humans became less reverent and more sophisticated. We see the increased dominance of male deities within pantheons and the emergence of masculine monotheism such as the Aten (briefly under Pharaoh Akhenaten), Judaism, Zoroastrianism and later Christianity and Islam.

It is perhaps no coincidence that as humanity moved away from the sacred feminine and an innate respect for the Earth itself, there is increasing evidence of exploitation of the natural world, overuse and depletion of resources and occasional collapses such as in Mesopotamia and the abandonment of Ephesus in Turkey.

No doubt, the deforested and soil-eroded Mediterranean region became that way due to the aggressive economies of Greece, Persia and Rome – societies that had abandoned earlier attitudes to the sacred Earth, in favour of imperial expansion and religious sensibilities that favoured aggressive and patriarchal gods.

So now we live in a time where, for most people, the Earth has lost its sacredness, nature is no-longer holy and soil is just dirt. Even our language in relation to soil is indicative of our lack of respect and value placed on it – seen as exterior to our every-day lives, unclean, annoying and 'dirty'.

Despite the negative perceptions about soil and a modern lack of understanding about what it actually is, the soil remains vital to life. An understanding of its composition and its role in life of humanity can restore soil to its rightful place as something not just essential but sacred.

## Soil Horizon

As I mentioned earlier, soil is not a homogeneous substance, unless it has been greatly disturbed, it is composed of several layers in what is collectively called the soil. Lying on the soil is a layer of organic matter, from leaves, broken stems, twigs and dead plant or animal material (O horizon). This organic material is constantly in the process of decomposing to become the top layer of the soil. The top layer is called humus (P horizon), similar in sound but totally unrelated to the popular food made from chickpeas! This is literally the organic layer of the soil, comprised of decomposed and decomposing organic material, in which lives a host of worms, grubs and insects as well as fungi and micro-organisms such as bacteria. There are literally millions of microorganisms living in the humus layer of soil and just below it and these have been found to be an essential ingredient to healthy soil and healthy plants.

Below this top layer is the surface or top soil (A horizon). This layer is composed of decomposed organic material and mineral fragments of varying size, derived from rock that have become disintegrated over time. This layer is rich in minerals and organic compounds derived from the matter within it and received from the organic layer on top of the soil, by the action of water dissolving soluble compounds that then pass down through it. This top soil or surface horizon is where the vast majority of biological life occurs in soil. It is here that various types of worms (including earthworms), arthropods (e.g. insects), nematodes, fungi, bacteria and single-celled organisms live in abundance.

This layer also provides home to plant life, where seeds germinate and the roots of plants begin their downward and outward journey. It is also home to an abundance of animal life that live in the soil, such as moles, or other animals that create a subterranean dwelling for themselves in this and lower layers of the soil.

At the bottom of this layer is the Eluvium layer (E horizon), which is generally only present in long undisturbed soils, created through the gradual weathering or leaching of the soil as water passes down through it. It is generally a thin layer of lighter colour than the top soil, often rich in silicates (sand and silt) with much of the clay lost to the lower layer through eluviation.

Below this is the sub-soil layer (B horizon), which is largely composed of minerals but also contains organic and mineral deposits carried down and accumulated due to the leaching action of water. It generally contains more larger fragments of rock (stones) than the layers above it. This layer is harder and less aerated than higher layers, with generally much less humus and organic material within it and can often have a reddish hue due to clay and oxides of iron that have accumulated in it from above. Nevertheless, plant roots penetrate and thrive in this layer but there is a much lower level of organic life present here than found in the topsoil layer.

Finally, below the layers of soil we arrive at the parent rock (C horizon) which, as the name implies, consists primarily of rock that been largely unaffected by the process of weathering that works upon higher layers. Although this will not be solid it consists of large lumps or sections through which water can usually percolate. This layer is usually the provider of parent material in the form of rock that was weathered and broken up over time in the formation of the layers (horizons) above it.

Underneath this is found the bedrock (R horizon) which is fairly solid, difficult to break up or excavate and less porous. It is generally not regarded as part of the soil but its presence has enabled the formation of the soil horizon above it over a huge period of time.

It is possible to see the soil horizon, without extraction, at coastal areas such as cliffs where erosion has exposed the land, often all the way down to the bedrock. Observed, in this way, as a cross-section one can see generally how the layers of soil, if they have been undisturbed, naturally exist. Unfortunately, the soil that is to be found in a modern garden may be quite different from the natural order of things.

Intensive agriculture and, more commonly, construction work often lead to the disruption of the soil layers and in some case total destruction of the soil horizon. In days gone by, before heavy machinery was readily available, the footprint of a building site was a small as possible, soil was removed down to the parent rock only as necessary. This made perfect sense not just in terms of leaving the surrounding soil intact but also avoided unnecessary use of limited energy resources.

Now, in the modern age, many builders have found it convenient to completely raze a site, scraping off all or most of the soil down to the parent rock or bedrock and dumping it in a convenient area. This makes building a house or office much easier for the builder and also enables the site to be re-landscaped entirely as required. Unfortunately, unscrupulous builders often sell off the majority of any good topsoil and bury building rubble and waste.

Worse still, some builders lay down 'hardcore' all around a site during construction for convenience and when re-landscaping will often put back soil that has been totally mixed up, all subsoil or only a thin layer of subsoil over hardcore and/or building rubble. I'm sad to say that in my work as a horticulturist I have all too often discovered that underneath what appears to be a 'normal' lawn is a horror story.

In the majority of cases I think that these things happen due to ignorance and expediency rather than any willful desire to destroy the land or defraud owners of any possibility of a vibrant and healthy garden. Nevertheless, it is devastating to discover a garden has only three inches of poor-quality soil under which are stones, broken concrete, plastic and electrical cables. In such cases, without massive remedial work, it is extremely difficult to grow more than grass, bedding plants and a few very tough shrubs; even growing ornamental bulbs can be very challenging in such circumstances.

A grass lawn can hide a multitude of sins and in some cases, I've discovered machinery parts, old tyres, a pit of used nappies, fridges and even a whole car! However, there are often tell-tale signs of trouble, especially in drought periods. The edges or border areas of drives, paths and buildings are often the least considered in terms of soil; often full of concrete or stone, it can even be as thin as three centimeters or one inch. Where this is the case, grass can turn yellow and die during a brief dry spell and will not look particularly healthy even at the best of times. This doesn't bode well for the rest of the garden and is often an indication of trouble elsewhere.

If one is lucky enough to live in either an old house or one built by responsible and knowledgeable builders, then the majority of these problems will not be there – the soil, good or bad will hopefully be in its correct horizons in most of the site, with all of topsoil in situ as nature intended. If this is the case you are off to a good start, if not then unfortunately the only options are to accept defeat, improvise (by creating healthy areas such as raised beds, elevated mounds or containers) or completely re-landscape to recreate a more natural soil.

Of course, where the soil horizon has been totally wrecked it is practically impossible to recreate it as it once was, the best one can do is to try to remove any waste/rubbish, hardcore and rubble in and above the parent rock and reintroduce subsoil and decent topsoil above that. Even so it can take many years for the soil to properly settle and build up soil organisms to a healthy level that is really suitable for growing more than a lawn.

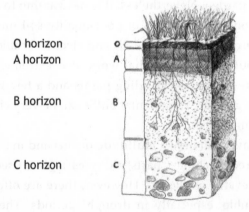

O horizon    O

A horizon    A

B horizon    B

C horizon    C

## Compaction

Another serious problem in the soil that is poorly understood and often overlooked is that of compaction. On many occasions

I've visited gardens where plants struggle to grow, mature trees are ill, dying or even dead for no apparent reason. After a few pertinent questions regarding groundworks or construction it is often easy to ascertain that the cause of this mystery is soil compaction. The root structure of a tree is in some respects like a mirror image of the canopy – a network of roots spreading out and down a considerable distance from the trunk, often as far as the canopy does above ground.

Often during building, ignorance of the extent of the roots leads people to think it might be acceptable to leave heavy piles of building materials, rubble or soil within a few feet of the trunk of a tree. This is very far from acceptable if one wishes the tree to remain healthy because what happens is that the soil is compacted by the weight above the surface of the soil, the heavier it is and the longer it is there then the more substantial the damage becomes. What compaction does is squeeze the airspace out of the soil as well as making water penetration more difficult. At the peripheries of roots are fine strands, which actually do the main work of absorbing air, water and nutrients from the soil, the thicker roots mostly carry it to other places within the tree.

As a result of compacted soil, the fine strands can die off, which severely impacts the tree's ability to absorb and transport what it needs from the soil. The effect is far from immediate, it can take months before any sign of trouble is visible but the long-term effect can be devastating – leading to permanent impairment of growth, general health and even death. For this reason, it is advisable never to leave heavy loads of any kind close to trees and it is a good idea to cordon off trees wherever building work is happening, in order to prevent irreversible damage from occurring.

The best way to deal with compaction is to avoid it happening in the first place, but unfortunately this is not always possible. Where soil is totally compacted, it may be necessary to dig up the soil to a quite some depth in order to create spaces and allow the air in again. Obviously where there are trees or large shrubs growing this is not practical to do unless you are potentially prepared to sacrifice plants. One can carefully dig between the major roots but with a wide network of roots in well-established plants this can be effectively impossible. Another alternative is to drill holes – known as aeration which can be done to a shallow depth with a garden fork or a machine with a series of metal spikes. Alternatively, a long spike or rod can be banged into the ground at regular intervals to create air holes. In both cases of shallow or deep aeration it is common to fill up the holes with sand or fine gravel, which can help with drainage and still allows air to penetrate. This technique is not likely to completely solve the problem but can at least improve the situation for suffering plants and certainly be beneficial for future planting.

## Soil texture and structure

Understanding the type of soil is extremely beneficial when it comes to choosing what to grow in your garden. In addition to knowing the pH (acidity or alkalinity) through a simple and cheap test, it is a good idea to establish what your soil texture and structure is.

Soil texture refers to the fineness or coarseness of the soil. The soil mineral composition can vary greatly from tiny particles to large grains and this affects the qualities of the soil such as nutrient and moisture retention. Fine soil is generally particles of 2mm or less and falls into three basic categories – clay, silt and sand. Clay is the finest and can be more than a thousand times smaller than a grain of sand, silt is in between. These differences are due to the parent mineral materials they consist of and also the extent of weathering over time.

Soil may consist of any one of the three groups or a combination of two or all three, in varying proportions. Loam, which is considered as friable (workable) soil, is generally valued by gardeners as desirable as it retains moisture but is also reasonably free draining, consists of roughly half sand with up to nearly half silt and a lower proportion of clay. Loam can be subdivided into clay-loam, silt-loam, sandy-loam, silty clay loam and sandy clay loam, depending on the more dominant proportions of each.

Soil can be analysed to give a breakdown of its constituent parts, which is costly, but there are two simple alternatives that you can do yourself at home. The first and simplest is to take about a dessert spoon size piece of soil and examine it in your hand. By the feel of the soil you can tell if it breaks apart, forms ribbons, clumps together in a sticky mess or somewhere in between. Also, by adding a tiny quantity of water you can test the soil between finger and thumb to feel if it is smooth or gritty. This test will not give you a breakdown of the soil but it will give you a general idea of whether the soil is mostly, clay, loam or sand. This is also indicated by the look of the soil and how well it absorbs water.

The second simple test requires about two cups of soil and a glass jar with a lid (preferably straight). After placing the soil in the container, fill the jar with water leaving a space of about an inch or 2cm at the top. If available add a small amount of water softening solution and with the lid on tightly, shake the jar for four or five minutes. Put the jar down and allow it to rest for one minute before measuring the level of soil in the bottom (without disturbing the jar) – this is the sand content. Leave the jar standing for 30 minutes and then measure the depth again – this minus the first reading is the depth of silt. Leave the jar for at least 12 hours and then measure the final depth of settled soil – this minus the first two readings is the depth of clay. From the three depth readings you can establish the relative proportions of clay, slit and sand in your soil. You can work out the percentage of each by dividing each reading by the total depth and then multiplying the result by 100.

The soil structure refers to how the clay, slit and sand in your soil groups together to form larger configurations or what are called aggregates or clusters. The aggregates that occur naturally in the soil are called peds and those that we see as a result of working the soil (tillage) are called clods. Aggregates are generally a result of the natural processes of weathering over time such as freezing and thawing, soaking and drying out, the action of plants and fungal organisms in the soil and also compaction caused by large animal and human activity. Aggregates are bound together by fine clay, organic matter (generally plant residues) and iron oxides, acting like a cement or glue - as organic matter often acts as cements. When soil microorganisms break down, plant residues descend, carried downwards by water (leaching).

Soil structure breaks down into eight primary types which are: blocky, columnar, crumb, granular, massive, platy, prismatic, and single grain. The illustration below gives an indication of the corresponding appearance, with the names also indicating their properties. Granular structure is the most preferable as it has the highest proportion of spaces between aggregates without being unable to retain water, like single grained sand.

## Soil structure

| Granular | Crumb | Platy | Prismatic |

| Massive | Columnar | Blocky | Single Grain |

So, why would we be bothered to know anything about the texture and structure of the soil? The reason is that the composition of the soil affects what will grow. Soil structure can change as it descends through the horizons, generally becoming more massive in the lower levels. Soils that are well aggregated are advantageous for growing – with air spaces and drainage. If the soil is heavily compacted the soil structure can be badly damaged, likewise if huge amounts of soil have been dug out and moved around or completely replaced then the soil structure can be completely wrecked, making it much harder for plants to become well established in the soil.

Soil texture is equally important in that it tells you what kinds of soil you have to work with – clay soils stick together and retain water but go hard in dry periods. It's important to sow plants that can tolerate sometimes waterlogged, low aeration conditions if you have clay soil – for instance many Mediterranean plants, such as lavender will struggle to survive in clay but a willow tree will do fine. Equally, sandy soil will present problems – plants with very poor tolerance to drought will suffer, as will those that require a lot of nutrients (which tends to leach out of sand).

Understanding your soil is essential for knowing what you should plant in the ground and how to improve conditions for the plants that you may already have. For instance if you have a succulent planted in clay you might want to move it into a container or add sand (unsalty); if you have a birch tree (shallow roots) in very sandy soil you might want to add organic matter or clay and ensure that it gets extra water in a dry spell. It is possible to compensate for the characteristics of the soil if you know what you are dealing with. Adding clay and organic matter to sandy soil is often somewhat easier than trying to transform clay soils. Often it is necessary to create drains to enable run off of water in heavy clay soils. Addition of horticultural lime to clay aids formation of clumps (flocculation) and addition of sand (never taken from a beach) and compost can also create spaces and improve drainage, however this often requires a major operation, which is not always desirable, affordable or practical.

If you can modify the soil conditions in certain areas of your garden then it widens the variety of plants that you can grow successfully. Of course, some people are lucky enough to have a good depth of loamy soil that has not been disturbed or compacted. However, the reality is that most people will not be this lucky and may have to think about modifying the soil to compensate or else use containers of various types to grow plants that don't suit the existing soil.

Soil is not simply dirt; it is an essential ingredient for life on Earth. In the sea, minute plant life can float but much of plant life still needs to be anchored to something; without plants in the seas, rivers and lakes there would be no higher organisms, such as fish. Likewise, on land, micro-organisms and almost all plants (except those in/on trees, such as mistletoe or orchids) rely on soil as a medium to live in - for anchorage and to obtain nutrients. Again, without soil there would be virtually no plants and with no plants there would not be any animal life forms, including us. So, clearly soil is much more than just brown stuff that things grow in – it is a basic building block of life and part of a complex ecosystem that has been built up over millions of years.

On a spiritual level it is part of the Earth itself, the skin of Gaia, the planet if you will. Soil or earth is one of the four neo-platonic elements of Western spirituality, earth is one of the three realms of Irish pagan spirituality (along with sea and sky). Earth is also to be found in many spiritual paths and indigenous religions across the world as one of the sacred building blocks of physical and spiritual life. Soil has been largely disregarded and downgraded in this age of technology but even there, without the silicon and rare earth metals (which are dug from the ground), none of electronic technology would be possible. Once more, people are beginning to realize the crucial importance of soil in human life and relearn that it is a vital and sacred part of life.

## Chapter 4

# Composting: Turning Death into Life

*"From the Earth we came and to the Earth we must return."*

Composting is such a vital part of life in the garden that it deserves its own chapter. A large component of decent soil is made up of the organic matter from plants and animals, without it, soil would be entirely mineral in nature. Obviously at some distant point in the Earth's past there were no plants and animals and hence very little organic matter. Huge changes in the structure of the Earth's surface meant that some of the organic matter that eventually became plants and animals ended up deep underground, where it decayed over huge time and pressure to become coal, oil and gas – the hydrocarbons that we have been using for fuel since the industrial revolution. These energy rich fuels are the compost from millions of years ago that although highly convenient are proving to be far from healthy for the planet. The compost that enriches the soil is made from the same materials as fossil fuels, only its decomposition is much shorter and in different conditions, where it can be made use of to create and sustain life instead of becoming the highly toxic but energy rich fuels trapped underground.

Composting is something that happens naturally all over the world on a continual basis, whether humans participate or not – dead plant matter, especially leaves, dead animals and animal feces all decompose (rot down) to form the organic matter in the upper levels of the soil, which gradually leaches downwards. This process can be replicated in the garden or you can buy compost commercially.

## Commercial Compost

Commercial compost has been available for thousands of years although in the past this was made entirely from naturally occurring organic sources such as waste food, plant material, animal feces and even human feces! Use of feces, especially human, is very dangerous unless it has been thoroughly decomposed in a manner that kills pathogens but until relatively recently it was common to collect and sell both animal and human waste for use as garden fertilizer.

Politely referred to as 'night soil', throughout the ancient world from Greece, Mesopotamia, to Asia, Africa and the Americas the use of human waste in agriculture was common. It persisted even in Europe up until the beginning of the 20th century and was still used by local government to create compost, which was sold to farmers.

Use of animal waste has traditionally been employed in making compost. In more recent centuries when horses were common for transport and agriculture and also Guano (from bird and bat faeces) were both utilised in commercial compost. However, the situation today is very different, surprisingly so. Industrial compost is big business and although companies that produce it would want you to believe that their product is natural, eco-friendly and healthy, that is not always as it appears.

Often commercial compost has colours added to it to make it more appealing as well as additional chemicals – salts of the basic elements Nitrogen (N), Potassium (K) and Phosphorus (P) that plants require as well as additional elements like Iron (Fe) and micro-nutrients. This will be advertised as a selling point e.g. 'fortified with Iron!' but in reality, artificial chemical supplements have been added because the compost would be deficient without it.

## Give Peat the Cold Shoulder

Peat compost is very common and has been popular for a long time due to its abundance and ease of use. Most commercial composts contain peat, sometimes almost entirely so, but 'peat free' composts are becoming more common. Peat is generally quite low in nutrient and may have artificial fertilizers added to it. Peat is also very hard to wet when bone-dry but becomes very waterlogged when soaked – not ideal and why sometimes wetting agent is included. Unless sterilized, peat may retain pathogens from the dead plants that it is formed from, which can then end up in your garden. Peat is also quite acidic (low pH), which is not great unless you particularly wish to grow acid loving plants or if your soil is already very alkaline (high pH). Finally, and perhaps most importantly, peat use has huge environmental impact. Peat bogs are a great carbon-sink and left to their own devices will continue to increase at a very slow rate (1mm a year). Most peat bogs have taken many thousands of years to form and cannot regenerate at any appreciable rate. Peat bogs have been and are still used as a fossil fuel (turf and briquettes) as well as for fertilizer but they are essentially a non-renewable resource.

Peat bogs are a limited but natural habitat for otherwise rare species such as dragonflies, waders and many mosses and flowering plants. In Britain 95% of the peat bogs are gone and they are fast disappearing in Ireland, mainland Europe and America. Commercial harvesting in peat bogs is ecologically destructive, which not only wrecks ecosystems and looks ugly but also releases massive amounts of carbon dioxide into the atmosphere in the process of making peat compost.

Many gardeners are completely unaware of the negative aspects of peat, but I've made a point of not using it for decades and I would personally like to see it banned outright – both as a fuel and as compost.

Commercial compost is very often sterile, it has no life in it all, which is not the case with compost you make yourself or certified Organic compost. Chemicals are added to the compost or it is heat treated (often using steam) in order to kill any pathogens and soil-borne diseases (such as Pythium), which sounds like a good idea. Heat treatment also kills off seeds that may be in the compost, which are generally considered undesirable. Because of excessive use of antibiotics in industrially farmed livestock, animal manure often contains antibiotic and growth hormone residues and also antibiotic-resistant organisms such as MRSA; this is another reason why commercial compost is sterilized. Unfortunately, sterilisation also kills off all of the beneficial microbes and bacteria that we do want for healthy soil – if your soil is already lacking in microbes then addition of most commercial composts will not really do anything to improve this, at least not in the short term.

In some countries 'sewage sludge' is used in the making of commercial compost – this is basically everything that goes down the toilet which has been decomposed into compost and sterilized to kill any pathogens. Although it will not contain any harmful diseases it may well contain heavy metals, artificial chemical residues, prescription drug residues and other contaminants, which will end up in your soil.

Very common today is the use of 'green' refuse from

restaurants and groceries, as well as household food and garden waste to make commercial compost. This is a much better idea than putting unused produce and compostable waste in land-fills but is far from perfect. Composting is often done anaerobically (no oxygen) because of the mixed content, and the high heat generated kills pathogens in the compost but does not necessarily destroy contaminants such as herbicides and pesticides, oil and chemical spillage (e.g. soaked into leaves) that enter through garden waste. Also, other contaminants through incorrect disposal in the green waste can end up in compost, such as bits of plastic, petroleum by-products and even asbestos. Obviously green waste is sifted first to remove 'rubbish' that has been accidentally put in the wrong container, but some of it is not detected and ends up in commercial compost bags.

A 1993 British study of 12 composts made from entirely, or some sewage waste, found that levels of heavy metals were high and all of the composts contained varying degrees of contaminants such as glass, plastic and metal. This situation has most probably improved in the last few decades but one can be sure that most commercial producers are unable to sell compost that is completely free of contaminants, which would just be far too expensive.

In truth, there are really only two ways to be sure that the compost that you use in your garden is healthy and free of contaminants – buy entirely organic, certified compost or make it yourself. In an ideal world we would all have the space, time and inclination to make our own compost but in reality, many people lack one or all three of the above and so have only one practical option. There are now some very good organic composts that are not made with peat, do not utilize sewage sludge or contaminated food and green waste and may not have been sterilized. As a result of an often longer process and a much greater level of care, these types of composts are relatively expensive, however, if you wish to grow ecologically sound and healthy plants (food especially) then this is an expense that is well worth paying.

If you buy commercial compost make sure to find about whether it is really eco-friendly or is just marketed to look as if it is, also be aware that compost that smells bad, either rotten or of ammonia is most likely not fully composted and should be avoided. Above all, try to avoid compost with peat in it, by doing this you will already be making a much lesser impact on the environment.

## Making Aerobic and Anaerobic Compost

There are two types of decomposition to form compost – aerobic and anaerobic, which basically means decomposing in airy or airless environments. Anaerobic decomposition tends to take longer and the results will be somewhat different from the aerobic process as it involves different micro-organisms, that do not require oxygen from the air.

Making your own compost makes a lot of sense – firstly it saves money, secondly because you've made it yourself you know what it's made from. Making compost also gives a sense of satisfaction in that you are making your garden grow better by effectively recycling waste that might otherwise end up in landfills or in commercial compost. It was a widely used and essential activity for gardeners and farmers up until cheap fertilizers and cheap commercial compost became available. It makes sense to make your own if you have the time and some would consider it a sacred duty as part of a commitment to protect and help the natural world.

### *The Compost Heap (Aerobic)*

The traditional compost heap is aerobic, it is exposed to the air rather than in a container that restricts airflow. It's generally a good idea to site the compost heap a good distance from the home itself but in a convenient location for use in the garden. It's possible to simply make a big pile on the ground, often 1 yard/ metre wide and high but usually not bigger than 2 yards/metres wide or high. Any bigger than this takes up a lot of space and becomes very difficult to manage when it comes to turning over the compost heap, plus the centre may get too hot.

Many people like to create an enclosed space for their compost, perhaps made out of old crates, wooden delivery pallets or even fence posts and chicken wire. Commercial composting bins, usually made from recycled plastic, are available with a network of air holes to allow oxygen to penetrate. Whatever way you choose to do it, the most important aspect is that the heap is open to the air and can be accessed to turn it over. The centre of the heap may not have much air percolating in it, in which case anaerobic decomposition may be happening, often at high temperatures. To ensure that the whole compost heap rots down evenly it is generally necessary to turn the heap at least twice during the six-months to a year that is needed to make it ready.

Turning the heap means basically mixing the heap inside out so that the centre becomes the outside and the outside ends up in the centre. To do this it is best to have a long garden fork and a rake that you use only at the compost heap, to avoid spread of pathogens into the garden, especially if your compost heap contains animal droppings. The advantage with an open heap is that it is easier to get at, although it might not be a compact or high as one that is contained. The disadvantage with a contained heap is that turning the heap is more difficult and the container often has to be removed in order to properly turn the contents. Using a container may discourage rats and mice from burrowing in or making their homes in the heap, especially if there are food scraps in the mix, however this is a distinct possibility and apart from smells and general hygiene, a good reason for locating it away from your home.

Another important aspect of a compost heap is what you are going to put into it and how it is layered. A successful compost heap is best constructed in layers of alternating soft material and more dense fibrous material, which helps air and water to penetrate throughout the heap and thereby helps the decomposition process.

The micro-organisms that break down the materials in your heap require heat (but not over 60°C), water, carbon, nitrogen and oxygen. In cold weather the rotting process drops to a crawl or stops, the hotter the weather the faster it goes and the rotting process itself generates some additional heat. The oxygen comes from the air and water from rain, the carbon and nitrogen from the organic matter to be broken down – generally an average ratio of 30:1 carbon to nitrogen is about right for the micro-organisms to prosper but anywhere between 20:1 and 40:1 is acceptable.

In order to achieve the right balance, it's important to vary the contents as you build up the heap. Food scraps tend to have the lowest ratio although grass clippings, animal manure, weed and vegetable/plant material are also relatively soft and low ratio contents. It is important to avoid certain problem contents:

- No diseased plant material - this spreads disease into the heap and into your garden
- No gone-to-seed weeds/plants - the seeds may survive and germinate in your garden
- No meat or fish – this will attract rodents
- No ash from coal fires – this is often full of sulphur, arsenic, cadmium, lead and aluminium
- No citrus peel – the acidity can harm both worms and micro-organisms
- No glossy/coated paper – this contains chemicals that may be toxic
- No cat/dog waste – feces from carnivores can be dangerous
- No sticky labels – these contain chemical glues and often are plastic rather than paper

- No pressure treated/painted/varnished wood – contains harmful toxins
- No large wood – sawdust and small chippings are fine but anything bigger will not rot quickly
- No fats/oils – these can upset the balance in the heap and take ages to break down

Apart from the above, pretty much any biodegradable stuff can go into your compost heap, although it is best to alternate the soft content, such as grass and vegetable waste with a thin layer of more fibrous material such as shredded paper, leaves, or sawdust. It is a good idea to immediately cover soft plant, vegetable and food scraps with the fibrous material, which discourages smells and discovery by rodents.

Maintaining a reasonable moisture level also makes a difference – in a wetter climate the pile can be dome shaped to encourage water run off; some may even cover the top surface with a waterproof sheet (temporarily), although this also generally reduces airflow. In a drier climate the pile can be made concave to encourage water retention and water can be added manually if necessary. Some people like to urinate or put urine on the compost heap, which introduces water and also urea, which is helpful in the decomposition process.

Another helpful addition to the compost heap is earthworms. Earthworms are great for the soil and also for helping to break down your compost heap and generally speed up the process. Vermicompost, which is made through extensive use of earthworms, is becoming increasingly popular both commercially and at home – worm casts are high in nutrients and lower in contaminants than the undigested materials. Earth worms tend to do well in already fertile soil – you can carefully dig them up and transfer them to the pile where they should have plenty of eat. If your soil is very poor then you might have to buy some worms to add, but make sure that your heap is already established, otherwise they may migrate to other gardens and areas that have more attractive food for them.

Depending on the warmth of your local climate, the compost could be ready in as little as six months, but be prepared to wait a year if necessary. Good decomposed compost should be crumbly and dark brown in colour with no visible signs of the original constituents – if you can still see what you put into the pile then it's not ready. Likewise, the pile should have a nice earthy smell, not a rotten one – if it smells bad then it's not ready yet.

## *Biodynamic Compost*

Biodynamic compost is basically made the same way as a traditional organic compost heap although it has an additional esoteric component that is believed to act as a catalyst for the absorption of nutrients by plants. There are six different preparations that are added to compost but one should note that these involve animal parts and so are not suitable for vegetarians or vegans. Six holes are made at a 45-degree angle near the top of the pile, facing towards the centre, and the preparations inserted at the same time they are believed to transfer their properties throughout the heap.

*Yarrow Preparation 502*: Yarrow flowers are placed in a stag bladder, hung up in a tree for summer and then buried for winter. Yarrow is said to be connected to the potassium and sulphur processes of the soil and helps draw in substances, to revitalize over-cultivated and tired soil.

*Chamomile Preparation 503*: Chamomile flowers are placed in a cow's intestine and buried over winter. Chamomile is said to be connected with living calcium processes and helps to stabilise plant nutrients, reduce excessive fermentation and stimulate plant growth.

*Stinging Nettle Preparation 504*: Stinging nettles are buried in wooden boxes or clay pots encased in peat for one year.

Stinging nettle is said to have a relationship to iron, developing sensitivity in the soil, helping to stabilise nitrogen and promote the formation of humus.

*Oak Bark Preparation 505*: Oak bark is buried in a sheep skull in a damp place over winter. With its calcium rich nature, oak bark is said to help increase resistance to plant diseases and fungal attacks.

*Dandelion Preparation 506*: Dandelion flowers are placed in the mesentery organ of a cow and buried over winter. Dandelion is said to be connected with living silica processes, activating light influences in the soil, and encourages natural relationships to be more effective.

*Valerian Preparation 507*: A solution of fermented valerian flowers is diluted and stirred in a special method for 15 minutes. Half of the solution is poured into the heap and other half is sprayed over the whole compost heap. Valerian is said to have a strong affinity to the activity of phosphorous. It is thought that it acts like a protective layer over the compost heap.

*Horsetail Preparation 508*: This is made into a tincture by boiling in water. It is said to help reduce fungal diseases and is added to the heap by spraying and is also sprayed directly onto plants.

Obviously, these preparations take significant time, effort and resources to produce, which is why many biodynamic growers buy the preparations ready made from Biodynamic associations or groups. Understanding how Biodynamics works is no easy business but it can be employed by gardeners successfully even if one doesn't comprehend the principles behind it.

## The Compost Bin (Anaerobic)

The other main way of making compost, one that is employed a lot commercially, is airless or anaerobic composting. To make it yourself you require a large container that has no holes, except for a few drainage holes in the bottom and a lid. Some such bins have a removable section in the bottom for easy access, but are otherwise fairly well sealed.

It is also possible to make an anaerobic heap by covering it completely with a tarpaulin but this tends to be very smelly and will attract rodents, especially if there are mixed food scraps including meat or bones. Because of this problem, it is generally best to use a container, which means that it's possible to compost a greater variety of items. The anaerobic environment does not tend to get as hot as one exposed to the air but there is a buildup of acidity which kills off pathogens just as heat does, although this process takes longer than aerobic decomposition.

Practically speaking, it's best to have two bins, one that can be left closed for up to a year once it is full and the other one that is being filled up. If your bins have holes in the bottom, they can either be elevated (to collect the liquid leaching out) or placed on/into the ground. Holes will mean the compost is dryer and the collected liquid can be placed on the garden as a fertilizer. Otherwise, if on the ground, the liquid will just leach into the soil and once the acidity has dropped a bit, earthworms are likely to make their way into the bottom layer of the compost.

The simplest method is to use a big plastic bag (like a heavy-duty bin-liner) with a few holes in the bottom and tied tight at the top. Also, old paint buckets (cleaned) or chicken pellet 20 litre containers can be used if a couple of holes are drilled into the bottom. These are best completely filled to exclude as much air as possible and left in a sunny spot, as the heat of the sun will help speed up the rotting process.

Unlike aerobic piles, with the exception of a plastic bag, you can add meat, bones, fish and cooked food without worrying about pests getting into it. You can even add pet waste as well as farm animal waste, but it is important that you allow the full time for everything to break down safely.

Anaerobic composting is less work, even if it takes longer, and should not require turning like a conventional compost heap. Hydrogen sulphide and methane are produced as gas, which will eventually dissipate by the time the compost is ready, so if you do not take off the lid ahead of time you should not be bothered by nasty smells.

Some people like to spread the finished compost on the ground for a month to ensure excess moisture and acidity is gone, also adding worms to the compost is popular to create your own vermicompost.

There are advantages and disadvantages to both types of composting and it's really a matter of what best suits you, although many gardeners may do both. Experience teaches us what works best, but one should be especially careful about using any kinds of animal waste, particularly human unless you are highly experienced and competent at producing compost. Poorly decomposed compost, especially from potentially dangerous material, can be deadly if used to grow fruit and vegetables. Creating compost is a wonderful thing but it should never be undertaken at the expense of your own safety.

Using compost that you have made is rewarding, but it's not simply a case of lashing it on everything. Converse to what one might expect, massive amounts of nutrients can be counter-productive, especially when it comes to newly germinated and young plants as these tend to grow better in a lower nutrient environment. One should never plant seeds in pure compost, it's much more sensible to sow in soil with none or no more than 10% compost added, as excessive salts limit the ability of seedlings to draw up water and can cause stunting or death. With soft (herbaceous) plants especially it is important not to put raw compost close around them or directly on the roots as the intense nutrients can cause damage to the young tissue both above and below the ground.

As a general rule, with less juvenile plants it's a good idea not to add more compost than will constitute one third of the total volume, that is one-part compost to two parts soil. Some hungry plants such as rose bushes and fruit trees can tolerate more compost as they will quickly make use of the available resources, but generally speaking it is better to err on the side of caution with any kind of fertilizing.

## *Alternatives To Composting*

Composting is a wonderful way of recycling, being natural, environmentally friendly and a great benefit to your garden, especially if you are growing fruit and vegetables, which make heavy demands on the soil. Even with rotation of crops, the soil will eventually become depleted of nutrients if you continually grow and harvest food on the same area of land – this is why replacing the nutrients is so vital.

However, many people simply do not have the time or the room to make compost or store it, especially those living in a more urban environment with small or no gardens, such as apartments. This is no doubt a disadvantage when it comes to gardening but that does not mean it is impossible – one can grow a significant amount in containers using window sills, terraces or balconies. In situations such as this there are ready made products that you can buy and some that you can still make yourself, such as:

- Chicken manure pellets – these are dried in a large tub and can be stored long term.
- Blood, fish and bone – a dry powder made from a combination of organic sources in a large tub.
- Organic liquid feed – many are available including some from seaweed extract.

Another old trick that has been used for centuries is to place a dead fish or a dead chicken in the hole where you are planting a tree or bush. The hole needs to be a bit deeper than normal because of this, and the fish or chicken needs to be covered over a couple of inches (6cm) with some soil before the tree/bush is put in, so that the roots are not directly in contact with the carcass. Over time the carcass will rot down and the roots will descend to begin absorbing the nutrients as it decomposes. This rather strange technique is one I have tried myself and it proved very effective for a sickly yew tree that began to recover rapidly after a couple months in the ground. One can imagine the life energy of the bird or fish being absorbed by the plant as this is a direct transfer of the components of one being into another. To me this powerfully symbolizes the process that is taking place through decomposition and composting all over the planet at any given time.

Even if you don't have a lot of space it is possible to use solid feeds from a tub or make your own organic liquid feeds at home. Liquid feeds give a more immediate 'hit' of nutrients to plants and so have more rapid results but these results are more short-lived, which means it needs to be used more often than compost. As with adding compost, care should be taken, especially with young plants, as making the feed too strong or using it too often can be damaging or fatal – err on the side of caution always. It's also important to avoid pouring liquid feed onto the stems and leaves of plants, which can cause damage, make sure it goes onto the soil and not the plant itself. Homemade liquid fertilizer will not keep for very long so it is best made in small batches to last a week or so.

## Making Quick Liquid Feeds

It's possible to make a successful feed in one or two days; these are not as strong as longer brewed solutions but are certainly effective and easy to prepare. There are a great many possible recipes that work, but here are just a few ideas that you can try out. In general, less is more – it is better to give a weak solution regularly (e.g. weekly or every two weeks) to plants than to give a big dose of liquid feed every six months. Many people forget to feed plants and so give an 'extra bit' thinking that a stronger feed will make up for it; this can have the opposite effect. Little and often is much better than lots every now and then.

Vegetable scraps: You can fill up large jar from a blender or food mixer full of vegetable scraps once processed. You may also wish to add a level teaspoon of Epsom Salts for each batch. For each litre of pureed scraps you make you will need to add 5L of clean water. It's best to stir up the mixture or shake it for a while to help nutrients to dissolve, also using warm water helps the process. Allow the feed you've made to sit for 24 hours and give it a final stir before you water, applying it to the soil at the base of your plants. For smaller batches scale down the amount of puree made e.g. 200ml to 1L.

Stinging nettle feed: Nettles are great for human health but also a good source of nutrient (especially nitrogen) for the garden. If you have access to these then make sure they have not been sprayed with chemicals and are not next to a busy road. Be careful not to take the leaves and stems from just one plant unless you are intending to get rid of it altogether.

Using a few handfuls (best done with gloves) bruise the leaves and stems and place in 500ml (1/2L) of boiling water for 5 minutes before allowing it to steep for an hour to make a tea. Remove the pieces of nettle and add the tea to 2L of water to make up a 2.5L batch, in the ratio of 1:4 tea to water.

To make a better version you need a bucket that you can cover with a plate or some form of lid (especially if outdoors). Fill the bucket with bruised nettle stems and leaves and then fill the bucket with water almost to the top and cover. Leave this to stew for at least a week, although two weeks is generally enough, stirring the contents at least twice during the stewing. It's best to sieve the mixture at the end of the waiting period using a garden or even a kitchen sieve, into another bucket or container. As before this tea (which might be a bit smelly) needs to be diluted in the ratio 1:10.

Comfrey leaf feed: this plant is sometimes grown as a green manure to add directly into the soil, but it also makes a great addition to any compost heap or liquid fertilizer as it is rich in nitrogen (good for leaves) and potassium (good for flowers and fruit). You can follow the above method using just comfrey, or some prefer to use a half stinging nettle and half comfrey mixture.

Grass, weed & trimmings feed: Put a handful of cut grass, a handful of weeds (not in seed) and a handful of cut leaves etc. into a large bucket or 20L tub with clean water, cover it over with a plate or board and leave it to steep for up to four weeks. As this can become smelly, leave outside. Sieve or strain the mixture into a watering can and use directly on the garden.

Manure feed: Using just a shovel or spade full of dry rotted manure from livestock such as pigs, horses, chickens or cows you can make up a batch of liquid feed in a 20L container (half a shovel for a 10L can full). Stir the contents with a stick and leave the bucket/container outside somewhere as it will smell, cover with a plate/board to keep off the rain. After a week it's ready to put directly on the garden, straining through a sieve or cloth if you wish. You can scale this down as needed – e.g. one cup of manure to 5L of water.

The longer the mixture stands and the more ingredient you add, the stronger the liquid fertilizer is, which is why it is important to dilute any strong feeds before use – so not to damage your plants. It's better to overdo the diluting if in doubt, you can always make it a bit stronger next time.

## Biodynamic Liquid Feeds

There are two special preparations that are used for spraying on the ground and plants. Again, these involve use of animal parts – in both cases the horn of a female cow. As with other Biodynamic preparations, these can be bought ready to use from Biodynamic associations.

*Horn Manure Preparation 500*: A cow horn is filled with fresh cow dung and buried in the ground (tip facing up) for at least 4 months over the winter period. This is thought to harness the fertile energies of the Earth and encourage beneficial microbial activity. Only about 25g is added to at least 10L of water and this stirred using a special method (to create a vortex) for an hour. The resulting liquid is then sprayed directly onto the plants and ground up to four times a year, usually in spring and autumn and preferably in the evening.

*Horn Silica Preparation 501*: Again, this uses a cow horn but this time it is filled with crushed quartz (silicon dioxide), which can be crushed with a hammer and a strong mortar and pestle. As with preparation 500, a cow horn is filled up. This is thought to increase light sensitivity and encourage photosynthesis, general vigour and resistance to disease. A tiny amount of water is added to the powdered quartz to make it into a paste consistency before filling the horn and this is then buried in the ground for six months between spring and autumn. The preparation when ready is used in small amounts – adding just 1g for 10L of water, mixed in the same special vortex method for an hour. The solution should be used as soon as possible, sprayed directly onto plants, preferably early in the morning after dawn, twice a year - in spring and autumn.

## Blessings

Saying prayers, invocations and blessings may be dismissed by science as mumbo-jumbo and pointless but it has long been a practice of farmers in cultures all over the world. In the late

1800s Michael Carmichael collected such like from the Gaelic speaking people of northern and western Scotland. In Ireland similar prayers, mostly in English, persisted into the twentieth century and some people still say agricultural prayers or bless animals to this day.

Given that organic compost is made from living or once living materials it is not such a strange thing to do to make invocations or prayers, both when making it or when using it. This does not have to be complicated and can be done silently or out loud. Here are a few suggestions but equally you can write them yourself to suit your own feelings, hopes and intentions.

*May that which once lived bless and nurture that which now lives and is yet to live.*

*May this compost/feed be blessed by the goodness of the rain, of the sun, of the wind and of the earth, may it bring health and vitality to the sacred soil and all that grows in it.*

*As this soil absorbs the fruits of death and decay, let it bring new life and growth, with the blessings of the Mother Earth and Father Sky, (or specific gods e.g. Anu or Lugh).*

*Let the Earth be blessed by this compost/feed.*

There are literally hundreds of possibilities, but what is most important is the feeling and intention put into it as you make or use the compost. A sense of commitment is more important than whether you use simple or complex language, your own words or someone else's. Connecting with the land and the things that we grow is a sacred part of agriculture that has been largely forgotten in these times. It was always considered vital in the past and perhaps it is even more vital now, as humanity struggles to reassess its relationship with nature.

*"Upon this handful of soil our survival depends. Husband it and it will grow our food, our fuel and our shelter and surround us with beauty. Abuse it and the soil will collapse and die, taking humanity with it."*

Sanskrit Vedic Scripture, approx. 1500 BCE

## Chapter 5

# Planning the Garden

*"The best place to find God is in a garden. You can dig for him there."*
George Bernard Shaw

In my travels in various countries I've often been shocked by the lack of biodiversity – huge fields of monoculture crops, often with fence or wall borders and fields of just grass, kept in check by the hungry mouths of sheep, cattle and horses. Twice, in southern France and in Finland, I have seen vast forests that reach as far as the eye can see, but this (at least for me) was a rare and powerful experience.

Equally shocking has been the lack of biodiversity in people's gardens. I noticed this in my travels to cities around the world, particularly in America and urban areas of Britain. Also shocking is the same pattern that I have observed in rural Ireland – sometimes large gardens of half an acre or more that are monocultures of grass, just like a field, except it is the lawnmower rather than animals that keeps it short. Often these 'wasteland' gardens are bordered with fences and walls instead of hedges, probably because they are easier to maintain.

Of course, I am making a huge generalization; there are plenty of people who enjoy gardening and have wonderful and bio-diverse gardens. However, I see the huge number of empty gardens as a terrible missed opportunity. A garden does not need to be a massive amount of work, in fact the less manicured and the more naturalistic it is the lower the amount of work is needed.

Having a real garden is aesthetically pleasing, it stimulates the senses and can be a very spiritually rewarding place, both in the creation and maintenance of it, as well as just being present in it. Apart from being a space to enjoy or to use for spiritual purposes, creating a garden that contains life is one of the best things any person can do to help our beleaguered environment.

The continual stripping away of wild spaces and biodiversity to make way for farming monoculture crops, grazing land and for housing developments has radically changed the landscape wherever it happens. In Europe alone there has been a devastating loss of insect and bird populations, which in turn affects larger mammals, that depend on these as food or as pollinators of plants.

As individuals there are limited options about what we can do to prevent farmland being 'improved', which often means just creating more production, or preventing new housing developments from happening. Social and political activism can and does have a positive effect in these areas, although this can take a long time and is not always directly evident. What individuals can do, with immediate and direct effects, is to transform a patch of land that is bereft of life (apart from common grasses) into a paradise for wildlife that is enjoyable and beneficial for humans too.

As with many aspects of life, a little bit of planning is helpful before beginning work. Understanding the conditions in your garden can save lots of wasted effort and time and help prevent heartbreaking failures that are totally avoidable. In an ideal world we would all have a perfect sized garden for our needs, facing south on a very gentle slope, full of fertile and free-draining soil. The reality of what we have to work with may be quite different and one has to take into account how things actually are before we think about how one would like it to be, and this process begins with observation.

## Orientation

If you have a compass or even a modern mobile phone with a compass app. then you can easily find out which way your garden is oriented. This first step is important as it will give you some indication of how much light your garden will get and where. It's generally accepted that the sun rises in the east and sets in the west but this is actually only strictly true around the time of the spring (vernal) and autumn (fall) equinoxes (at the latitude of Britain and Ireland). The position of sunrises and sunsets changes throughout the year - with slowest changes at the solstices and fastest changes around the equinoxes. For the northern hemisphere, in mid-winter at the solstice it's southeast rise to southwest set, which gives a very short day, with the sun's midday height at its lowest in the sky. In mid-summer at the solstice, it is northeast rise to northwest set, which gives a very long day, with the sun's midday height at its highest in the sky. Where your garden is, relative to the cardinal directions, and to the position of your house, will make a huge difference to the amount of light that your garden receives.

Given that light is the primary factor that affects the level of growth of plants, understanding the orientation of your garden makes a big difference to what you can plant in your garden. This is especially evident in more northern or southern countries such as Finland or Chile, where the extremes of the seasons are far more pronounced than in countries close to, or within the tropics. If your garden is facing south that is ideal, however if all or most of your garden is behind a two or three storey house then you might experience a lot of shadow, except in summer. If your garden is on the north side of a hill then you are in the worst possible position for light, which is a reason why agricultural land in such positions is usually cheapest.

If you are lucky enough to have a garden that is well lit for all or most of the year then you have far more flexibility with plants than if you have a dark garden. Obviously, other factors will have an effect on light, such as surrounding trees, buildings and local topography. If you know that your garden is dark or has dark areas then you can adjust your planting scheme accordingly. Understanding the light in your garden can save you time, effort and money when choosing what to plant and where to plant it – for instance it is pointless to try to grow fruiting cherry trees or sunflowers in a dingy spot.

## Location
Knowing where your garden lies in the local topography is also important. Of course, the biggest factor is your geographical location on the planet and the local climate – the intensity of sun and rain being crucially affected by this. Even within the same country there can be different climatic zones and micro-climates. However, more local considerations also can have a considerable effect. If you live less than a kilometre from the coast, without some kind of a barrier between (e.g. woodlands) then this will likely restrict what you can grow, due to salty winds. If you live

at high altitude it is likely to be colder and windier, which again may affect what you can grow successfully. If you are located at the bottom of a valley, you might be prone to shade and possibly water-logging and even flooding, which again has a restrictive effect. All of these different conditions, or combinations of them, will have some bearing on what you can expect to grow successfully in your garden.

## Soil

As discussed earlier, there are many different soil conditions, which will favour certain types of plants and not others. If your soil is extremely high in sand or clay, lacking in depth or badly degraded then you will be restricted in what you can grow. If this is the case then be prepared to either extensively modify the soil or look at growing plants in raised beds and containers. Knowing if your soil is alkaline or acid will also affect what you can grow. Neutral soil, or fairly close to it, is ideal but not always available. High levels of acidity or alkalinity are difficult to change over a large area, but can be achieved in a small area or in raised beds/containers if you are not satisfied with only acid loving/alkali loving plants. Again, with extensively depleted or damaged soil you might be forced to consider raised beds or containers if large-scale regeneration is either too difficult or too expensive.

## Water

The availability of water makes a crucial difference to your garden. If you have sandy soil on a slope, in an area with low rainfall you may find yourself having to do a lot of watering. Water butts connected to rain gutters can be very useful and help reduce the amount of water needed from the domestic system or a domestic well, also rainwater does not contain chlorine and fluorine found in domestic water of some countries. If you have access to a stream or river on your land that may be helpful, although if you have low-lying boggy ground this may be the last thing that you want.

## Space

What you can do with your garden is very much determined by how much physical space you have. One of the common problems of gardeners is overplanting – the tendency to plant too much, putting plants too close together and sowing plants that will become too big for the space they are in. Overcrowding can have a serious effect on the growth of plants and where trees and bushes become too large it can severely restrict or even kill off plants around them.

When picking what and where to plant it's important to consider what space you have, how fast and large plants may grow and make choices appropriately. For instance: if you have only a balcony it is going to prove impractical to grow a large oak tree but that doesn't mean you cannot grow any trees – there are dwarf trees (such as Mugo Pine) and Bonsai to consider.

## A Druidic Garden?

Once you have a good understanding about the space you intend to use then you can begin to plan what you will do with it. If one is intending to follow the example of the Druids, then knowing what the Druids actually did would be a helpful place to start.

We know that the Druids worked in nature, venerated and had knowledge of the trees and of the medicinal and spiritual usage of plants; this has been confirmed by Greek and Roman writers in their commentary on the Gauls in particular. Unfortunately, if there were any texts written about the horticultural knowledge of the ancient Gauls, Britons, Iberians or Irish, they have not survived. What has survived of any use comes mainly from Ireland, from Brehon Law, which continued in use well after the Pagan era and long after the Norman conquest. Brehon Law describes the four categories of trees, which were of immense practical and economic value to the native Irish and also gives punishments for unlawful damage to them.

Mythology also gives clues about the uses of herbs and other plants for healing and magic, the importance of livestock (cows mostly) but with very little detail that would be of specific use to modern gardeners. Most of the lore relating to plants has been carried down generations by oral tradition and some of this undoubtedly survived in Celtic societies such as those found in Ireland, Scotland, Wales, Brittany, the Basque region of Spain and a few parts of other European countries.

It is known that gardening was happening in many urban civilizations that were concurrent with the Druids, but the Celts had a semi-nomadic civilization and may not have had any concept of keeping a garden in the way that we now understand it. Archaeology yields the bulk of the information about what the Celts did in terms of agriculture – they certainly grew food and kept animals but there is little evidence to suggest that gardens were kept. In most of Europe the Celts were eliminated or absorbed by the Roman empire and it is their ways, not the ways of the Celts, that are best preserved by historical records. Likewise, in Ireland there is almost nothing recorded about how people farmed until after the Norman invasion, although there are a few mentions of food produced in poetry and in law texts:

'We reached a fort wonderful
With ramparts all custardy
On the lake's far shore;
Fresh butter, steps' construction,
The stone rampart wheaten-white,
Palisade of pork.
Pillars of cheese barnyard
And broad beams all bacony
Alternately spread;
Jolly joists of heavy cream

Bright rafters of cottage-cheese:
They support the house.'
From *Aislinge Meic Con Glinne*, Gaelic c. 1100 CE

'...a calf valued at a sack of wheat for summer roasting... a
cauldron of new milk for cooking as sweet cheese with butter,
a vessel of ripe cream, 20 loaves of bread... two fistfuls of
Welsh onions and two leeks as summer render, a bacon flitch
36 inches long...'
Extract of payments to a Lord from *Críth Gablach*, early Irish
law text.

This certainly gives an idea of what the ancient Irish ate, but tells
us little about their fields, animal enclosures or how they grew
food. Certainly, cattle were of vital importance in ancient Celtic
countries, particularly Ireland. Much of the clearing of trees
in Ireland began around 5000 years ago with the introduction
of cows, sheep and goats. This was to create pasture land for
large herbivores to graze on, which gradually transformed the
landscape. Even so, it was not until the Elizabethan period that the
vast forests that had characterized Ireland disappeared rapidly,
leading to the largely denuded landscape that is evident today.
Cattle had a huge social significance, being indicative of wealth
as well as providing meat and a whole host of dairy products.

Dairy was one of, if not the most important foodstuffs in
ancient Ireland – there were a large number of types of milk,
curds, cheese, buttermilk and butter, even bog butter which was
stored in the anaerobic conditions of a bog. Early Irish cuisine
revolved around 'white foods' or *banbidh*, although people also
ate grains. Oats and barley were the main grains, although wheat
was also grown but in smaller quantities due to the difficult
climate. Wheat bread was a luxury so bread was more often
made on stones or a griddle (as there were no ovens) from oats
or barley.

Wealthy people with livestock would have been able to eat meat regularly – mostly pork, as cows were too valuable to eat often. The less wealthy would have to rely on occasional hunting or fishing if near to the sea. Some vegetables were grown such as cabbages, leeks, carrots, onions, turnips and garlic but it has been suggested that this was not common before the 8th century CE. Prior to this people would have relied on foraging for wild leaves, roots, berries, fungi and seaweed (near the coast). Fruits and nuts were not generally cultivated before about 1500 CE, apart from the apple tree, although blackberries, rowan berries and especially hazelnuts were popular.

Ancient Celtic communities generally lived within ringforts of varying sizes, remains of which can still be found extensively across Ireland as well of parts of Britain and western mainland Europe. There were usually earthen banks or circular stone enclosures, sometimes with wooden palisades. Legal texts from Ireland indicate people lived in round thatched houses surrounded by a *les* (enclosure) within which were often outbuildings for their livestock such as pigs, cattle, hens and sheep, a manure storage area and rarely areas for growing food - one account mentions four raised beds, or a few fruit trees. Fields would have surrounded the enclosure, in strips like petals on a daisy, and in some cases a series of circular walls or mounds protected the fields outside of the main fort – an interesting example of which can be found just outside Tullow, county Carlow, in Ireland. A fascinating insight into Celtic agriculture can be found in Fergus Kelly's *Early Irish Farming*, for those with a desire to explore this area further.

In mainland Europe and Britain dramatic changes in agriculture and food were instigated by the Roman colonization. Likewise, the Norman invasion of Ireland had a dramatic effect on food and agriculture in the areas that they controlled. Chickens arrived before the Normans but the Normans introduced rabbits to Ireland, new breeds of sheep, fallow deer and inadvertently, the black rat and house mouse. The Normans also brought wine, previously unknown plants and herbs as well as more modern farming methods and the detested feudal system. The Norman system, which is itself a descendant of Roman farming, was based on the Manor and was well organized, with many surviving records that inform us of what they produced.

Over centuries more plants and trees, as well as animals, were introduced for the wealthy by aggressive colonization, as the Celtic way of life became eroded. The arrival of the potato dramatically changed native Irish eating habits as they became increasingly impoverished, ultimately leading to the tragedy of the mid-19th century famine.

## Making A Plan

Most of what we know about gardening and farming in western Europe relates to Roman and renaissance influence, the ancestor of the practices that are most common today. Due to the lack of information about what the Celtic peoples of western Europe did in relation to farming it is very difficult to recreate a Druidic garden in any literal sense.

Given this difficulty one can only truly create a Druidic garden in the spirit of Druidry/Druidism rather than a literal garden that emulates the practices of the ancient Druids. This same problem applies to the creation of Druidic ritual and ceremonies as no precise details survive about the exact content and style of Druidic practice. Even so, just as modern Druidic rituals honour the spirit of Druidry and reference as much of Celtic survivals as possible, the same can be applied to creating a Druidic garden.

Many of the techniques used by the ancient Celts and much of their knowledge has been retained through the writings of scribes in medieval times and through oral transmission in folklore and traditional knowledge. The Druids lived in a time when organic gardening was the only option as there were no artificial fertilizers or pesticides. Biodiversity was much greater than it is now, despite the fact that huge numbers of non-native species are now readily available – the huge areas of monocultures we see today simply didn't exist. This meant that despite deliberate clearing and planting, far more mixed species of plant were likely to coexist within the landscape, both in the wild and in human communities.

A Druidic garden should aim to reflect the biodiversity of the wilderness, which in doing so can provide a home not just to a wide variety of plants but also birds, insects and other animals as a direct result. Features such as walls or fences can be made from all-natural materials – utilizing the ancient technique of dry-stone walling or fences constructed from willow or hazel branches (which can also be bought). Depending on the size of land available, the garden can be divided into specific areas – such as an orchard, ornamental plants, fruit bushes, vegetable garden, woodland, rockery, pond, poultry coop, beehives, wild meadow, human-free wilderness. Alternatively, for the ambitious, you may wish to integrate the many specific areas by creating a Permaculture garden, although this does require acquiring specific knowledge in that area. If you have a substantial plot of land you may be able to incorporate all of the different areas I described or a large proportion of them. Even if your garden is small you can pick areas that most appeal to you and which will be of most benefit to the natural environment – even a tiny woodland or meadow can be of significant benefit to wildlife.

## *Woodland*

Trees were of great practical and spiritual significance to the ancient Celts and particularly for Druids. Even if you have a fairly small garden it is possible to create a mini woodland. In a smaller garden you should select smaller trees such as hawthorn, hazel, blackthorn, rowan or trees grown on restricting rootstocks – such as many fruit trees. Even with smaller trees one should be careful where they are sited as they will create shade as they grow larger and also their roots will spread out. In a larger garden you have more options but again one must consider the typical height and spread and extent of the root system – something that can easily be overlooked. Poor planning can lead to overcrowding, too much shade on your house or garden and undermining of foundations by vigorous roots (e.g. willows). Another thing to consider is the use of native trees – for instance in Europe oaks may support hundreds of species but non-native trees such as sycamore support relatively few species. Trees will be discussed in detail in a subsequent chapter.

## *Orchard/fruit bushes/vegetable garden*

One of the best ways of connecting to and gaining an appreciation of nature is to grow your own food. As a general rule, one should locate all of these in the sunniest part of your garden as sunlight is the engine that fuels growth. Ideally this would be south facing. If there is plenty of room these areas could be completely separate if preferred. If space is limited you should create an area facing towards maximum sunlight with the highest growing plants (trees) at the back, fruit bushes in front of these and vegetable beds/raised beds at the very front. Herbs would also be grown here but they might equally be grown in containers close to the house, in a sunny spot. There are many techniques for growing food, much of which will be discussed later.

## *Rockery*

Apart from being an attractive feature, alpines, succulents (depending on climate) and some herbs will tend to do well in a free draining environment such as this. This can be an interesting way of creating a well-drained area for plants in an otherwise damp or boggy garden and is quite easy to achieve with just large stones, sand, soil and suitable plants.

## *Ponds*

With climate change frogs, toads and newts have become increasingly endangered, exacerbating threats to their existence from loss of habitat. Creating a pond can be a vital life support for amphibians and insects as well as a home for aquatic plants. Plastic liner or concrete is the most common way of sealing a pond but neither are environmentally friendly. This can be achieved without either by using a mechanical whacker to compress the soil or by making a layer of heavy clay, it's more work but more natural. Also, it's not necessary to have electrical pumps and filters to keep the water oxygenated. If you really want to go down that route then consider solar powered aerators or fountain pumps instead of running electricity to the pond. Natural ponds don't need these, so neither does your pond – oxygenating plants will do the job and a layer of stones in the pond will provide a home to beneficial bacteria. Marginal water plants, that grow in the shallow edge of the pond, will also help reduce excess nutrients that would otherwise encourage algae growth. A reasonable amount of shade (near to 50%) will restrict algal growth, water lilies are especially useful in this respect.

## *Wild Meadow*

Most people have a large area of their gardens dedicated to lawns – this is very much a feature of modern times, inherited from when renaissance gardens of the wealthy had them. Irish legal texts do mention a *faithche (green)* outside the *rath* or enclose, on the land of kings and wealthy lords. This was an area set aside for ball games, horse-racing and gatherings and may also have featured a sacred tree (*bile*) or several of them. It would appear that the ancient green was for practical rather than aesthetic purposes. Apart from being somewhere to sit or play they are today of little practical use and are often a monoculture wasteland as far as nature is concerned. This is certainly the case with maniacally kept lawns which are dosed with herbicides and fertilizers to eliminate weeds and moss while keeping the grass lush green. Perfect lawns also need frequent cutting and as a result need feeding in order to replenish the soil that becomes depleted from obsessive mowing. The modern lawn is pretty much the epitome of unnatural gardening – it needs constant maintenance and interference to stay looking perfect. The wild meadow is the antithesis of the lawn – what happens when you let nature take over. The grass or grasses will grow tall and set seed, weeds and wild flowers will take off although you might need to sow some wild flowers initially. The chaos of unbridled nature can be joy to behold and will be a haven for bees, butterflies and other insects as well as small mammals such as mice and hedgehogs. You don't have to get rid of your whole lawn – you could still maintain a small area for sitting out or for ball games etc. as well as allowing a meadow to thrive. If you are prepared to accept some weeds and don't cut your lawn excessively tight or often then keeping a lawn does not have to be tiresome. Meadows are something I remember seeing much more often as a child – obsession with order in fields and along roadsides has meant they are a relatively uncommon sight and as a result many wild flowers are endangered or becoming extinct. Creating space for even a small meadow is one of the best things a gardener can do to increase biodiversity.

## Poultry

It's possible to keep chickens, ducks, geese, pheasants etc. in a very small space, but to do so goes very much against the ethos of modern Druidry and environmentalism. While they don't need much space in terms of a coup, shed or hut they do need space in which to wander if they are to have a decent life. Most people in 'first-world' countries are completely alienated from the raising, keeping and slaughter of animals for food and many are completely ignorant of the horrors of industrial farming that condemn chickens and many other animals to a miserable and short existence. Keeping birds for eggs and/or meat is a good way to reconnect with this age-old partnership. While they have little choice in the matter, keeping poultry should be respectful of the fact that they are living, conscious beings that should have a right to a decent life, free from suffering. Done well it should reconnect us with the cycle of life and death – everything we eat must die, be it plants or animals but this fact is easily forgotten when everything comes packaged in supermarkets.

If you have sufficient space it is nice to let them roam free during the day when they are far less likely to be attacked by foxes etc. Although they are not discerning and will eat whatever plants are convenient, they also help out by eating insects and molluscs (slugs and snails). If you have only room for a small enclosure it will become rapidly denuded and they will rely on humans to keep them fed. In addition to a mixture of grains they will happily eat cut grass, weeds, slugs, vegetable peelings which might otherwise end up in the compost heap. Poultry tend not to lay all year round unless given 'layers pellets', which encourage unnatural over-production of eggs. An organic diet is better for the birds as well as better for you if you intend to eat them or their eggs, or indeed if you wish to use their dung as fertilizer.

## Beehives

Pollinating insects, bees especially, are under threat, which in turn threatens the future of much of life on this planet. Some plants, such as grasses, are pollinated by the wind but the vast majority of plant species rely on bees (primarily) and other insects to do the job that ensures that there will be future, genetically diverse generations of plants. If bees suddenly disappeared from the world then it would be an ecological disaster of unprecedented proportions creating a vast loss of plant species and a subsequent vast famine across animal species, including humans.

Bees were clearly of economic importance to the Celts, as honey was the primary sweetener before sugar became in common use and it was also used to make the alcoholic drink mead, which had a higher value than beer in ancient times. In Ireland there was a special Brehon law legal text devoted to the subject of beekeeping, *Bechbretha* (bee law), known to date at least as early as the seventh century CE. Although they may not have fully realized the huge importance of bees in the greater environment, the Celts greatly valued them.

One really cannot emphasize enough how important bees are to the land life of this planet and so I cannot encourage you enough to help them out. Avoiding or completely refraining from using toxic weed-killers and insecticides is a first step to assisting them; growing flowering plants is a second, but keeping bees is the third and best step in aiding their recovery. Modern industrial beekeeping is at best of no benefit to the bees, it's just a means of making honey as cheaply as possible. However, natural beekeeping is becoming increasingly popular – one can make a beehive in many ways out of wood, including a hollowed-out log. Both horizontal and vertical top-bar designs exist that are easy to make. The Warré hive (French design from early 20th century) is a design that mimics the bees' natural tendency to create a vertical nest and is becoming increasingly popular. Bees have managed fine without our help for some 10 million years, only being 'kept' in the last few thousand years and in the last century kept in increasingly detrimental ways. Bees don't need artificial organization (foundation), they do much better if they are left to build and organize their combs themselves. Provided with a suitable space they don't really need human interference and there is plenty of evidence to suggest that regular inspection and intervention is damaging to their colonies. The main objective of a natural approach to bees should not be the obtaining of honey. In fact, the best thing to do is not to take any honey from them at all – after all they create it for their own sustenance, not ours. By depriving bees of their honey, it forces them to work harder and endangers them if they are left with insufficient honey to provide for the hive in cold weather or other times of scarcity.

## *Boundaries*

The Celts used natural materials for walls and fences, they didn't really have any other options. However much of their ancient methods can still be seen today, particularly in Ireland and Wales. They constructed four main types of boundaries – ditches and mounds, stone walls and two types of fencing. Irish legal texts describe these boundaries and certainly the ditch and the dry-stone wall can still be found all over the country (in modern farms) as well as the remains of ancient boundaries. The basic mound and ditch (often just referred to as a ditch) consists of excavating soil to build up a long mound in front of it, which was and is still often planted with bushes or small trees such as hawthorn, gorse and blackthorn which provide a natural barrier. These ditches can also be left bare or be topped with a stone wall or fencing.

Stone walls that don't make use of cement often slope inwards slightly, and are constructed so as to remain stable solely by placement of the stones, a skill that can still be learned today through classes or online. Ancient fencing is not so different from the modern variety, the common height was about 4 feet above ground as now. The main difference with these ancient fences is that they were constructed with interwoven branches between posts (often willow or hazel). In some cases, the top of the fence would be interwoven with light hawthorn or blackthorn branches, a form of natural defence akin to barbed wire. Natural fences are making a comeback and it is possible to buy them readymade as well as constructing them yourself.

## *Wilderness*

As humans become increasingly numerous across the world the number of wild spaces is rapidly declining, particularly in places that are fairly hospitable to us. Most farming practices are degenerative, they do not help the land or the environment in any way and do not encourage biodiversity. Systems such as Biodynamics aim to be regenerative and it is common for a portion of land (e.g. 10%) to be set aside as unfarmed land where nature can just do its own thing. If you have a portion of land that is empty it might need some help to get started by sowing pioneer trees such as birch, transplanting a few rare specimens or scattering some wild flowers seeds, but even without our help a barren patch of ground will eventually become home to plants and animals. It has become hard for modern man to leave nature alone to be itself – this mania for controlling the environment has become a collective compulsion, a form of madness. Wild areas are very important to biodiversity so creating even a small one can really help.

One should also be very careful when visiting truly wild areas to do no harm. I've dug up some wild plants such as three wild garlic plants that prospered and multiplied in my own wild area. Personally, I am very much against wild foraging unless there is a huge abundance of a particular plant. This activity has become quite popular in recent years but risks depleting already stressed and threatened wild plants. One should never take entire plants (except to transplant), one should take leaves or stems from multiple plants rather than denuding a single plant. If there are only one or a few of a particular plant then leave it alone – damaging what few specimens there are in an area could lead to them disappearing completely. A Druid colleague of mine explained her rule of never harvesting more than a third – a third for myself, a third for the animals and a third for the earth. This makes a lot of sense, but better still is to leave the wilderness alone and try to grow desirable wild plants in your own garden instead.

## *Sacred Space*

A sacred space within the garden is desirable to many spiritual paths, for instance Taoism, Zen Buddhism, some forms of Christianity as well as Druidry. From a Druidic point of view, one might wish to create such a space within a wilderness area or within a woodland, although ultimately one should choose a space that instinctively feels right. This space might be completely empty, it could include a special tree, a standing stone or even a stone circle. Creating a stone circle can be simple enough if the stones are not gigantic, using a stick and a rope for spacing. Aligning stones to the four directions is relatively easy, using a compass, but aligning to say the summer solstice sunrise is a matter of observation at the right time and will be specific to whatever your location is. There's no reason why a sacred space might not be multi religious e.g. Buddhist & Druidic if that suits your own intentions. What is advisable is to try to commune with the spirit of the land and any entities that might live on it (e.g. sídhe/fairies) to gain permission for this.

## Before You Start - Blessings

A common practice among humans all over the world, regardless of their religion/spirituality is to pray for success or ask for blessings upon their chosen activity. Apart from being a pleasant beginning, a ritual, or even a simple prayer, is an acknowledgement that we are part of a larger world that is not entirely controlled by us and recognizes a connectivity between humanity and the divine and (hopefully) our dependency on the world of nature that surrounds us and which we are also part of.

Once you have a plan for how you will go about creating your garden it is a good idea to invoke the permission and support of whatever you perceive to be spiritually important. Going about this task will vary greatly from person to person and should reflect your own beliefs and preferences. One might ask permission of what the Romans called *genii locorum*, spirits of place, the ancestors of the place and your own family, specific gods and goddesses or something vaguer and more ethereal altogether. There is no rule about how this is done so long as it is heart-felt, meaningful to you and respectful of the land on which you will begin work. Some people may also feel it is appropriate to make an offering to the land, usually symbolic, as part of this process. Remain open to feedback from the land and spirit realms, a negative response is unlikely given a genuine intention to create and support a refuge for nature. However, it is possible to make mistakes even with the best of intentions and so one should be mindful of any omens or supernatural communications about your project. Below are a few simple examples of prayers and blessings, but I believe that is best to write your own, specific to your own circumstances if possible.

*I/we ask the blessings of the goddess of the land, Danu, upon this garden and all that grows it in it, may it be a place of joy and life and the bounty of nature.*

*May this garden be blessed by the four elements – by the waters of the rain that falls upon it, by the fire of the sun that shines upon it bringing new growth, by the gentle wind that carries the air, the pollen and the seeds of new life, and by the nurturing soil of the earth itself. May the elements be in balance in this garden bringing abundance to all that lives here.*

*We pray for the guidance and inspiration of the spirits of place, of the ancestors and the sídhe, that this garden become a refuge of nature and all that is for the highest good.*

## Chapter 6

# Plants as Living Beings

*"Green is the prime color of the world, and that from which its loveliness arises. For in the true nature of things, if we rightly consider, every green tree is far more glorious than if it were made of gold and silver. It seems very safe to me to be surrounded by green growing things and water."*
Pedro Calderón de la Barca (1600 – 1681)

Before doing anything in the garden it is a good idea to have some understanding about plants – what they are and how they work, otherwise it is a lot more difficult to nurture them and sustain a positive environment for them to prosper in. After all, only a fool would think to become a medical surgeon without first studying medicine. It's not necessary to become a botanical expert, but gaining a basic understanding is helpful both in practical and spiritual terms, when interacting with the world of plants.

Many people regard plants as little more than objects and not truly alive in the sense that humans and other animals are alive. While it's true that plants do not have or need a brain that does not mean that they have no awareness or no ability to receive sensations, or to communicate; in fact, scientific research demonstrates the opposite.

Plants are not simply a mass of vegetative flesh; they have been shown to have an awareness of when they are being eaten (e.g. by caterpillars) and will produce a chemical response to try and protect themselves and also to communicate danger to surrounding plants. A low-level noise is emitted with the release of gas; plants nearby can sense the sound waves when a plant is injured or sick and respond to a perceived threat. Plants are also able to move – they are heliocentric and gravitate towards the sun. They are also able to sense objects around them, which many climbing plants put to good use to grab supports, or obstacles can be avoided. Time lapse photography clearly shows the ability of plants to move of their own volition. Injection of carbon isotopes into trees enabled scientists to trace communication through the root system with surrounding trees – within days the isotope could be detected in all the trees within a 15m radius of the injected tree. Trees are able to communicate through their root systems and even pass nutrients to weaker or younger trees, in order to help them mature.

Pioneering works such as *The Secret Life Of Plants* (by Tompkins and Bird), although still controversial among botanists, has done much to change our understanding of plant biology and in recent times the new field of 'plant neurobiology' has taken a deeper look at how plants function, attempting to understand what their bio-chemical and bio-electrical signaling does. Plants are able to sense light, water, gravity, pressure, temperature, soil structure, nutrients, toxins, objects, microbes, animals as well chemical signals from other plants although they do not possess a brain. Plants may not be able to experience pain or emotions in any human sense but they appear to possess a rudimentary intelligence and consciousness – they are aware of themselves and their surroundings.

Plants produce a vast array of chemicals that have proven to be highly useful in many areas of human life - medicine in particular is based primarily on plant extracts and even today new and useful naturally occurring chemicals are being discovered in plants from the world's rainforests. Plants are able to perform very simple and limited examples of short-term memory – carnivorous plants like the Venus Flytrap, not wanting to waste precious energy in rapid movement, sense insect movement but can wait up to twenty seconds for another trigger to be sure that a significant sized insect has landed. Equally intriguing is the apparent ability of a moving fern (Mimosa pudica) that folds its leaves when touched, to learn when to ignore non-dangerous encounters. In an experiment plants dropped a short distance of 15cm initially reacted by closing their leaves but after four or more drops had 'learned' that the stimulus was not dangerous and stopped responding. Repeated tests, a week later, showed that the plants remembered what they had learned and it took a whole month before the plants 'forgot' their learned non-reaction.

The spiritually minded and esoteric savants have long believed plants to possess physical and spiritual properties that contradict their rather simple and static appearance – qualities that scientific researchers are increasingly exploring as areas worth investigation. As a bare minimum we should respect plants as living entities that have consciousness and awareness, a body, albeit very different from humans and animals, the ability to feel, communicate, move, procreate and even kill.

## Some Basic Plant Anatomy

It is not absolutely necessary to understand plant anatomy but it certainly helps one to understand how plants work and how best to look after them. Unlike animals, the parts of a plant do not immediately correspond to human body parts. As we tend to anthropomorphize the world around us maybe this explains a common lesser affinity and less close relationship with plants. We are unable to communicate with plants, except perhaps on a spiritual/psychic level, or at least it appears that way to us, plus they do not have similar anatomy.

Despite that, we can visualize certain parts of the plant as equivalent to parts of our own body in function, which may

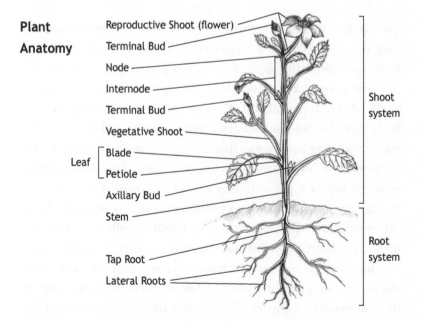

**Plant Anatomy**

Reproductive Shoot (flower)
Terminal Bud
Node
Internode
Terminal Bud
Vegetative Shoot
Leaf — Blade
Leaf — Petiole
Axillary Bud
Stem
Tap Root
Lateral Roots

Shoot system

Root system

also be helpful in relating to them as living creatures. The first major difference between plants and animals is that plants are generally fixed to the ground, there are a few exceptions such as orchids and mistletoe, but this is usually the case. Plants have more parts than one might expect, some of which have similar functions to our own body parts.

## Roots

The root system is all the parts of a plant below the ground and, apart from the absence of leaves, has a very similar shape to most structures above ground. The root system anchors the plant and absorbs both water and nutrients. Roots support a plant's parts above ground and also play an important role in the senses of the plant and in communication between one plant and another. We might visualize roots as equivalent to our feet, which connect us to the ground, support the rest of our body and are actually quite sensitive if not covered with socks and shoes.

## Stem

The stem of the plant is the strongest 'limb' of a plant and may vary enormously from a grass stem to a tree trunk, although the basic function is the same. The stem supports the above ground or aerial parts of a plant and from it shoots the main bud, known as a leader or terminal bud. The stem also supports the auxiliary buds that become secondary stems, leaves and flowers. We might visualize the stem as like the human torso or trunk, which supports our head, arms and major organs. The terminal bud is at the top of a plant, like our head although it is in no way similar, its sole function is to continue growing upwards – if cut off, new buds will replace it, but it will usually result in less upward growth and a bushier appearance (except in grasses).

The secondary stems of a plant can be likened to arms, and the leaves that grow on them like hands. As with our own limbs, they do much of the work of day to day life – in the case of plants it is for collecting food, but in some cases (e.g. ivy) stems can grab hold of or grow around other objects.

## Leaves

Both leaves and stems can have green colour due to chlorophyll, which has a very special function, unique to plants, and they also can contain stomata, which are basically tiny holes that are involved in gas exchange (breathing) and release of water. Stems also have stomata but it is primarily the leaves that do this job. Leaves have a miraculous capacity to 'eat light', turning light energy from the sun into storable energy that, combined with nutrients from soil, enables plants to survive and grow. No other organisms on the planet have the capacity to do this and plants in the sea (especially phytoplankton) and on land are the basis of all life on earth because they produce oxygen that we and other animals need and are also a vital source of food. Without the miracle of photosynthesis (making food from light) the seas would be empty, as would be the land. Leaves act as the world's lungs, creating the oxygen we need, as well as collecting the solar 'food' that plants need to thrive.

## Flowers

All plants need to reproduce and flowers are basically the sexual organs of plants, even grasses that might appear not to have them, do produce tiny flowers. Just like animals, plants can have male and female sexes but they are in many cases also capable of being both sexes at the same time. Bisexual flowers produce functional male and female sexual parts – the stamen that produces pollen equivalent to 'sperm' and an ovary (entered by the stigma) that contains one or more ovules in which a female 'egg' is found. The situation can also be that plants are monoecious – meaning that it produces individual flowers that are either male or female, on the same plant. In this case the corresponding opposite sexual gender parts on a flower are missing or non-functional, good examples are Birch and Alder trees. Plants can also be dioecious, meaning that individual trees produce flowers of only one sex, much like humans and other animals that have one set of sexual organs (usually). A good example of this is the Holly tree, both produce flowers but the male tree produces pollen and the female tree ovules to receive them; only the female trees produce fruit (berries).

In the vast majority of plants sexual intercourse occurs with the assistance of insects, primarily bees. In order to encourage this, flowers produce scent and nectar which is sugary and attracts insects to enter the flower petals and make contact with the stamen and/or stigma. It's through the physical activity of insects that sticky pollen is transferred on the insect's body (via the plant's stigma) to the ovary and pollination or fertilization then takes place.

Wind pollination is the sexual method found in most grasses and their flowers have somewhat different characteristics as a result. The flowers are smaller and often green or brown, have no nectar or scent, the pollen isn't sticky and is smaller and lighter. This type of pollen is produced in great quantities as luck is very much a factor in fertilization, this is a major factor in human 'hay fever' or pollen allergy. The stigma is outside the

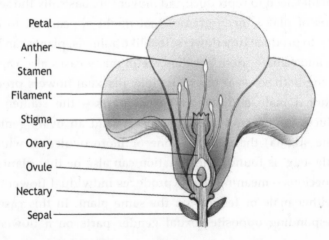

Petal
Anther
Stamen
Filament
Stigma
Ovary
Ovule
Nectary
Sepal

flower in this instance instead of inside the petals and there are usually many of them in an arrangement so that passing grains of pollen can be captured from the air.

So, we can see that plants have sex, just like animals and humans do, although the sexual organs are not a permanent fixture and there are more variations in how these sexual organs occur. Because plants are rooted and not able to physically move to have sexual intercourse they rely on either insects or the wind to help them do this, nonetheless, they have sex to reproduce. We can visualize flowers as sexual organs because that is exactly what they are and they exist solely for this purpose.

## Fruit and Seeds

Seeds are in fact the children created through plant sexual intercourse; although this is a rather obvious fact it is easy to avoid seeing the simple truth of this statement. In truth the seed is more than that, it is equivalent to an external womb containing the dormant child. We know that planting a seed should lead to a new plant but we can often fail to regard the seed as the unborn child of a previous generation of plants because the life-cycle of plants is different and not so obvious as that of animals.

Once the ovary has been fertilized with pollen the life of the flower comes to an end, the sexual organs can only fulfill their destiny once. The flower will wither away leaving just the ovary, which in many cases develops into a fruit and the ovule(s) become seeds. In some cases, fruit is not necessary and the seed develops externally or partially enclosed by the ovary. Seeds can be dispersed into the environment in a number of ways, away from the parent that carries them. Wind is a common form of dispersal, the bare seed is blown away, maybe with a parachute or wings or a pod (fruit) opens to allow the same. Some fruits are designed to cling onto passing birds and animals (e.g. Burdock) which will fall onto the ground eventually and seed will be released. Seeds can be propelled by the explosion of the fruit, usually a pod which will burst open and thereby scatter seeds (e.g. Pea). Lastly, the more familiar kind of fruit is one that is eaten by animals, including humans. These are often much larger, brightly coloured and of attractive flavour in order to encourage them to be eaten. The seeds inside these fruits are generally indigestible through having a tough exterior (testa) or a coating that protects them (e.g. tomato). Once the seeds have passed through the digestive system of an animal they are often far away from their parent. Some seeds may still germinate if the fruit just rots on the ground but in many cases, this will not happen and the seed has to be ingested first.

## Germination

Seeds can vary enormously in size – from barely visible (Welsh Poppy) to as big as a coin (broad bean) but basically, they all have a similar composition. Three is an important number in Druidry and Celtic culture generally, so it is interesting to note that seeds have three main components. These parts include a tough outer layer (testa), a starchy food store that enables it to begin growing, and the embryo itself. The embryo is the living part of the seed, the testa is akin to a womb containing the food store and the 'baby' itself. The embryo can itself be divided into three parts – the cotyledon which is one leaf (grasses) or two leaves (everything else). When the plant emerges, it will have either one or two very basic leaves with which to begin life. The embryo also has a plumule (stem) and a radicle (root) already formed. When the seed germinates it usually requires heat and water to do so – the water softens the testa to enable the embryo to emerge and the heat is necessary to facilitate growth. Initially the plant will use the store of starch inside the seed to grow, this is because the seed is very often underground. Like animals that gestate in darkness and emerge into light at birth, plants usually emerge from the darkness of the soil, struggling themselves to be born rather than the mother struggling to give birth.

The size of the seed directly affects the embryo's ability to emerge, with a larger store of energy, big seeds can emerge from deeper underground and feed a greater initial spurt of growth of tiny root, stem and leaf. It makes sense not to sow tiny seeds deep in the ground as they will never make it to the surface, planting depth should be relative to the size of the seed.

Seeds are quite amazing as they can survive in a dormant state for huge lengths of time. Narrow Leaf Campion (Siberian plant) found to be over 30,000 years old were germinated in-vitro by biologists but even naturally germinating seeds have managed to endure hundreds of years before emerging. As humans we can be either a help or hindrance to the process of a plant being born (germinating) – we can break the dormancy by weakening the testa (scarifying in peas), soaking it in water, or providing heat. Once germinated the new-born plants will need water, nutrients, air and most importantly light to continue their journey and a medium to live in (usually soil).

## *Breathing*

Breath is such a basic part of life that we often fail to think about it, even though it is the most essential part of our existence. On a spiritual level the breath is vitally important as is evidenced by it being linked with 'life force' in nature, which is found in Indian *prana*, Chinese *qi*, Polynesian *mana*, Greek *pneuma* and in Druidry it is the Welsh *nwyfre* or Irish *neart*. In the spiritual beliefs of Hinduism, Taoism and many others apart from Druidry, this force is not just the breath, it is part of spiritual and physical vitality, that can be influenced and developed with the aid of the breath as well as other physical and metaphysical exercises.

All animals, including humans, have the necessity to breathe to stay alive and so do plants, although how it happens is somewhat more complicated in plants – they create their own food as part of the process. Plants do not possess lungs but they are covered in tiny holes called stomata that serve the same function of letting gases in and out, as well as water vapour. Plants absorb carbon dioxide from the air through their stomata, which they convert into glucose sugar using water and sunlight. This 'breathing in', which is really called photosynthesis, can be expressed in the following way:

**Carbon dioxide + Water + Light > Sugar + Oxygen**

Most of this oxygen is not needed by the plant and so all the excess is released through their stomata back into the air. However, just like humans, plants need to use the glucose to provide energy, which is called respiration and plants also store excess sugars in the form of cellulose, while animals can convert it into fats. Respiration or 'breathing out' can be expressed like this:

**Glucose + Oxygen > Energy + Carbon dioxide + Water**

What is particularly different about plants is that, not only do they make their own food (glucose) during the daylight, they continue to respire at night releasing some carbon dioxide and water, using up the oxygen they have retained to make energy. Most of the oxygen they create is released during the day as they need only about 10% of it to consume at night. Most of the carbon dioxide the plant took in is converted into energy and building blocks of the plant's body, only a small amount is exhaled, hence plants are an amazing 'carbon sink'. As part of this process, plants transpire, releasing water into the air; in fact, about 10% of water vapour in the atmosphere comes from plant transpiration. Apart from plants like cacti, they hardly transpire at night, although in very hot conditions plants close their stomata to prevent water loss if dehydration occurs, but this (except for cacti and succulents) also means that the plant cannot photosynthesize or respire while this is happening.

Although plants don't have lungs, they most certainly breathe. Fortunately for us, they use up far more carbon dioxide than they emit (which is useless to us and causes global warming) whilst producing far more oxygen than they use – a great benefit to us and all animals that rely on oxygen to survive. One might visualise the multitude of microscopic stomata on plants as thousands of tiny lungs that help keep every one of us alive!

## *Fluids (Xylem & Phloem)*

Like humans, plants rely on fluids. In humans and other animals, it is blood that is transported around the body, carrying water, oxygen, sugars and other nutrients to where it's needed via our veins and arteries through the pumping action of the heart. Plants do not have a heart but they do have a delivery system not so different from veins and arteries, which serve a similar purpose. Plants are able to move water without a heart by capillary action and they have two types of cell structures for transport of liquids.

Xylem is made up of vessels which are a continuous network of tubes running from the roots upwards throughout the plant. The walls of these vessels are strengthened with lignin which is created from carbohydrates. As well as water, soluble nutrients are transferred from the roots to the stems and leaves of the plants, the xylem vessels work in one direction only, which is generally upwards. Xylem is not living tissue; it can be visualized as basically a tubular water delivery system that has a secondary function of strengthening the stems of plants.

Phloem is made up of living cells and its purpose is the translocation (movement) of the products of photosynthesis – sugars and amino acids dissolved in water, around the plant. Unlike xylem, this delivery system works in both directions, up and down. Sieve tubes are connected to each other allowing the liquid (cytoplasm) to be transferred from one to the other with the assistance of energy from companion cells, which one could visualize as tiny pockets of liquid that pump from one to another.

So, we can see that plants have a circulatory system just as humans do, although it works somewhat differently. Plants also have a skin, like us and if you cut the tubes of xylem and phloem under the skin or epidermis (bark in trees) liquid will flow out. The same happens in animals if you cut veins or arteries, although it is much more dramatic because of the constant pumping action of the heart. In both animals and plants, the circulatory system is a vital part of life, so much so that in some human belief systems the blood is sacred and thought to carry the soul. For this reason, some religions do not allow blood to be consumed or blood transfusions to take place.

What I have outlined in this chapter is very basic botany but it clearly shows that plants are not just 'stuff in the ground', they are very much alive and sentient beings, although very different from humans. In the Druidic worldview, plants fit into the mosaic of life just as much as animals and humans do. Classical writers reported that the ancient Druids followed and taught the equivalent of the Pythagorean belief of metempsychosis or the transmigration of souls. Human souls could be reincarnated in trees or animals as well as in human form. The sacredness of trees is well known in Druidry, as demonstrated by worship in sacred groves, the symbolism of the world-tree (*bile buadha*) and the tribal/clan totemic tree. Animism permeates Druidism, as it did the early Celtic Christianity – a belief that divinity exists in all living things. With that in mind, a Druidic approach to the world of plants embraces them as sacred, along with human and animal life. We are part of a huge web of life on this planet, one that is interdependent and interconnected, not just physically but on a spiritual, metaphysical level too.

# Chapter 7

# Connecting with Plants

*"He Himself is the tree, the seed and the germ. He himself is the flower the fruit and the shade."*
Kabir

While this book is primarily intended to be a practical book, describing a more harmonious way of gardening with the Earth, it is coming from the spiritual perspective of modern Druidry/ Druidism, namely an animistic viewpoint that sees divinity in all of creation. With that in mind, after looking at the basic foundation work, I feel that is important to say something about connecting with the plant world before we explore specifics of growing and working with plants.

Connecting with plants can be approached on many levels and in many different ways, from physical to emotional and spiritual, although all of these helps develop a sensitivity and empathy for our plant relatives. This is something that is hugely lacking across many parts of the world both in terms of perception and in how they are treated. Obviously, with a more enlightened perception of what plants really are, their role in the world and how useful and vital they are, more appreciative and caring treatment of the plant realm is likely to follow.

## Physical connection

The most basic and obvious method of connecting with plants is physical, which most of us have had an instinctive ability to do since very early childhood. Plants are very often beautiful and hence very attractive to even the youngest child. Despite what seems like a hard-wired and completely natural affinity with the natural world, this is very often lost in people by the time they reach adulthood. Even so, the most hardened, concrete-loving city dweller will still most likely be able to enjoy a vase of beautiful flowers. For some people, that is as close to appreciating the plant world as they ever get and they usually fail to realize or care that their flowers, doomed to a short life, may have been grown in and transported from environmentally degraded lands on the other side of the world.

Cut flowers are lovely and provide a wealth of sight and smell for us to enjoy, however there is a huge world-wide industry behind this that is far from beneficial to the plant world and biodiversity. So, I would suggest that buying cut flowers is one of the worst ways of appreciating the plant realm; even picking wild flowers or flowers from the garden is somewhat dubious if it is done frequently. Isn't it better to buy a flowering plant to keep and grow on the kitchen table? Better still, one can venture out into the garden, the hedgerows, the woods and the seashore to experience the wonders of plants without having to cut them down or dig them up – why destroy their beauty when it can be left for others to enjoy and to fulfill its purpose in existing?

Just being around plants is therapeutic for humans. Japanese, British and German scientific research has shown that being physically present in a forest has multiple health benefits before you even consider any kind of intentional connection. Cancer killing cell production is stimulated, trees have beneficial effects on stress, mental health and high blood pressure as well as the typical benefits of some fresh air and exercise.

However, there is much more to physical connection than just being there – the passive benefits of being around plants can be greatly enhanced by taking an active role. I've often been struck by the apparent lack of connection of people out walking in nature who seem to be storming through the experience as quickly as possible, taking no time to actually engage with the physical sensations around them, in anything but the most superficial way.

To really connect with plants in a physical way takes more than a few fleeting seconds – one needs to spend some time with the plant world. Plants have an abundance of time, even the short-lived (ephemeral) plants are not going anywhere in a hurry, they are not consumed with our ideas about time and how it should be used.

If you already have a garden with plants in it, allow yourself the time to go out into it and just connect – not to read a book, drink tea or do a bit of gardening. One can go and lie down on the grass, perhaps in bare feet and allow yourself to relax and let the weight of your body sink into the ground, breathing slowly. Be aware of the sensations in your body, of the grass, dampness in the ground, the air and feel of any wind. You might then sit up and choose a place to sit next to a plant, shrub or tree and begin connecting by looking at it.

This might sound rather silly to some people – hanging out with plants and staring at them, but if you find yourself feeling somewhat cynical about this, please remember that you probably could do this as a child without feeling silly and doing it now is for a good purpose. Most people don't really look at plants properly – having gained some understanding about plant anatomy, begin to look not just at the whole plant but its different parts. Spend some time looking at the main stem from its tip to the roots, at the texture of it, at its different stems or branches, the leaves and flowers and fruit if they are present. As you look deeply at the parts of the plant, think about the plant as a living being and try to visualize the processes that are going on inside it – the harnessing of energy, the flow of liquids and gases that keeps it alive. This might come easily to some, especially those who are already keen gardeners, but for some this might be the first time of looking at a plant in detail and as a truly living creature.

After a good look at the plant and really studying it you might wish to touch it, although be careful of some plants that are toxic, such as foxgloves and ragwort, poison ivy and members of the nightshade (Solanaceae) family. It's a good idea to wash your hands after touching plants and if your skin becomes at all irritated it is best to wash immediately. Most plants are safe enough to handle – touch the leaves and stems, on trees feel the bark. If there are flowers, smell them, touch berries or fruit and perhaps even taste some if you are 100% sure they are safe.

The more time that you spend around plants, looking at them and touching them the more familiar you will become with their anatomy and their status – with experience one can tell if a plant is healthy, stressed or ill, just from looking at it, and often know what it needs – e.g. more water, less water, light, help with a pest or disease.

Some people also like to talk to plants, although some might consider this to be crazy, plants are able to sense our presence, including our breath if we speak very close to them. Talking to plants certainly will do them no harm, it might help us establish a spiritual and empathic connection with them and better intuit their needs, so one should not be embarrassed to give it a try.

If you don't currently have a garden it's a good idea to go to a woodland or even a public park, one can also connect equally as well with house plants in the home. So long as you are not interrupted and can concentrate on what you are doing, anywhere where plants grow is fine.

## Spiritual connection

For some a physical connection is sufficient, this alone will help develop empathy for the plant kingdom, although for many there is a desire and a benefit to develop a spiritual connection. Trees and plants are mentioned throughout the mythology and literature of the world's religions and clearly have a symbolic value in spirituality. Trees in particular pervade spiritual writings and ideologies – for instance the tree of life and tree of knowledge in Judaism, the banyan/bodhi tree under which Buddha sat to become enlightened, Yggdrasil the ash world tree connecting the nine realms in Norse cosmology, the oracle oak tree of Zeus, called Dodona, the Egyptian sycamores of the afterlife and countless other examples. The idea of a world tree can be found in many cultures across the world, in native North America, Pre-Columbian South America, Siberia, China, Mongolia and India as well as northern Europe. In a Druidic context the Celtic tree of life (*crann bethadh* in Irish), while not clearly evidenced in literature is thought to be similar to the Norse Yggdrasil, connecting the three realms of earth, sea and sky – representing the lower, middle and upper worlds of Celtic cosmology. The sacred tree or *bile buadha* is well known and documented in ancient Irish culture and is believed to be the physical representation of the world tree and a tribal totem. Connecting with the world tree is a good way to connect with the plant realm as well as creation in an animistic sense. Connecting with it through meditation is quite simple through visualization, although this can be aided by sitting against or under a large tree that would act as a suitable symbol.

*Find a comfortable position sitting down, if you like with your back leaning against the trunk of a large tree, cross your legs if it's comfortable to do so. Shut your eyes and take a series of deep breaths. Say to yourself, or out loud, "I take three breaths – together with the earth beneath me, the sea around me and the sky above me." As you take each of the three breaths in and out as slowly as you can visualize each realm, the ground and the planet you are sat on, the seas and oceans that stretch across the planet and the sky that wraps the planet like a protective blanket.*

*You should be feeling relaxed now and if you are leaning against a tree allow yourself to sink into it, imagining that you are merging with the tree. If you are sat alone then imagine a huge tree and visualize becoming merged with it. Visualize the roots going deep down into the earth and that you can travel deep down through them, down into the dark where it's warm. You may wish to visualize the creatures in the earth and the network of mycelium and roots that connect across vast distances. You may wish to visualize yourself connecting with the otherworld of ancestors and the sídhe or shining ones, but only if that feels right to you.*

*Now when you are ready visualize returning into the tree trunk and beginning to ascend, as you do this imagine you can look out across a vast expanse of land all the way to the sea shore. Visualize the plants and animals and people on the earth and feel your connection through the tree with all living things on this planet, that breathe the same air, rely on the same water and the warmth of the sun. Visualize beyond that the seas and all the animal and plant life that lives in it, which you are also connected to.*

*When you are ready imagine yourself ascending the tree all the way to the top of its uppermost branches. Visualize yourself touching the sky, above the clouds where you can see the sun or the moon and stars shining brightly. Imagine the highest mountains below you far away and bird's way below you and all the trees also reaching upwards towards the sky. You might wish to visualize the divine energies, a singular god, gods and goddesses or angelic beings, whichever fits with your conception of the divine.*

*Now visualize that all the world is connected through the roots and trunk and branches of this tree and that all manifest creation is connected and part of this tree, including yourself. You might want to visualize this as a golden light that shines within all beings and connects between them.*

*Allow yourself some time just to feel this connection and sense of oneness before slowly imagining yourself descending to ground level. Now imagine your body becoming separate from the tree and take a few deep breaths. Become aware of your body's weight on the ground and slowly move your fingers and toes. As you become more aware of the sounds and sensations around you, return to your everyday consciousness and open your eyes. Take your time to get up and move around, it is a good idea to drink some water and eat a snack to ground yourself.*

For thousands of years another way of connecting with plants has been to ingest them. Psychoactive plants are thought to have been used for spiritual purposes for millennia and use for purely recreational purposes would seem to be a relatively modern idea. There are many spiritual paths where psychoactive plants and fungi have been used to induce altered states of awareness, for shamanic and prophetic journeying – an area that has been discussed and written about extensively. I am not going to recommend that anyone undertake ingesting of psychoactive plants or fungi as there are very obvious risks in doing so which may diminish or completely counteract any perceived benefits.

It is often the case that psychoactive plants and fungi are poisonous and can possibly kill the recipient if not taken with appropriate knowledge and extreme care, and misuse or overuse can lead to permanent psychological or physical damage or even death. Although many people have experimented with plants such as marijuana and ayahuasca, apparently with no harm and many benefits, many others have had negative experiences. With that in mind, one should think long and hard about using psychoactive plants and accept full responsibility for whatever outcomes occur, it is a very personal decision that should not be made lightly.

Spiritual use of plants is by no means confined to psychoactive plants. Ceremonial or ritual use of plants can be undertaken with no end of plants, although taking care to do so in a safe manner that avoids any possible risk of poisoning. This generally involves ingesting a small amount of a plant or an elixir made from the plant in a sacred manner, usually involving some form of meditation or journey.

## *Connecting Through Meditation*

Before undertaking a ritual or journeying with a plant it is perhaps a good idea to try and connect – first physically and then through meditation. Try to cultivate an open heartedness and gratitude towards the plant. Through your thoughts or spoken out loud, express your intentions to connect spiritually with the plant and be open to any response. Plants are generally open to communication with humans but if you feel negative, suddenly cold, sick or any sense that this is unwanted or inappropriate at this time then do not proceed. If you feel the plant is not resistant or communicating approval then begin trying to connect on an inner level. Having established a physical connection through your senses, close your eyes and visualize the plant and yourself becoming connected through your emotions, plants do not have an intellect so this is most often how they can communicate with us. Communicate your thoughts and feelings directed at the plant and be as open as you can to receiving whatever it may wish to communicate to you. Allow yourself to be as blank as possible but if your thoughts wander to making dinner or what the weather will be tomorrow then gently return your thoughts to the intention of connecting and communicating with the plant. What you receive in the form of communication may vary considerably from person to person just as it does when communicating with spirits or deities. You might receive conversation, feelings or physical sensations, some people might be able to see or sense the aura of the plant and changes in it during communication. If nothing happens at all don't be put off, it may take several attempts to successfully connect.

## *Offerings*

Afterwards say thank you to the plant for its connection and you may wish to leave an offering. Care must be taken in expressing gratitude as not all offerings are truly appropriate. Some typical traditional offerings are milk, flour or pork. A small quantity of pork (chopped up) left by the plant will not be likely to do any harm and most likely it will be eaten by an animal of some sort before it can decompose. Likewise, a small quantity (a handful) of flour scattered around a plant is unlikely to cause damage. However, one should be very careful with milk, the fatty solids can clog the soil and milk will encourage mould and bacterial growth that can cause serious harm to plants. If you decide to make an offering of milk it should be low fat and diluted 1-part milk to about 10 parts water, this way some nutrients can be absorbed without the negative consequences. Leaving a small amount of foodstuffs such as a bit of homemade cake or bread is fine as this will rot safely or otherwise be eaten, but be careful to avoid chocolate as this is toxic to many animals. Some people like to leave dried flowers or herbs, which I personally find rather strange, as these are parts of another plant and I don't feel particularly comfortable leaving them as an offering, although others might be entirely ok with it. Leaving small rocks or crystals is a safe enough offering. One offering I strongly advise avoiding is alcohol – research has shown that all alcoholic beverages are toxic to plants, even weak beer, if not hugely diluted, will slow their growth. Strong alcohol, such as vodka or whiskey, can seriously stunt or even kill plants. If you insist on making an alcoholic offering it should just be a few drops dissolved in a glass of water. Other possibilities might be to give some water (assuming it is not already very damp) or some appropriately diluted liquid feed – this is quite likely what would most benefit the plant, at least in a physical sense. Alternatively, one can make a symbolic offering by gently touching or kissing the plant, saying thank you or even singing a song. One should go with whatever feels appropriate at that moment and for the particular plant, so long as there is no possibility of it causing harm to the plant. Offerings are particularly appropriate when part of a plant is harvested for ingestion ritually, it is also good practice to give thanks when plants or parts of plants are harvested for food and when eating them in a meal – after all their sacrifice is what benefits us and as with all living things we should be grateful for any sustenance they provide to us.

## Ritual ingestion – ceremonial plant diets

A great many plants can be ingested in a spiritual manner, to gain insight and connection, without resorting to psychoactive plants. This can be done by eating parts of the plant or by consuming an elixir made from an infusion in boiled water, a decoction using boiling of water or a tincture in alcohol, although there are other less common methods such as wines, vinegars and oils. Describing how to make an elixir is beyond the scope of this book but there are a wealth of methods that can be found on-line or in books on herbalism, one can experiment with different methods before settling on the one that suits you best. Preparation of the elixir will take some time, varying hugely depending on the method so it is sensible to prepare it an appropriate time in advance of when you intend to undertake the ritual ingestion.

There are many ways in which one can perform a ceremonial plant diet, a particularly good guide to doing so is given in Carole Guyett's excellent book *Sacred Plant Initiations*, which also gives significant details about individual plants and their properties and is an indispensable read for those with a serious interest in this activity. She gives a detailed outline of the general procedure for performing a ceremonial plant diet, which I will now discuss together with specific Druidic practices.

1. *Making a sacred intention for your plant diet* – i.e. deciding on the purpose of diet, this will include making a connection with a plant and accepting their spiritual and physical gifts in a grateful way, honouring their place and contribution in the world. It may have some specific purpose for yourself or in pursuit of the highest good for yourself and of all. This intention is bound to be reflected in the next step.

2. *Deciding which plant to ingest* – there are literally thousands of plants that you could avail of but it is important to know something about plants and their physical and spiritual properties in order to make a choice. Some are drawn to a decision instinctively and may be sensitive to a perceived calling from a particular plant. I would advise that one investigate the properties of any particular plant to see if it is indeed a good fit with your sacred intention. Once the plant is chosen one might be able to tune in with it on a spiritual or psychic level before the actual ritual takes place.

3. *Harvesting the plant and making the elixir* – this may be done very quickly, as is the case with a simple decoction, but in some cases where say both flowers and fruits or seeds are required then preparation will inevitably take far longer, perhaps even months. How one goes about this may vary enormously, it could be based on spiritual guidance, including from the plant, from your own intuition or even from practical considerations. For those doing this for the first time it is probably best to prepare an elixir that does not require a huge waiting time and with a plant that is not hugely challenging to work with. With more experience and greater knowledge of the plants one can vary techniques and depth of the work. As regards harvesting, this should be done with the utmost of respect to the plant, taking only the minimum quantities necessary. If appropriate, materials should be taken from several plants instead of just one to minimize the damage inflicted. It is a good idea to give thanks to the plant(s) and give an offering of some form. Approaches to harvesting vary differently from picking early in the morning when dew is still present, picking in full sunlight, to picking by the light of a full moon. Follow your own intuition or from the guidance of herbalists or your own spiritual path. Generally speaking, from a biological point of view, it is best to pick the plant almost immediately before you prepare the elixir. From the moment a part of a plant is removed it will begin to decompose, unnoticeably at first but increasingly so as time passes. Unless you intend to dry out the part(s) keep them cool and out of sunlight before and during preparation.

4. *Self-preparation* – assuming that you have the elixir prepared, you can now begin preparing yourself for the ritual. This may include a period of prayer and meditation, perhaps for several days in advance of actually taking the

elixir. This might also include a period of fasting before and during ritual. This could be as severe as not eating or might involve abstaining from certain foods such as meat or dairy or might just involve eating lighter meals than usual, it's entirely up to the individual to decide what is appropriate. Remaining hydrated is important and is often a part of physical cleansing so water should be readily available at all times.

5. *Conducting the ritual* – in an appropriate space, where you can spend the timeframe decided on without interruption by people, phones, radio, television etc. one should open a sacred space for the ritual to take place. In a Druidic scheme of things this generally involves the casting of a circle using the mind, a finger or a wand/staff in a clockwise direction. This might be done silently or with spoken words stating exactly what you are doing. Some traditions involve the blessing of the space with water, incense or smoke from a dried plant such as sage, vervain or rosemary. Some like to use these items on themselves or all those present, as well as on the sacred space. If you open a circle then it should also be closed at the end of your ceremony, going anti-clockwise.

6. *Altar* – It is suggested that an altar is set up with the plant on it, together with representations of the elemental model you are using. The most common form, using the neo-platonic elements of Air, Fire and Water and Earth, generally are placed in the East, South, West and North respectively. Starting in the East you go clockwise around the circle and at the end anti-clockwise to close, giving thanks. A typical way to invoke the elements would be:

*I call upon the blessings of the element of Air, upon the powers of the East and of the wind, the blessings of the hawk in the sky. I call upon the time of spring and new growth, the sword of Nuada, the inspiration of thought. I ask your presence and blessings for this ceremony.*

*I call upon the blessings of the element of Fire, upon the powers of the South and of the sun, the blessings of the stag in the forest. I call upon the time of summer and warmth, the spear of Lugh, the power of magic and creation. I ask your presence and blessings for this ceremony.*

*I call upon the blessings of the element of Water, upon the powers of the West and of the sea, the blessings of the salmon of knowledge. I call upon the time of autumn and decline, the cauldron of Dagda, the wisdom of the ancestors in Tír Na nÓg. I ask your presence and blessings for this ceremony.*

*I call upon the blessings of the element of Earth, upon the powers of the North and of the land, the blessings of the northern star Polaris and the Great Bear. I call upon the time of winter and rest, the Lia Fáil, the strength and nurturing of the goddess Anu in the deep dark soil. I ask your presence and blessings for this ceremony.*

There are many ways to do this for each direction with a multitude of correspondences for each element or just a simple calling in, depending on your own preferences. It could be as simple as *I call upon the blessings of Air, Fire, Water and Earth into this sacred space.*

Less common but equally valid is the use of the three realms of Sea, Land and Sky and the corresponding nine elements which are sea, moon, wind; land, plant, stone and sky, sun, cloud. These nine elements also correspond respectively with parts of the human body – blood, mind breath; flesh, hair, bones and head, face, brain. One can simply call upon the three realms with a simple sentence such as *I take three breaths together, with the sea around me, the land beneath me and the sky above me.* Equally one can devise something far more complex if you feel it appropriate, including marking three circles clockwise below, around and above. For instance:

*I call upon the realm of the sea, of the otherworld and the wisdom of the ancestors, may your blessings be with us. I call upon the realm of the land, of this middle world of physicality, may your blessings be with us. I call upon the realm of the sky, the domain of the gods and their guidance, may your blessings be with us. I call upon the blessings of the 9 elements of dúile and the nine directions, above, below, though, east, west, north, south, inwards and outwards.*

As with the four elements, the three realms and/or nine elements and nine directions should be thanked if invoked and any circles closed in reverse direction at the end of the ceremony. For more information on the three realms and nine elements and nine directions it is worth reading the work of Searles O'Dubhain at summerlands.com. Once the preliminaries are over the elixir can be drunk. Sometimes this might happen several times during the ritual. Alternatively, elixir can be applied to the skin, especially if it is an oil. Care is advised with regard to pregnant and breast-feeding women or anyone with any health issues that might be problematic. What happens during the ritual will be unique each time for all people involved and is greatly dependent on which plant is chosen. This might involve just being in a meditative state for a long time, journeying with drumming, dancing or singing. The length of the ceremony can be a few hours or several days, including sleeping in the sacred space. It may involve a total fast (apart from the elixir) or eating some food – common sense is required to decide what is appropriate and risks should never be taken with one's health, especially with regard to dehydration and blood sugar levels. In group ceremonies the ritual would often include sharing of experiences and insights gained. Prayers and blessings and giving thanks to the plant and all spirits invoked should also be done at the end. Before a formal end, elements and realms invoked should be thanked and dismissed and a circle closed if it was opened.

7. *Integration* – It is advisable to allow oneself time to integrate the experience before resuming everyday life. Effects of the ritual may be felt for several days after, especially if you continue to ingest a low dose of the elixir for some time afterwards. It is best to try to avoid pressured or stressful situations, if possible, spend some time in nature and avoid eating heavy meals. Taking part in plant rituals can have a transformative effect on a person and as well as developing a deeper relationship with a particular plant, it may well develop a deeper affinity with the whole plant realm and nature in general.

There are many different options for creating a spiritual connection with plants, whichever method you choose the aim is to gain a greater understanding of them and deeper empathy for their existence. This may not be of any practical use in a physical sense, but it should make some difference in how one relates to plants and this in turn will affect how you interact with them spiritually, emotionally and physically – treating them with greater respect and being more aware of their needs and their vital role in the existence of life on Earth.

# Chapter 8

# Trees

*"For in the true nature of things, if we rightly consider, every green tree is far more glorious than if it were made of gold and silver."*
Martin Luther

Trees feature heavily in world mythology and religion; it is no wonder really considering their vital role in providing oxygen for all animal life and in retaining water and soil on the land. Discussing the metaphysical symbolism of trees is worth a whole book in itself and there are a wide variety already available on the subject, hence this book will concentrate on the practical uses of trees and how to look after them. Trees played a very important role in ancient Celtic societies, which is clearly evidenced by the recording of veneration of trees by the Druids in Gaul and Britain and by the ancient literature of Wales and Ireland. The story of Mad Sweeney (*Buile Suibhne*) gives extensive detail of trees during his wanderings and the Brehon law of Ireland (particularly *Bretha Comaithchesa*) gives great detail of the value and usage of trees and the heavy fines for their unlawful damage or destruction. Likewise, in Wales there is similar mention in *Cad Goddeu* (Battle of the Trees), from the *Book of Taliesin* and in Welsh law documents such as *Llyfr Iorwerth*. In late medieval Scotland trees are also shown to be of great value as is clear from *Leges Forestarum* (Laws of the Forests), which dates from the 11th century CE.

What I will focus on in this section is the individual properties of trees, how to grow and look after them, while also discussing some of their spiritual and practical aspects. First though I shall give a general overview of trees and their physical properties, how to plant and care for them. For an organism that is so vital to our very existence and has a vast array of practical and medicinal uses, I am often shocked by how little most people know about trees, their value and importance and how to look after them.

## Sacred planting

Whether planting a seed, a seedling or more established sapling, I like to say a short blessing in acknowledgement of gardening as sacred work. This can be applied to pretty much any plant with a small bit of adaptation if relevant. You may wish to write your own blessing(s), that better suit your own spirituality. It doesn't need to be long or complicated so long as it conveys your intentions effectively. Say this or your own blessings as you put the seed/plant in the ground/pot as it can help foster a good relationship with the plant and help it to make a good start.

*May you be blessed by Earth and rain and wind and sun.*
*May you grow straight and strong and true.*

It might also be a consideration to plant by the phases of the moon, in broad terms it is better to sow seed or plant on a waxing moon. In terms of Biodynamic gardening, different days are advantageous for leaf, root, flower and fruit crops or in fact for doing nothing. This is not easy to work out as it requires astrological knowledge, but practically this can be implemented easily with the aid of a yearly *Biodynamic Sowing & Planting Calendar*, such as that produced by Maria Thun or by checking biodynamic websites on-line for short-term information. Another excellent work that explains how this works is Elen Sentier's *Gardening With The Moon & Stars*.

## Growing From Seed

The first area worth looking at is tree planting – an activity often filled with mishaps that can have a very long-term negative effect on the life of a tree. The obvious place to start is with the seed, as this is what happens in nature. There are two ways to go about growing from seed, the first being the natural way and the second being to emulate natural conditions to precipitate germinations.

In nature seeds are usually dispersed in late summer through to autumn and in most cases, germination will occur the following spring as the weather warms up. Depending on the type of tree the seed will need to undergo dormancy of one or more types. Some seeds will simply need what is called scarification – the softening of the testa (shell) and breaking down of the impermeable coating over the winter. Some will require cold moist stratification – a period in damp and cold conditions over winter before germination can begin. Some seeds will also require warm moist stratification over summer, followed by cold moist stratification – which means that the seed will lie dormant for over a year, this is typical of Hawthorn and Mountain Ash (Rowan) or Lime. If you wish to emulate these conditions to stimulate germination then it's necessary to find out how seeds for individual species are propagated. A good source of information on seed propagation is the *Plants For A Future* website database; as well as general information about thousands of species it gives details of the germination process so one knows what to expect.

If you are growing the natural way this can be done either in situ – where you want the tree to grow or in a pot. Of course, not all seeds are viable and how successfully the seed will grow depends on the conditions of the year and the strength of the seed, generally speaking seeds from a weak tree will become weak seedlings.

If the seed is viable and conditions are favourable the seed planted in the ground or in a pot will germinate in spring and hopefully survive to become a healthy and mature tree. In both cases it is wise to make sure the seed is not planted too deep, generally the larger the seed the deeper it can be planted. If the seed does not have enough stored energy to send its shoot all the way up to the surface and expose its first leaves to the sun then it will die. The seed is totally reliant on its stored carbohydrates in order to do this as it cannot photosynthesize under the soil, so planting too deep is a guarantee of failure.

Do not plant seeds in a compost heap or put a large amount of compost in a pot – too much nutrient is more harmful to new seedlings than too little, causing it difficulty in absorbing water due to excessive salts. Seeds should be planted individually in a pot to avoid competition and damage in separating them later on. Only a small amount of compost should be added to the soil, which should be reasonably free draining as too much moisture can cause the seed to rot. Both in situ or in a pot the seedling might need to be protected from damage by animals – this can be achieved typically with a bit of wire mesh that will prevent them being crushed or eaten.

To artificially stimulate germination one can emulate the conditions of winter and summer to trick the seed into germinating early. Warm stratification can be done two ways – the quick but less reliable way is to bathe the seeds in hot water (about 60°C) and leave them to soak for up to two days, disposing of any seeds that immediately float as they are most likely unviable. The second method is to wrap the seeds in damp tissue paper and store them in a warm place (e.g. airing cupboard at 20°C) or in a plastic bag for a month to three months.

Cold stratification can be done by storing seeds wrapped in damp tissue paper in the fridge in a plastic bag for at least a month, perhaps three months for some species. If the conditions are right, the seeds can be planted outside where the warmth and moisture should enable them to germinate. Spring conditions can be emulated inside with the help of damp soil seed trays or small pots on a warming mat. Once the seeds have germinated, they will immediately need light, otherwise they will die.

Newly germinated trees can be very vulnerable to sudden changes in the weather, that can often happen in spring. A period of extreme cold, drought or extreme wind is very likely to kill some or all of your seedlings so it is a good idea to protect them. Seedlings grown inside will need to be 'hardened off' or acclimatized to the outside weather once strong enough. Seedlings outside can be protected from extreme cold with horticultural fleece, from drought by watering and from the wind by a windbreak or by putting them in a sheltered position. What is most important is not to just abandon them if you want their chances of survival to be good. One cannot just leave a new-born baby to fend for itself and trees have a much better chance if they are checked on regularly and given a little help through initial hardships.

Some people believe it is best to grow only in situ, but that can make taking care of the tree more difficult. Of course, it is better for a tree if it does not have to be transferred from a pot to the ground but if this is done carefully then there should not be any real problems.

It is worth noting that growing fruit trees from seed can often yield greatly varying results as usually the seed will be a combination of two or even three parent trees. One cannot always guarantee that the parent trees (particularly with Apple) will be of the same variety and so it is likely that the seedlings grown will not be identical to any parent. To guarantee that a particular variety is retained many gardeners use grafting or buy grafted saplings, which are essentially clones.

## Cuttings

Many trees can be grown from cuttings or from suckers. Suckers are generally easy to manage if transplanted in the dormant season (winter) but cuttings require far more care. It's advisable to use rooting hormone powder in order to promote root growth, only a tiny dusting is required so a small pot should last for many years. An alternative to artificial hormone powder is to leave the cuttings in a solution of chopped up fresh willow bark or chopped fresh young roots from a briar (blackberry) both of which contain natural hormone. Also, the young shoots of the black poplar can be used in the same way. A few hours or overnight will be sufficient but this is not as effective as the artificial powder. A common mistake is to use large sections of plant, a smaller section requires less water (bear in mind it has no roots!) and so has more chance of surviving. It is especially important not to leave cuttings in direct sunlight or strong wind as they are guaranteed to die! Also, it is essential to make sure that the soil of the pot or bed does not completely dry out at any point. It is also inadvisable to try and move cuttings before there is signs of considerable growth. The cutting will not grow until it has developed adequate root and obvious leaf growth is a sure sign that roots have grown. Even so, it is sensible to protect these young and still vulnerable clones from extremes of the weather for the first year.

## Planting Seedlings

Depending on the species and the strength of the individual seed, trees can grow at vastly differing rates. A seedling is usually defined as having a trunk of 2.5cm diameter or less. Once you've a fair idea of whether you've a fast-growing tree or not, this should give you some idea of the size of pot you will need. Some people prefer to sow directly in the soil, but this has risks as it is more difficult to protect the tree from damage from animals or extreme weather. It's best if the tree can go straight from a pot to its final location in the ground, so one should allow a big enough pot for the tree to grow for at least two years. If the pot is too small the tree will become 'potbound' meaning that the roots will fill the pot and go around in circles, becoming entangled in themselves. In such cases the tree has almost definitely exhausted the soil and is suffering from a lack of nutrients and possibly water too. If becoming potbound happens, it can sometimes do irreversible damage to the tree and so planting out or repotting should be done well before this is a problem. Once more than one or two roots start to come through holes in the bottom of the pot then you know that the tree is ready for a bigger space. Trees such as Willow, Sycamore and Alder can grow very quickly. Many trees do better if started off in a coldframe, which is cheap to buy or can be easily built at home. An alternative is to make a long cloche from two old shower doors, bolted or screwed together to make a triangular glass cover.

## Container Grown Trees

In some cases, if you don't have any garden or if there is only a hard surface then it might be necessary to grow the tree from a seedling in a pot for its whole life. In this case it's best to select a tree that is not likely to grow very big, such as a Hawthorn, Blackthorn, miniature Pine (e.g. Pinus mugo), Rowan or a grafted fruit tree on a restrictive rootstock. Such trees are better suited to living in containers and can still be healthy and happy if well looked after. In such cases the seedling can be transferred from its initial pot to a larger one with plenty of well-rotted compost as well as soil. Container grown trees will need watering, even in winter and especially during extended warm periods in summer. After a few years in the final home the tree is likely to have exhausted the nutrients in the soil and so will need to be given fertilizer from that point onwards. Liquid feeds are the most convenient method of ensuring the tree continues to receive nutrient. One can also put a layer of compost as a mulch on the soil surface in autumn, being careful not to put it all the way up to the trunk to avoid damage. The compost will gradually break down and be absorbed. As with any mulch, e.g. bark, stones or dried leaves it will help with reducing weeds and aid water retention, preventing the soil underneath from being dried out as quickly by sun and wind.

## Planting in the Ground

It's important to pick the right location for a tree, as ideally you want to plant the tree once only and not have to come and dig it up and move it years later, or worse still, be forced to cut it down. It's important not to plant too close to a building, path or road (especially Willow) where it causes issues when it gets towards maturity, a bit of forethought can avoid the unfortunate felling of the tree later in its life. Another important factor is locating the tree where it is likely to do well – planting a Willow or Elm in a bog is fine as they love water, many other trees may struggle or die as a result. Some trees, such as Holly or Hazel will do fine in a shady spot, others (especially fruit trees) prefer the full sun. Trees such as Birch have quite a shallow root system and so might do badly in quick draining sandy soil unless you are prepared to water them. Understanding what conditions your tree prefers will determine where you plant it, as well as factors such as growth habit. It's pointless to grow a Giant Redwood in a small garden or where it will overshadow everything else – trees chosen should be appropriate to the size they will eventually grow to in height and spread, with adequate space left between them.

## Growing From Saplings

A sapling is a young tree, generally regarded as having a trunk of less than 10cm diameter. This fairly broad definition includes trees that might be 3 years old or perhaps even 15 years old. This all depends upon the growth rate of the species and also on the climatic conditions in your area. It is possible to obtain saplings in several different conditions – barerooted, rootballed, burlapped or containerized (potted). General folk wisdom (in UK and Ireland) is that any month with a letter 'R' in it is ok for planting trees – that means September to April. This is a pretty good rule of thumb but it also depends on the individual weather conditions. It's advisable to avoid planting during frost or snow, during stormy periods, during drought or hot periods. If any of these conditions arise after planting then special care might be required such as protection with horticultural fleece or extra watering.

Generally, it is a good idea to add some compost to the soil, especially if the soil is sandy and low in nutrients, however be careful not to overdo it as this can do more harm than good to the roots. If the soil is especially boggy you may need to add non-salty sand and possibly some horticultural lime to aid clump forming. With certain trees such as willow and elm, that love the damp, you will not have to concern yourself with improving drainage. With acid loving plants such as conifers, adding lime is a very bad idea, in fact you might need to add acidic compost if your soil is already alkaline.

## Bareroot Trees

These can vary greatly in size from perhaps less than a metre, up to perhaps 3 metres. These trees have been grown in loose sandy soil or gravel so that they can be removed with the root system intact. They are usually available in early winter (e.g. late October or November) when the weather is cold and the tree is in a dormant state. They are not usually available after mid spring when new growth is beginning – to plant any later than that is quite risky. Usually these are planted in the ground but it's also possible to plant them in a decent sized container.

Opinions differ about whether it is best to plant in early winter or in mid spring. By planting in early winter, one allows the tree the maximum amount of time to acclimatise to its new home and gets its roots re-established. Even in winter, trees are able to use stored energy to expand their roots. The downside of this is that the tree will have to endure the whole winter and spring in a new environment and may suffer if the weather conditions are especially bad. Planting late may avoid the worst of the bad weather but the disadvantage is that the tree has less time to acclimatise before it 'wakes up' and sends out new growth above the ground. On balance I would suggest planting in early winter if the conditions are mild and are predicted to remain so for a few weeks at least.

When planting bareroot trees it's wise to dig a hole that is at least 1.5 times deeper and wider than the extent of the root system. It's a good idea to break up the soil a little and mix in some good well-rotted compost, but not more than one third as excessive compost can 'burn' young and tender roots. It's extremely important to keep the roots of a bareroot tree damp and covered up from both the sun and wind – if the roots dry out, they begin to die rapidly! It's also important to handle to roots carefully, try not to damage them. Generally speaking, it's best to plant the tree the same day that you get it, to minimize the amount of time spent out of the ground. Be careful not to plant the tree too deep or too shallow, the top of the root system, where the bark starts, is where it should meet ground level. Also be careful not to 'firm in' the tree too lightly but more importantly, not too vigorously. Stamping the ground can squeeze all of the air out of the soil and also damage the roots. It's important to water the tree well and keep an eye on it in the coming weeks as its ability to pull up water is diminished initially after replanting.

### *Rootballed and Burlapped Trees*
This is essentially the same thing, although burlapped trees are often in a larger sack rather than a bag, usually made of natural fibre such as hemp or hessian. Often the roots have been trimmed but the bag/sack will also contain some of the original soil that the tree was grown in before it was lifted. Sometimes the roots will also be contained within a mesh of metal wire and may also be bound up with natural or synthetic twine. On occasion the fibre bag might be synthetic or be natural fibre treated with a preservative such as copper sulphate, which stops the bag rotting quickly. Be careful not to drop the tree or put unnecessary pressure on the roots, although they are contained, they are still fragile.

In my opinion it is best remove all twine, bag/sack and wire mesh/basket but this should be done carefully once the tree is lowered into the hole using sharp scissors or a sharp knife. It's best to carry the tree from the bottom of the ball and not by the trunk. The hole should have slanting sides and be 2-3 times the width of the root system. Again, the collar, where the bark starts, should be at ground level at not below the soil. If you cannot get rid of every last piece of natural bag under the roots don't worry, it's better to leave a small bit rather than damage the roots. If at all possible, remove all metal, synthetic or treated material as this can impede or damage the roots.

Often soil may have built up around the base of the trunk, it's best to remove this by gently washing or scraping it off, this also makes it easier to see the collar where the bark ends and the roots start. As with barerooted trees, the roots must be protected from sun and wind and not be allowed to dry out – watering after planting is also essential. In fact, this is often even more vital than with bareroot trees as frequently the roots have been chopped back quite severely and the capacity for the tree to absorb water has been greatly reduced. As with all planting, be careful not to compress the soil by over-eager firming in. With larger saplings you might want to consider a stake for support, although this depends on the likelihood of exposure to strong winds.

## Containerized Trees

Most trees that are for sale to the general public are containerized, grown in pots of varying sizes. This can be very convenient for both the seller and they buyer but isn't the ideal growing medium for the tree. Within a period of months, a tree is likely to exhaust the nutrients within the soil of the pot. In addition, the tree will expand its roots to fill the available space, after which the roots will go around in circles, becoming 'potbound'. If a potted tree has a number of roots trying to escape through holes in the bottom of its pot then it is severely 'potbound' and could possibly struggle to recover for the rest of its life – do not buy such a tree unless you are prepared to accept that.

When planting a containerized tree, you should give it a good soak first and leave it in the pot until the last moment. Again, the hole should be much larger than the size of the pot, a bit deeper and twice as wide. When you remove the tree from the pot inspect the roots to see if any are tangled or entwined. If necessary, cut away the pot to release roots rather than force them out and do whatever you can to gently loosen and untangle roots. Keep all of the soil from the pot and plant that with the tree. Once again, mix some compost with the ground soil and be careful with the 'firming in'.

## *Staking Trees*

Staking is a contentious issue for any tree, barerooted or otherwise. Trees do not come with stakes so obviously the most natural thing to do is avoid them. With very small trees they are less likely to be knocked over by wind and will hopefully develop a strong root system that can withstand heavy winds. Some people believe that a stake only discourages their root strength and is a detrimental support. With saplings over a metre there is a good case for staking as wind can tip them at an extreme angle, cause wind rock root damage or even completely uproot a vulnerable tree.

A major problem with staking is that people often do it incorrectly, which ends up harming the tree, they also often forget to come back and attend to the tree, causing more harm. One should be careful with single stakes not to hammer them in right next to the trunk as this can badly damage the roots, plus as the tree widens it will soon grow into the stake, causing compression (fasciation) of the trunk and damage to the bark. It is better to use a single stake at an angle of 20 to 30 degrees to prevent damage. It is important to pick a stake that is the right size for the job – a stake that is of smaller diameter than the tree is not likely to give much support and within a year or two will certainly be of no use. It doesn't make sense to use a stake that is three or four times wider than the tree either, as this unnecessarily disturbs the root space. For larger trees it is often a good idea to use two stakes with a cross-member, to which the tree is attached.

A common mistake is to attach trees to stakes with a bit of wire, rope, cable ties or other abrasive, inflexible and nonexpansive materials. The result of this is damage to the bark and if left long enough, major abrasions and growth around the offending article. The wounds left by poor tying can also be a source of entry for infections and diseases as well as making an unsightly scar on the tree. All this can be easily avoided by making a trip to a garden centre to buy proper tree ties, preferably those made from recycled rubber or recycled plastic. Tree tape can also be used but this is less flexible material and does not expand – so more caution is required and earlier inspection to avoid damage.

I have witnessed many trees severely damaged by stakes, inappropriate ties and tree tape/ties that have been left on a tree for years too long, sometimes the damage has a permanent impact. The same is true also of collars applied to deter hares, rabbits and other animals from damaging the bark. If left on for excessive time they too will cause damage in a similar way to stakes and ties. A rather bizarre remedy to deter animals is to mix up a strong paste from mustard powder and smear this over the lower region of the tree. The unpalatable taste will deter them from coming back, hopefully long after the mustard eventually washes off.

As with good practices in general, returning to inspect your trees on a regular basis is a good idea. By doing so you can eliminate problems before they become major problems. You will notice if the stake is too small, needs removing or replacing, if the tree tie is too loose or tight and hopefully any other problems such as pests and diseases or unwanted new growth in a rootstock. If you return and spot problems then they can be dealt with, neglect means that you cannot do anything about problems that you are unaware of – the result of which is that the tree suffers. One always has to remember that these are living beings and if we are not going to just 'leave it to nature' and pure chance then it is necessary to actually take care of plants, just as one would a small child or an elderly relative.

## Trees of the Druids

There are thousands of wonderful trees from all over the world, but in some cases growing them in a non-native environment can be very problematic. This is certainly the case of Rhododendron plants in Britain and Ireland. These beautiful plants, that eventually grow into medium sized trees, were introduced from Asia and thrive in the European climate. They are vigorous and hardy, are not attractive food for deer, sheep, goats and other animals and with about 7000 seeds per flower head are extremely good at propagating themselves. In less than two hundred years they have become a major problem in some areas of Europe, crowding out native species and spreading in a way that can be best described as invasive. For this reason, as well as the limitations of space, I am concentrating on the native species of Europe where the Druids once lived.

Many books concentrate solely on the trees of the *ogham* alphabet list, which of course only relates to Ireland. The Druids did not exist just in Ireland, they existed throughout Britain, Gaul (what is now France, Netherlands and Belgium) and parts of Germany, Switzerland and even as far as northern Italy (Cisalpine Gaul) and central Europe around the Danube river. As a result of this fact, I have included trees that are native to Britain and western Europe as well as Ireland, as these would have been known to, and probably used by, the Druids of ancient times.

Much of the general principles of tree care apply to all trees, but it is worth knowing something of the physical and spiritual properties of any individual tree species you have the pleasure to look after. The best source of information about trees in Celtic times is from an eighth century CE Irish law text *Bretha Comaithchesa* (judgments of neighbourhood), which details four classes of trees. Sadly, Ireland had relatively few native trees compared to the rest of Europe and most of what we know about those historically is derived from Roman or Roman influenced sources. As one would expect, fines for the destruction of (other peoples) trees were highest for the most valuable class of tree, deceasing with each category.

The Irish tree list is as follows, as given by renowned academic Fergus Kelly, however there remain differing opinions about which trees or plants should be on this list:

*Lords/Nobles of the wood (airig fedo)*

| Dair | 'oak' | (Quercus robur, Quercus petraea) |
|------|-------|----------------------------------|
| Coil | 'hazel' | (Corylus avellana) |
| Cuilenn | 'holly' | (Ilex aquifolium) |
| Ibar | 'yew' | (Taxus baccata) |
| Uinnius | 'ash' | (Fraxinus excelsior) |
| Ochtach | 'scots pine' | (Pinus sylvestris) |
| Aball | 'wild apple-tree' | (Malus pumila) |

*Commoners of the wood (aithig fhedo)*

| Fern | 'alder' | (Alnus glutinosa) |
|------|---------|-------------------|
| Sail | 'willow' | (Salix caprea, Salix cinerea, etc.) |
| Scé | 'hawthorn' | (Crataegus monogyna) |
| Cáerthann | 'rowan' | (Sorbus aucuparia) |
| Beithe | 'birch' | (Betula pubescens, Betula pendula) |
| Lem | 'elm' | (Ulmus glabra) |
| Idath | 'wild cherry?' | (Prunus avium) |

*Lower divisions of the wood (fodla fedo)*

| Draigen | 'blackthorn' | (Prunus spinosa) |
|---------|--------------|------------------|
| Trom | 'elder' | (Sambucus nigra) |
| Féorus | 'spindle-tree' | (Euonymus europaeus) |
| Findcholl | 'whitebeam?' | (Sorbus aria) |
| Caithne | 'strawberry tree' | (Arbutus unedo) |
| Crithach | 'aspen' | (Populus tremula) |
| Crann fir | 'juniper?' | (Juniperus communis) |

*Bushes of the wood (losa fedo)*

| Raith | 'bracken' | (Pteridium aquilinum) |
|---|---|---|
| Rait | 'bog-myrtle' | (Myrica gale) |
| Aitenn | 'gorse' | (Ulex europaeus, Ulex gallii) |
| Dris | 'bramble' | (Rubus Jruticosus aggregate) |
| Fróech | 'heather' | (Calluna vulgaris, Erica cinerea) |
| Gilcach | 'broom' | (Sarothamnus scoparius) |
| Spín | 'wild rose' | (Rosa canina, etc.) |
| Eidenn | 'ivy' | (Hedera helix) |

Note: according to Niall Mac Coitir *spín* should refer to gooseberry rather than wild rose.

Finally, below is a poem from *Aidedh Ferghusa meic Léide* (The Death of Fergus), which comes from Ireland in the middle ages, translated by Standish O'Grady in the mid-18th century. The king of the fairies (Iubhdán) advises Fergus mac Léide (who ruled Ulster) on the special properties of trees, including which ones should be burned. It gives an interesting insight into the knowledge of and reliance on trees in ancient Ireland.

*The pliant woodbine/honeysuckle if thou burn, wailings for misfortune will abound,*
*Dire extremity at weapons' points or drowning in great waves will follow.*

*Burn not the precious apple tree of spreading and low-sweeping bough;*
*Tree ever decked in bloom of white, against whose fair head all men put forth the hand.*

*The surly blackthorn is a wanderer, a wood that the artificer burns not;*
*Throughout his body, though it be scanty, birds in their flocks warble.*

*The noble willow burn not, a tree sacred to poems;*
*Within his blooms bees are a-sucking, all love the little cage.*

*The graceful tree with the berries, the wizard's tree, the rowan burn;*
*But spare the limber tree; burn not the slender hazel.*

*Dark is the colour of ash; timber that makes the wheels to go;*
*Rods he furnishes for horsemen's hands, his form turns battle into flight.*

*Tenterhook among woods the spiteful briar is, burn him that is so keen and green;*
*He cuts, he flays the foot, him that would advance he forcibly drags backward.*

*Fiercest heat-giver of all timber is green oak, from him non may escape unhurt;*
*By partiality for him the head is set on aching, and by his acrid embers the eye is made sore.*

*Alder, very battle-witch of all woods, tree that is hottest in the fight*
*Undoubtedly burn at thy discretion both the alder and whitethorn.*

*Holly, burn it green; holly, burn it dry;*
*Of all trees whatsoever the critically best is holly.*

*Elder that hath tough bark, tree that in truth hurts sore;*
*Him that furnishes horses to the armies from the sídhe burn so that he be charred.*

*The birch as well, if he be laid low, promises abiding fortune;*
*Burn up most sure and certainly the stakes that bear the constant pods.*

*Put on the hearth if it so please thee, the russet aspen to come headlong down;*
*Burn, be it late or early, the tree with the palsied branch.*

*Patriarch of long-lasting woods is the yew sacred to feasts as it is well known;*
*Of him now build ye dark-red vats of goodly size.*

# Alder

Latin: Alnus Glutinosa

Irish: Fern, Fearnóg. Welsh: Gwernen/Gwern. Breton: Gwern.

3rd letter of the Ogham alphabet.

The alder tree is fast growing tree that can reach up to 30m in height, but usually lives around 60 years - a relatively short life-span. It very often has one stem, but can have multiple stems, giving a bushier canopy. It can be found throughout Europe and even as far south as North Africa. Its leaves are round and similar in appearance to those of the hazel, although it produces flower catkins similar to the birch and small cones as does the larch. In Irish tradition, the first man sprang from an alder tree but this tree is also associated with death, war and the otherworld god Donn. This association may be because of the red, bloodlike, colour the felled wood takes on and also the fact that it was often used to make shields for battle.

Scottish stories also associate alder with death and fairies and in Ireland it was considered to be an unlucky tree. Despite this alder was often used in the construction of *crannogs* or artificial island dwellings on lakes, due to alder's tremendous resistance to water; hence it was extensively used in the construction of Venice.

Despite its negative association's alder was referred to positively by the 7th century Irish king Mad Sweeney and St. Brigid blessed an alder which thereafter magically bore apples and sloes. In folklore and myth alder is associated with war and often recognized as the 'red branch' of the Red Branch knights of Ulster. Alder also features in the Welsh poem Cad Goddeu, alder is referred to as in the front line of the battle and also in relation to King Bran (the blessed). Bran's nephew, who becomes King of Ireland to restore peace between the Britons and Irish, is named Gwern, meaning alder in Welsh. Alder is also associated with the Celtic cult of the severed head, which was thought to contain the person's soul or spirit and was often collected by warriors. Bran's severed head continues to speak years after his death until shortly before his comrades bury it at London, facing Europe to ward off invasion. Alder may be used spiritually for purposes of protection and as a shamanic aid to overcome inertia.

## Uses

Because of its resistance to water it has been used for making barrels, bowls and other containers as well as fence posts or poles and clogs. Although it does not burn well, it can be used to make good charcoal. Alder can produce several dyes – red from the bark, green from the flowers and brown from twigs, black from catkins and bark. A mixture of bark, young shoots and copper powder creates a yellow dye. Rubbing leaves on the skin acts as an insect repellent.

Medicinally it is associated with clearing and unblocking and with the blood. An infusion if applied as a wash soothes burned skin due to its astringent properties. An infusion from dried bark is a cure for a sore throat. Alder makes a good anti-inflammatory and has been used to treat rheumatism and aches and pains. The fresh leaves are applied directly to the skin or they can be laid on or applied in a cloth bag or pillow case to the affected area. Inner bark boiled in vinegar can be used against lice and skin conditions such as scabies. Traditionally a decoction is helpful in the treatment of several cancers. Alder leaves were placed in the soles of shoes on long journeys to prevent swelling of the feet. It is of great value to wildlife, especially moths, butterflies, bees, crane flies and several species of bird. In wet conditions it provides a home to lichens, mosses, fungi and even otters.

## Cultivation

Alder will grow in a wide variety of conditions but it does best of all in damp soils and will often be found around river banks and lakes. It can grow well in heavy clay and depleted soil with low nutritional content and across a wide variety of pH. It will also do fine in semi-shade and along coastlines, being very salt tolerant. It is often planted as a windbreak or used for hedging and also coppicing.

Alder has a symbiotic relationship with certain soil micro-organisms called Actinomycetes, these form nodules on the roots of the plants and fix atmospheric nitrogen. Some of this nitrogen is utilized by the alder itself but some can also be utilized by other plants growing nearby, hence it is a useful tree for improving the soil conditions and supporting other plant life.

The seed contains air pockets which means they can float on water for up to a month before sinking. Growing from seed it can be planted in autumn in the soil or in spring on the surface of the soil. Because of the nitrogen fixation seedlings can grow very rapidly which means that potted specimens will need potting on quickly or should be transferred to a permanent site as soon as possible. Alder can grow several metres in the first few years and like birch is a pioneer tree that is useful for establishing new woodland.

## Apple

Latin: Malus domestica, Malus pumila, Malus sylvestris
Irish: Úll, Aball, Quert. Welsh: Afal. Breton: Gwez-Avalou.
10th letter of the Ogham alphabet.

The apple tree of the ancient Celts was quite different from the domesticated apple varieties that we are used to now. Generally, the wild or crab apple is what is referred to, which produced very small apples with a fairly bitter taste. Domesticated apple varieties were introduced into western Europe by the Romans and into Ireland by the Normans.

There is a vast amount of folklore and legend associated with the apple, particularly connecting it with the otherworld

– Tir Na nOg (land of the young), the isle of Avalon or Eamhain Abhlach (region of apples). Various stories featuring Manannán Mac Lir, St. Brendan, Lugh, Merlin/Myrrdin, Aongus Mac Og, Mad Sweeney, Lailoken etc. refer to apple trees, the otherworldy apples or an apple branch. Apples as such are symbolic of the otherworld or otherworldly experience and can provide spiritual sustenance. Apples also feature extensively in other ancient cultures such as Greece and Scandinavia, in a positive aspect. Perhaps most famously, apple features in the Hebrew story of the Garden Of Eden as the forbidden fruit that tempted the first human couple – a rather negative connotation for a wonderful and valuable tree. It's interesting to note that when you cut an apple in half horizontally one can see the shape of a five-pointed star or pentagram in the core – indicative of its metaphysical aspects and its connection to the elements and the world of spirit. Apples are also connected with Halloween (*Samhain*) which is clear from the apple games that still endure in the British Isles at that time.

Apples are also connected with fertility, good health and healing – hence the well-known phrase 'an apple a day keeps the doctor away.' Apples have long been a source of food, fruit juice and cider and are a great source of vitamin C, which is vital for health and especially needed to fight off colds and flu.

## Uses

Apple trees have primarily been used as a food source, for eating and drinking. The wood burns well but is rarely used for this purpose. The bark can be used to make a yellow dye, but again this is rarely used due to the tree's value in producing fruit. The fruit is a great source of pectin, which is particularly useful in the making of jam – it helps the jam solidify (set) and is added to fruit that would otherwise not set. Pectin is said to help protect the body from radiation. The seed can be used to make an oil which is edible and can be burned in a lamp for light. The seeds however contain a small amount of hydrogen cyanide which can be beneficial to the digestion, respiratory system and cancer treatment in tiny quantities but is highly toxic if consumed to excess. Apple wood is hard and fine-grained and is sometimes used for walking sticks and handles of tools.

Medicinally apple is used to treat inflammations and small wounds, as a poultice. It has astringent and laxative properties and the leaves have antibacterial properties. The bark can be used to treat parasitic worms and also acts as a soporific (inducing sleep) and a treatment for fevers. Although they contain significant amounts of sugar, apples can be used to clean the teeth and gums through the action of eating, but drinking water is advisable after to wash away residual sugars. Apple juice, although containing some acids, becomes alkaline carbonates in the stomach and so can help reduce excessive acidity.

## *Cultivation*

There are a wide number of ancient cultivars (varieties) that are no longer widely available in garden centres but these can still be obtained from specialists such as Seedsavers. Native varieties generally fare better than imported common varieties which are generally clones grown on a root-stock that controls its growth rate. Native varieties are often more resistant to disease and local climatic conditions (e.g. lots of rain) than many popular varieties that are not at all well suited to a wetter climate with unreliable sun levels – a perfect example of this would be Cox's Orange Pippin which often does badly in Ireland, Scotland or Wales.

In many cases apple trees are not self-fertile, they are often diploid (needing a tree of another compatible variety) or triploid (needing two compatible varieties), a good example of the latter is the Bramley cooking apple. Fortunately, the crab apple, the ancestor of all domestic apples, is compatible with all other types of apple trees and so can be a useful addition to the garden. Crab apples are also a great benefit to birds and a large number of insects. Domestic apples are hybrids and so the apples they produce are generally not true to type – the seed will produce apple trees that are not identical to their parent varieties.

To grow from seed, it's best to sow in Autumn outside, cold stratification is required. Germination usually happens at the end of winter, although it might take over a year for germination to occur. Protection from wind is a benefit, although they can tolerate cold well. Once a few inches high they can tolerate fairly strong compost, which will encourage rapid growth. Most commercially available apple trees are propagated from cuttings which are then grafted on a rootstock. If taking cuttings yourself, these are best taken in late spring, being about 14cm long with at least one bud. Apply rooting compound or soak in homemade rooting solution (willow bark or blackberry root). Plant in well-draining moist soil, with half (7cm) in the soil, with no direct sunlight.

Apple trees are fairly easy to grow, reaching heights of up to 10m if unrestricted by being grafted onto a root-stock. If you have a small space available it is advisable to buy a variety on a root-stock that will slow down the growth, thereby preventing your tree from becoming an unmanageable size. Apples prefer a loamy soil that is slightly acidic and free draining. It is advisable to do a top dressing with compost every year, in order to maintain a good supply of nutrient for production of flowers and fruit (potassium in particular). They will grow in heavy, damp soils such as clay, but they tend to do less well and will be more prone to diseases such as canker.

In order to get the best results, so far as fruit is concerned, apple trees require plenty of sun, ideally south facing, with not too much exposure to frost and wind, especially in late spring when flowering. Depending on which varieties you pick, fruit can be available from July until early winter and apples store very well in a dry and aerated place so long as they are not bruised. It is advisable not to store apples near potatoes or carrots as this can affect the flavour of the apples and the carrots. Companion plants (i.e. beneficial) are foxgloves, wallflowers and dandelion, which are thought to improve the flavour and aid ripening.

## *Training & Pruning*

This subject is particularly relevant to fruit trees and this information can be applied to other fruit trees generally speaking. The basic rule of rule of training is to begin while the tree is young – this is only really relevant where space is of a premium in which case it might be advisable to train your apple tree in a cordon, fan, espalier of column arrangement.

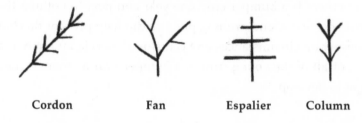

| Cordon | Fan | Espalier | Column |

This is achieved by careful pruning which, should be done at least annually in this case. As a general rule it is a good idea to do some light pruning on free standing (not trained) fruit trees every year. To start with you are looking for the 'three Ds' – dead, damaged or diseased branches. What is called formative pruning is carried out in the early years, to give the tree an open and uncrowded shape, with particular attention being paid to crossing branches that can rub together and create an easy entry point for disease. If a tree that is not too tall is desired the 'leaders' or central uppermost branches can be pruned, which will encourage more lateral (sideways) growth and a bushier shape. Depending on what type of tree you have fruit will appear as tip bearing - at the tip of the branches or on fruit spurs (clusters). Flower buds can be differentiated from leaf buds by their size, i.e. larger size, which should help in avoiding removing them – remember every flower is a potential apple fruit. It's best to either prune in late spring/early summer before flowering, or late winter before the new growth starts, either way it's wise to avoid pruning fruit spurs, which grow on wood two or more years old, unless the spurs are very congested in which case they can be thinned. Tip bearing apple trees bear fruit on the tips of branch growth from the previous year. It's very easy to tell the difference when the trees are in fruit, otherwise it's easiest to spot spur bearing from the short branches with clusters of buds that grow off the main branches.

Sensible pruning generally leads to better and bigger fruit on a regular basis. What is most undesirable is biennial bearing – where there is a bumper crop one year and next to nothing the following year. Good pruning practice can help prevent this but in desperate circumstances one can stop the cycle by removing most or all of the young fruit in a bumper year as soon as they begin to develop.

## Ash

Latin: Fraxinus excelsior
Irish: Onn, Fuinseóg /Nuin, Nin, Uinnius. Welsh: Onnen.
Breton: Onn.
17th or 5th letter of the Ogham alphabet (depending on interpretation of source material).

Ash is one the most important trees in ancient Celtic culture, as was also the case in Norse culture. There is a huge wealth of myth and folk custom associated with this tree – in Ireland it was linked with fertility of the land and childbirth. In Norse myth it is sacred to the father god Odin, who hung himself on an ash tree (for nine days and nights) to gain insight, and the world tree Yggdrasil was a huge ash tree connecting the nine realms of existence. It is also considered sacred to the pan-Celtic god Lugh, who possessed a magical spear. Spears were most often made of ash in Ireland. Three of the five sacred trees of Ireland were ash trees – *Bile Uisnigh* in Meath, *Craobh Daithi* in Westmeath and *Bile*

*Tortan* (the most sacred of all) also stood in Meath. It was great age and size and is believed to symbolize the world tree; when it fell a calamity fell upon Meath, so much was the prosperity and sovereignty of the land linked to it.

Superstitions around ash include that it is the first tree to be hit by lightning. Ash twigs placed under milk vessels were thought to deter theft by fairies. Ash keys (winged seeds) when carried were thought to protect against witchcraft, although ash was also used by witches in magic. Various folk cures especially for children existed and in Scotland a green ash stick was held in the fire and the resulting sap that came from the other end was the first liquid fed to newborns to give them the strength of the ash.

Ash is strongly associated with holy wells, including those that predate Christianity. Ash is associated with St. Brigid, who herself is associated with children and their protection. The ash wand of the Druids was used in healing, surviving as a tool of the fairy doctors in Ireland who would place it on their knees during invocations and prayers.

In myth Queen Maebh is associated with the ash, in the epic *Táin Bó Cúailnge* every place that she planted her ash horsewhip became known as *Bile Maedhbh*. The poem Cad Goddeu mentions the ash as particularly exalted and in Gaul the goddess Onniona was worshipped in ash groves.

### *Uses*

The immature seeds were pickled in vinegar and eaten as a condiment and an edible oil can be extracted from the mature seeds. Ash makes great firewood and is a species that can be burned 'green' i.e. without being seasoned, it was often used for the traditional yule log. It was often used in building and fencing as well as for tools, boats and furniture. It was also used in Ireland for spears and hurley sticks (to play hurling); due to a shortage of ash (and ash die-back disease) it is mostly imported by hurley makers. Ash bark was also used for tanning leather, and dried leaves could be used as animal fodder. A fungus growing on ash (St. Anthony's buttons) was formerly used as firelighters. A green dye can be obtained from the leaves, and lengths of bark were used like short ropes for ties. Ash can be coppiced and grows back quickly; it is often found in hedgerows.

Medicinally ash bark extract was used for cuts and for fever. It can also be used as a laxative and purgative. Ash buds or roots were used to cure liver problems. Young tips and leaves were dried and powdered and used to treat rheumatism, jaundice and gout. As an essence it is used to give endurance and resilience. Both the leaves and the bark can be used as an astringent. The seeds can be used to treat flatulence and a gassy stomach.

Ash has been used magically to make wands as well as spears, thought to harness solar energy, associated with the god Lugh. It was widely used to make witches' brooms as well as Maypoles at *Bealtaine*/Beltane. Ash can be used in healing, love and fertility magic as well as in divinatory fires or as an aid to prophetic visions or dreams.

## *Cultivation*

Ash is a fast-growing tree despite the fact that it is late to come into leaf and early to lose its leaves. It is a hardy tree that can grow to around 30m tall with a wide canopy. It is usually dioecious which means that you need both male and female trees in order to obtain seed from the female, however they can also be hermaphrodite and even change sex yearly. It grows well in virtually any soil type and can tolerate both alkaline and very acid soils but grows best in loamy, damp soil. It does not grow well in shade but can tolerate windy locations, coastal areas and polluted conditions.

Young growth can be vulnerable to late frosts in spring and are best protected from early morning sun although they should never be grown in a shady spot as they are liable to do very badly or die as seedlings or saplings. They are resistant to honey fungus but are being decimated across Europe by the fungus Hymenoscyphus fraxineus, commonly called ash die-back. This is incurable, although efforts are being made to breed resistant trees. Diseased trees should be felled and burned in order to reduce the spread of the fungus.

Seed can be collected while it is still green, before it dries out and turns brown. It can be sown immediately in autumn, preferably in a coldframe outside as it requires cold stratification, and usually germinates in spring. Much of the seed will not germinate until the second spring in soil. Seedlings should be grown in full sun, of course ensuring that they are also well watered regularly, especially during dry spells.

## Aspen

Latin: Populus tremula
Irish: Crann Creathach, Fiodhadh, Edad, Eadha. Welsh:
Aethnen. Breton: Unknown.
21st letter of the Ogham alphabet.

Aspen, with its flat leaves that rustle in the slightest wind, is associated with death and misfortune and considered an unlucky tree. The sound it makes is reminiscent of the sound of the sea, leading people to associate it with the otherworld beyond the western ocean, in Ireland it was referred to as the trembling tree.

In both Wales and Scotland, it was believed that Jesus' cross was made from aspen and so it was particularly reviled. The wood was never used for tools but it was acceptable to burn it. Despite its fearsome reputation it was used in medicine and magic. Folk cures included nailing a piece of hair to an aspen for fever, drinking mare's milk from an aspen spoon for whooping cough and also to expel evil forces. Due to its association with death, the funereal stick used to measure bodies (*fé*) was made from aspen, the stick would only be touched by the undertaker and it was generally regarded with dread. In Irish myth aspen is associated with approaching death, such as the death of Oscar of the Fianna (son of Oisin and grandson of Finn). It is also referred to negatively in the story of Oisin's return from Tir Na nÓg and in the Fate of the Children of Usna. Aspen is also associated with witches and magic and bronze age burials such as in Denmark and earlier still in Sumer.

## Uses

Apart from its ancient use in association with death aspen has very few practical uses, although in desperate times the inner bark could be ground up to be used in flour. Aspen is very wind tolerant and can be used as a windbreak to provide shelter. They can also be planted to help improve heavy clay soils. The wood is soft and flexible and can be used to make high quality paper or charcoal.

Medicinally it has been used to treat fevers, the bark and leaves are a mild diuretic and expectorant. Aspen is sometimes included in medicines for chronic prostate and bladder disorders. The bark contains salicin, a glycoside that probably decomposes into salicylic acid, giving anti-inflammatory, pain relieving and fever relieving properties. It is used especially in treating rheumatism and fevers, and also to relieve the pain of menstrual cramps. It is used in Bach flower remedies for fear and anxiety. Magically it is used in relation to shielding, overcoming fears and to aid communication with the spirit world. It has been used in 'flying ointments' to aid otherworldly travel and vision.

## Cultivation

Aspen is part of the poplar genus and is a fast-growing tree that can reach up to 20m in height. Aspen can colonize ground by sending out suckers, in some cases creating a whole woodland in which most of the trees are directly connected. Aspen is dioecious, meaning that both male and female trees are needed in order to produce any seed. The flowers are long catkins, similar to those on birch or alder. Aspen grows in most soils, including heavy damp clay but it is not especially drought tolerant and does not like limey (alkaline) soil. It will struggle badly in salty coastal conditions but does well in exposed sites inland. It is generally not hard to grow and grows rapidly, but like alder, is a short-lived tree. Because of its extensive and invasive root system it is not a good idea to plant them near drainage areas or within 10m of a building.

Aspen are a benefit to wildlife, especially insects, including butterflies. Aspens flower in early spring before fully in leaf. The female trees produce seed that ripens in late summer, which is dispersed by the wind. The seed is not viable for long and if it dries out much will not germinate. Seeds should be planted when ripe in damp conditions and the seedlings will need to be well watered until they become established.

An alternative way of growing an aspen is to dig up root suckers and transfer them to a new site, branch cuttings can also take easily if kept in moist conditions without direct sunlight. Aspen can breed with other members of the poplar family, producing some interesting hybrids.

## Beech

Latin: Fagus sylvatica
Irish: Phagos. Welsh: Ffawydd. Breton: Faou.
25th letter of the Ogham alphabet (depending on interpretation of source material).

Beech probably should not be in the *ogham* alphabet at all, as it was only introduced to Ireland in the Norman period. It is native to Britain and all of Europe. The Welsh goddess Cerridwen in the form of Henwen (the great white sow) gained divine insight from eating nuts from a sacred Beech tree. It is said that, like hazel nuts, beech nuts symbolised ancient wisdom to the Druids. In

Greek legend Jason built his ship the Argo from beech and Helen of Troy was said to have carved Paris' name upon a beech tree. Altars dedicated to the Gallo-Roman god Fagus have been found in France, who was the god associated with beech trees. The Taliesin poem *Cad Goddeu* refers to the beech as a tree associated with magic and it was believed that saying spells or incantations by a beech tree or writing them on beech wood increased their efficacy. In Saxon tradition *boc* (beech) was used to carve the first runes and is root of the word 'book.'

## *Uses*

Beech wood is hard and heavy and very durable. The beech nuts are edible and have been widely eaten in the past, raw or roasted. The seed can be ground into powder for flour as a coffee substitute, however the outer casing of the seed is poisonous. A delicate oil can be pressed from the seeds which can be used in dressings and cooking. The oil can also be used as a lubricant, fuel for lamps and for polishing wood. Young leaves are also edible can be used in salads and are also used in making a liqueur.

Traditionally leaf buds harvested on the twigs and dried were used as toothpicks. Brown leaves gathered in autumn were used to stuff mattresses. The wood is excellent for furniture but not for outdoor use as it is often attacked by beetles. The wood burns well and is also used for turning, flooring and to make creosote, methylated spirit and acetic acid as well as charcoal.

Magically, water from a hollow in a beech is said to be efficacious for any spells. Words written on beech wood or leaves were thought to take on the power and magic of the gods. Beech is associated with divine wisdom and learning generally.

Medicinally, Beech Bach Flower Remedies is considered effective for mental rigidity, intolerance, criticism and lack of sympathy or empathy. Beech bark is antacid, antipyretic, antiseptic, and expectorant. A tar made by dry distillation of the branches has stimulating and antiseptic properties. It is used internally as a stimulating expectorant and externally as treatment for various skin conditions, such as psoriasis.

## *Cultivation*

Beech grows to around 30m and can at times be as wide as it is tall, but is slow growing. The species is monoecious (flowers are either male or female, but both sexes can be found on the same plant). It is pollinated by wind. It can grow in most soils but prefers well-drained soil. It can prove highly dangerous in drought conditions, when beeches are prone to drop large individual branches in order to conserve water. It can tolerate a wide range of pH and will also grow in full shade or full sun. It is tolerant of windy sites and high levels of pollution but cannot tolerate coastal salty air.

It is noted for attracting wildlife, including insects, and the 'nuts' are also a valuable food source. The immature tree retains its dead leaves in winter and is commonly used for hedging, however it cannot be coppiced and does not re-grow well when heavily pruned.

The seed has short viability and is best sown as soon as it is ripe in the autumn in a coldframe. It is advisable to protect the seed from mice and other rodents. Germination takes place in the spring although it is best to protect seedlings from frost for their first winter. They can be planted out permanently in late spring or early summer when risk of frost has passed. Young trees grow slowly and are susceptible to damage to new growth from frost.

# Birch

Latin: Betula pendula, Betula alba, Betula pubescens
Irish: Beith, Beithe. Welsh: Bedw. Breton: Bezv.
1st letter of the Ogham alphabet.

Birch is a tree of beginnings and is a pioneer tree, colonizing new ground, hence it is the first letter of the *beith-luis-nin* or ancient Irish alphabet. Birch has wealth of folklore and myth associated with it – it was particularly thought to be protective of small children and was placed over cradles for this purpose, it was also associated with promoting fertility. Birch was regarded as purifying and protective against evil, it was often placed in graves as a symbol of rebirth and is associated with funeral rituals in Ireland, Scotland and even ancient Celtic burials discovered in Germany.

Birch is a symbol of femininity and maidenhood and the white birch (alba) being compared to a beautiful young woman while the weeping birch (pendula) was compared to an old woman with wisdom and experience. It is also very much associated with the goddess Brid (Brighid), particularly in Scotland and Ireland, where twigs were used in ceremony around *Imbolc* (St. Brigid's day). There is also some evidence to link it with the Irish god of love, Aongus Mac Óg. Strangely birch was also used for corporal punishment of children (apparently also used to beat Jesus), in which a thin branch or tied branches was used like a cane, presumably to purify them of their wickedness! This bizarre form of punishment persisted in Scotland until the 1980s when it was banned.

Birch features in tales as a symbol of love, the famous lovers Diarmuid and Gráinne slept on a bed made of birch tips and rushes. Birch features in both Irish and Welsh poetry alluding to the beauty of women and also as a symbol of romantic love.

It was thought to protect people from malign fairies and it is said that the first use of *ogham* was seven letters representing

*Beith* written on a birch branch as a warning to the god Lugh whose wife was in danger of being abducted by the *sídhe*.

## Uses

Birch was traditionally used for brooms but has a large number of other uses. Because it is waterproof, durable, tough and resinous the bark has many uses- drinking vessels, canoe skins, roofing tiles etc. If only the outer bark is removed, this does cause excessive damage or kill the tree. Tar-oil is obtained from the white bark in spring which has fungicidal properties and can also be used as insect repellent and as shoe polish. The bark was used for kindling or firelighters and it also produces a high-quality charcoal favoured by artists.

A decoction of the inner bark was used to preserve ropes and fishing lines, as it contains a large amount of tannin. The inner bark is also used to make a brown dye. Strips of the inner bark were twisted to make cords or ties. Glue can be made from the sap. The young branches are highly flexible and were used in fencing (wattles), thatching and to make implements such as a whisk.

The wood is soft, lightweight and flexible but fairly durable. It has been used extensively for tools, furniture, toys and ornaments and is also pulped to make paper.

An oil from the inner bark can be used medicinally and also makes a refreshing tea, as does the young leaves. It can be cooked or dried and ground into a meal or added as a thickener to soups etc. or can be mixed with flour for making bread, biscuits etc. The Sap, raw or cooked, has a sweet flavour which is best harvested by tapping the trunk in early spring, before the leaves become established. A drink and a syrup can be made from the sap and it can also be used in beer making and to make a wine. The young leaves are edible both raw or cooked.

Birch has many medicinal uses. It is anti-inflammatory, stimulates bile flow and promotes sweating. The bark has diuretic and laxative properties. An oil from the inner bark is astringent and is used in the treatment of various skin afflictions, especially eczema and psoriasis. A decoction of leaves and bark is used as bath for skin irritations and spots.

The inner bark can also be used to treat fevers. The buds produce an aromatic and oily balsam. The leaves are acidic and diuretic and reduce cholesterol levels. They also contain anti-bacterial agents – phytoncides. An infusion of the leaves can be used in the treatment of gout, dropsy, urinary tract infections such as cystitis, rheumatism and to dissolve kidney or bladder stones.

It is said to be a cure for impotence, exhaustion, general fatigue by calming the adrenal glands and stress. As a magical or healing tonic, the sap, tea or essence is meant to provide renewed vigour, purification and revitalized mental and spiritual states.

*NOTE: It is recommended that pregnant women do not ingest birch. The aromatic and aliphatic hydrocarbons in birch tar can irritate those with hypersensitive skin. It is advisable not to be consumed by people with chronic kidney or heart conditions.*

## Cultivation

Birch is fast growing, but the European varieties rarely live over a hundred years, although some species of birch can live up to 300 years. If they are able to grow in drought free conditions, they are likely to live far longer. As a pioneer species, it readily invades fields, wasteland, brownfield sites, cleared or burnt land and creates conditions suitable for other woodland trees to grow. Since it is relatively short-lived and intolerant of shade, it is often eventually out-competed by longer lived and more shade tolerant trees.

Betula pendula reaches around 20m tall and grows quickly. It is hardy and frost tolerant and is in flower in April, producing catkins, and the seeds ripen from June onwards. The species is monoecious (individual flowers are either male or female, but both sexes can be found on the same plant) and is wind pollinated. It is beneficial for wildlife, supporting over 200 insect species.

It will grow in most soils but due to its shallow root system is often prone to suffer in light sandy soils that drain very quickly. It does not do well in drought conditions and is considered likely to become extinct from much of southern Europe and other areas that are becoming increasingly short of water.

Birch will grow well in exposed sites and in soils of a wide range of pH but it is not able to tolerate salty coastal conditions. It makes an excellent nurse tree for seedling trees, although its fine branches can damage nearby trees in a windy location. Its root action helps improve the soil and makes a good companion plant. The young tree is brown in colour, eventually turning white and black as it matures. They generally don't produce seed until around 15 years old.

To grow from seed, it is best sown as soon as it is ripe (summer/autumn) in a light position ideally in a coldframe. The seed should be sown very close to the soil surface and spring sown seed does not need to buried at all. In all cases, sow in a sunny position where the warmth will aid germination. It's advisable to keep seedlings in a coldframe for at least their first winter. Plant them out into their permanent positions in late spring or early summer, after the last expected frosts. If you have sufficient seed, it can be sown in an outdoor seedbed, either as soon as it is ripe or in the early spring - do not cover the spring sown seed. It is important to monitor moisture levels with birch as although they need plenty of sunlight, they are intolerant of drought, especially when they are juvenile.

In relation to using parts of the tree, some care is required to ensure continued good health.

Bark is best obtained from cut branches or felled trees, to avoid killing the tree. Leaves and buds should be taken in spring for use immediately or stored for later. Sap, taken in spring, should be taken from mature trees only. It's advisable not to take more than 5 litres and this should not be repeated for several years otherwise the tree may die. The tap hole must be plugged after tapping.

## Blackthorn

Latin: Prunus spinosa
Irish: Straif, Draighean. Welsh: Banadl. Breton: Irin.
14th letter of the Ogham alphabet.

Blackthorn, from the cherry genus, has more in common with hawthorn and buckthorn having thorns and bitter sloes (berries). This is a small tree much associated with evil and fierceness but also strength and protection, in Ireland a blackthorn stick was thought to protect one from harm, including warding off fairies. Blackthorn has ambiguous qualities being able to cause harm or help to animals or crops in folk tales. In Scotland it was regarded as an unlucky wood to use. As with the buckthorn it was superstition that Jesus' crown of thorns was made from blackthorn.

In Irish tradition the blackthorn was protected on the 11th day of May and November by 'lunantishees', probably a corruption of the term for fairy lover *Leannán Sídhe*. Perhaps because of its attractive flowers it was associated with feminine beauty, and unlike hawthorn, is considered a female tree. It is linked to the *Leannán Sídhe*, a female fairy that bewitches men with love causing them to waste away.

In myth, Mad Sweeney is tormented by thorned trees, including blackthorn. It is referred to in the story 'The Intoxication of the Ulstermen', in which advancing warriors are compared to the tree. Other references in stories emphasize its warlike or malevolent nature such as the tales of Conn and Sadhbh, in which a horrific worm monster emerges from the head of their son as a result of eating blackthorn sloes. Blackthorn is also associated with witches, the Cailleach, powerful females and most probably the pagan war goddesses of Ireland.

## *Uses*

It was often used for walking sticks (shillelaghs) in Ireland. The berries are used to make sloe gin that was traditionally drunk at Halloween (*Samhain*). It is also popular to this day as a hedging plant, particularly in farm hedgerows.

The fruit (sloes) are very astringent, it is normally cooked but once the fruit has been frosted it loses some of its bitterness and can be eaten raw. The fruit is more usually used in jellies, syrups, conserves etc. and as a flavouring for sloe gin and other liqueurs than eaten on its own. The seed, inside the sloes, can be eaten cooked in small quantities but is very bitter and contains toxins. The leaves are used as a tea substitute, but they also contain some toxin. The dried fruits can be added to herbal teas or are served in gin cocktails. The flowers are edible and can be crystallised or sugared.

The flowers, bark, leaves and fruits are mildly purgative, astringent, depurative, diaphoretic, diuretic and febrifuge. An infusion of the flowers is used in the treatment of diarrhoea (especially for children), bladder and kidney disorders and stomach weakness. It can also be used to treat inflammations of the mouth and throat. In very small amounts hydrocyanic acid from this plant, although exceedingly poisonous, stimulates respiration and improves digestion.

*NOTE: pregnant women, people with heart problems, allergies or high blood pressure should avoid ingestion. The toxin Hydrogen cyanide is found mainly in the leaves and seed and is highly poisonous unless consumed in very tiny quantities.*

## *Cultivation*

Blackthorn is a small deciduous tree growing to 3m at a medium rate. It is hardy and wind tolerant. It is in flower from the end of

February to April, making it an early source of food for bees. The fruits ripen in October. The species is hermaphrodite (has both male and female organs) and is pollinated by insects.

It will grow in most soils of variable pH including very alkaline soil, but it prefers well-drained soil and does badly in very acid peat soils. It is highly resistant to honey fungus. It can grow in semi-shade or full sun and in coastal exposed sites. It prefers moist soil. The plant can tolerate maritime exposure.

It is an important food plant for the caterpillars of several species of butterfly as well as bees. Plants are shallow-rooted and produce suckers that can form dense impenetrable thickets, which are ideal for nesting birds. They regenerate quickly after cutting or after fast moving forest fires, producing suckers from below ground level. The flowers, which arrive early, are often damaged by late frosts.

The seed needs 2-3 months cold stratification and is best sown in a coldframe as soon as it is ripe in late autumn, to protect the seed from mice and other rodents. The seed can take up to 18 months to germinate. Leave them in a coldframe for their first winter and plant them out in late spring or early summer of the following year. Cuttings can be made of new growth from strongly growing plants in spring to early summer in a frame, protected from direct sunlight. They can be grown by digging up and dividing suckers during the winter and planted in their final position.

## Broom

Latin: Sarothamnus scoparius, Cytisus scoparius
Irish: nGetal, Giolcach. Welsh: Banadl. Breton: Banal.
13th letter of the Ogham alphabet (depending on interpretation of source material).

As a small tree of about 3m in height, broom is probably the correct interpretation although some *ogham* lists give dwarf elder or the small herbaceous plants fern or reed instead. The oldest source material, *Auraicept na n-éces* (Scholar's Primer) favours broom, which I would consider to be most likely to be correct.

Broom is an attractive, fragrant tree associated with purification and indeed was commonly used as the brush on brooms, hence the name of the cleaning tool. Broom is associated with maidenhood and feminine beauty and in England, Wales and Brittany it has connections with marriage. It was also adopted as the flower symbol of Brittany. In May it was common to bring the yellow flowers into the house. In Ireland a single broom bush was regarded as a likely place for the *sídhe* (fairies) to live. In Welsh myth broom relates to female figures: Olwen's hair is compared to the broom flower and Blodeuedd is created from broom, oak and meadowsweet flowers. The tree is also associated with astral travel and flying witches, although it was also considered to offer protection from witches.

## Uses

The branches were used in thatching and the bark fibres can be used to make paper. The branches were also used in fencing and to make baskets. Tannin from the bark can also be used to tan leather. In ancient times the flowers were eaten. The seeds have disinfectant properties as does the ash from burned broom. In Ireland rooms were fumigated using the smoke of burning broom twigs. The flower buds can be pickled and used as a substitute for capers or be added to salads. The tender green tips of the plant have been used like hops to give a bitter flavour to beer. The roasted seeds make a reasonable coffee substitute. A yellow and a brown dye are made from the bark, a yellow dye from the flowering stem and a green dye from the leaves and young tips. An essential oil from the flowers is used in perfume.

Broom is a bitter narcotic herb that depresses the respiration and regulates heart action, slowing its pace and as such should only be used by an expert herbalist. The young herbaceous tips of flowering shoots are diuretic, emetic and a vasoconstrictor. The plant is excellent for stimulating urine production and thus countering fluid retention. It has been used to prevent blood loss after childbirth as it causes muscles of the uterus to contract. In Cornwall a diuretic drink was made from the corresponding sexed tree for both men and women. A drink made from the flowers was used to treat gout.

*NOTE: Use this herb with caution since large doses are likely to upset the stomach and also affect the heart. This herb should not be prescribed to pregnant women or patients with high blood pressure. Flowers and young tips are collected in late spring but they should not be stored for more than 12 months since the medicinally active ingredients break down.*

## *Cultivation*

It is a small hardy tree and is not frost tender. It usually flowers May to June, and the seeds ripen from August to November. The species is hermaphrodite (has both male and female organs) but the plant is not self-fertile. It is pollinated by bees and the seeds are dispersed by explosive action when the seed pods burst open. It can grow well in most soils but is well suited to low-nutrient sandy soils, especially along coast lines as it tolerates salt very well. It can tolerate a range of pH, pollution, drought, severe cold and will grow in semi-shade as well as full sun. It does not like highly alkaline soils.

Growing well on dry banks and on steep slopes, it is an effective sand binder and soil stabilizer and is also able to fix nitrogen in the soil. Broom is one of the first plants to colonize sand dunes by the coast. It also attracts insects away from nearby plants and is a benefit to wildlife, especially bees, ants and butterflies. Broom has deep roots and will regenerate after being cut back. It is often killed by fires but this prompts rapid germination of seeds.

This tree is best grown in a permanent spot and does not like to be transferred, especially when more than 25cm (1 foot) tall. To grow from seed, it is best sown as soon as it is ripe in the autumn in a coldframe. The seed stays viable for a long time. Pre-soak stored seed for 24 hours in warm water then cold stratify for one month and sow outside, preferably in a coldframe. Seeds germinate in spring when warm temperatures resume. Seedlings should be potted up quickly, since plants quickly become intolerant of root disturbance, and transferred to a permanent location as soon as possible in summer. It can be grown from cuttings in autumn using short lengths (5cm) if protected from direct sunlight and drought.

## Buckthorn

Latin: Rhamnus cathartica
Irish: Muin, Ramh-dhreighean. Welsh: Rhafnwydd.
Breton: Unknown.
11th letter of the Ogham alphabet (depending on interpretation of source material).

Buckthorn was an important medicinal tree in ancient times due to its purgative properties. There is not a lot of folklore relating to this tree. In England it was superstition that Jesus' crown of thorns came from buckthorn. It was considered to offer protection against evil but was often confused with blackthorn that was generally regarded as a malignant tree. The name *ramh-dhreighean* was often confused with *draigen,* meaning blackthorn.

### *Uses*

A green dye is obtained from the immature berries. If they are mixed with gum arabic and limewater, it makes a green pigment used in watercolour painting. Yellow dye is made from the bark and orange and brownish dyes can also be made from buckthorn but are not long lasting. It has been used in the past to colour paper and maps. It has been grown in hedges, like hawthorn or blackthorn as a barrier for livestock. The wood is hard and has a pleasant grain and has been used in turnery for small items.

Both the bark and the fruit of buckthorn have been used for their purgative effect upon the body, however they can be rather violent in their action and so are rarely used in modern medicines although it was commonly used by apothecaries and physicians in the British Isles. The ripe berries are cathartic, depurative, diuretic, laxative and violently purgative. About 8 - 15 of the mature fruits chewed, are a strong and effective laxative for adults, but they should not be used by children. An infusion of the not quite ripe fruits is milder in its purgative action. It can be an effective cure for constipation.

NOTE: *Should be used with caution, in large doses the fruit can cause vomiting and violent diarrhoea.*

## Cultivation

This small tree grows to around 6m and about half that in width. It is hardy and not frost tender. It flowers from May to June and the seeds ripen in October. The species is dioecious (individual flowers are either male or female, both male and female plants must be grown if seed is to be produced). It is pollinated by insects and the plant is not self-fertile. It is a benefit to wildlife including insects. It can grow in full sun or semi-shade and it grows in most soils and will tolerate any pH including highly alkaline soils.

Seeds are best sown as soon as they are ripe in the autumn, in a coldframe. Stored seed will require 1-2 months cold stratification and should be sown as early in the year as possible outside in a coldframe, where they should remain for their first winter. Plant them out in late spring or early summer of the following year. Cuttings of half-ripe wood can be made in later summer, kept out of direct sunlight.

# Cherry

Latin: Prunus avium
Irish: Nin, Nuin, Silín, Fidach, Idath. Welsh: Ceirios.
Breton: Kerez.
5th letter of the Ogham alphabet (depending on interpretation
of source material).

With its beautiful flowers, attractive bark and sweet fruits this
tree is symbol of beauty, love and youthfulness. It is a popular
tree worldwide, especially in Japan where it is the centre of an
annual spring festival. Cherry was associated with the cuckoo,
especially in England and is connected with forbidden love, and
cherry stones were used in children's divination games.

In Celtic legend and lore, it is referred to as *Idath* in the old
Irish tree listing, although this term was later replaced leading
to its confusion with Ash, within the *ogham* tree lists. This same
term is used in relation to youthful love rivals to an older man
and indeed some stories of Irish love god Aongus Mac Óg
include references to the cuckoo, linked to this tree.

In the 'Cattle Raid of Fraoch', Fraoch son of Idath (cherry),
the handsomest warrior in Ireland and Scotland, seeks the
hand of Findabair, the daughter of Connacht rulers Maebh and
Ailill. In Scottish highland folklore, wild cherry had mysterious
qualities, and to encounter one was considered auspicious. Many
varieties of cultivated cherry exist, with Pliny describing their
introduction by Rome into Gaul and Britain in the 1st century
CE, most probably as a sweeter and larger fruited alternative
to the wild tree. It is said the fairies love flowering cherry trees,
although its brief flowering period is symbolic of the fleetingness
of both youth and often love.

## Uses

Cherry fruit has been gathered as food since ancient times. In
county Offaly, Ireland, excavations of a bronze age *crannog*

revealed cherry stones. It is highly valued for the fruit but all other parts of the tree except the flowers are poisonous to humans. The fruit is used to make alcoholic beverages. The wild cherry is often used as a rootstock for cultivated cherry varieties as well as other fruit trees. Its wood is strong and durable but there is little evidence of it being used much in ancient times, although it has been popular for furniture and instruments in more recent eras. A green dye can be made from the leaves and a dark grey to green dye can be made from the fruit. The bark usually only contains small amounts of tannin, but this sometimes rises making it suitable for tanning leather.

The fruit stalks are astringent, diuretic and tonic. A decoction can be used in the treatment of cystitis, edema, bronchial complaints, loose bowels and anemia. An aromatic, edible resin/gum can be obtained by making small incisions in the trunk. This has been used as an inhalant in the treatment of persistent coughs. The seeds should not be eaten as they contain compounds that form hydrocyanic acid which is toxic.

## Cultivation

This deciduous tree grows to around 18m at a fast rate although many modern varieties are grown on rootstocks that restrict the growth. A large number of commercially available varieties are purely ornamental, being infertile and producing no fruits. It is hardy to zone and flowers from March to possibly May, and the seeds ripen from July to August. The species is hermaphrodite (has both male and female organs) and is pollinated by insects, it is not self-fertile. It will grow in most soils of a reasonable pH range but does very poorly in heavy clay or boggy soil. In damp countries it prone to diseases such as bacterial canker, hence does less well in Ireland, Scotland and Wales than other countries of western Europe. For good fruit production trees are best located in full sun. They can produce quite a lot of suckers and can form thickets, especially if the main trunk is felled.

Many modern cultivars may be trained, such as on an espalier, or against a south facing wall, at least two trees are required to obtain fruit. Cherry is attractive to both insects and birds. Use of nets is quite popular to prevent birds from stripping the trees of ripe fruit, which can occur in less than a day. It makes a good companion plant for potatoes, reducing their susceptibility to blight. They are best grown away from plum trees as the roots of plum are antagonistic towards cherry.

To grow from seed needs 2-3 months cold stratification and it is best sown in a coldframe as soon as it is ripe. Protect the seed from mice and other rodents. The seed can sometimes take 18 months to germinate. Leave seedlings in a coldframe for their first winter and plant them out in late spring or early summer of the following year. Softwood cuttings can be made from strongly growing plants in spring to early summer, protected from direct sun. Suckers can be dug up and divided in the winter and replanted in their permanent positions.

## *Training and pruning*

See this section under 'apple' for general information. Cherry should only be pruned in mid-summer during a dry warm spell in damp countries such as Ireland or Scotland. This is to reduce the chances of infection such as bacterial canker or honey fungus, which this tree is vulnerable to. Avoid damaging the bark if at all possible as this is another entry point of infection.

## Chestnut (Horse)

Latin: Aesculus hippocastanum
Irish: Crann cnó capaill. Welsh: Castanwydden y meirch.
Breton: Kistin-Moc'h.
Not native to Ireland or Britain.

There is no Celtic myth or lore related to this tree, as it was only introduced to Britain and Ireland around 1600 CE, although it is native to the Balkans and was in western Europe at the time of the Druids. The most known use of horse chestnut is the game of conkers in which the seed is hung on a string to try and smash an opponent's conker, the game is still played today.

## Uses

The seed is not suitable for human consumption without removal of the saponins which are toxic, which can be done by slow roasting and rinsing in water for at least two days. The roasted seed can used as a coffee substitute and also to make a porridge, although due to the effort involved, they are rarely made use of.

Saponins extracted from seed are used as a soap substitute, extracted by soaking the diced seed in hot water. A yellow dye is obtained from the bark. A starch obtained from the seed was used in laundering. The bark and other parts of the plant contain tannin, which can be used to tan leather. The wood is fairly soft and not durable but is used for furniture, firewood, boxes and charcoal. It can be pollarded and re-grows strongly when cut back.

Horse chestnut is an astringent, anti-inflammatory herb that helps to tone the vein walls which, when slack or distended, may become varicose or haemorrhoidal. It can be used to treat fluid retention. The bark, harvested in spring, is anti-inflammatory, astringent, diuretic, febrifuge, narcotic, tonic and vasoconstrictive. The plant is taken in small doses internally for the treatment of a wide range of venous diseases, including hardening of the arteries, varicose veins, phlebitis, leg ulcers, haemorrhoids and frostbite. It is also made into a lotion or gel for external application. A tea made from the bark is used in the treatment of malaria and dysentery, externally in the treatment of lupus and skin ulcers. A tea made from the leaves is tonic and is used in the treatment of fevers and whooping cough. An oil extracted from the seeds has been used externally as a treatment for rheumatism. In Bach flower remedies it is used for mental ailments such as unwanted thoughts and difficulties with learning from past experience.

*NOTE: this tree is potentially toxic and should only be used medicinally under expert supervision.*

## *Cultivation*

Grows to around 30m and with a wide canopy at a fast rate. It is hardy and is not frost tender. It produces attractive flowers in May, and the seeds ripen in September. The species is hermaphrodite (has both male and female organs) and is pollinated by insects. It can grow in almost any soil of variable pH and can grow in nutritionally poor soil. It will grow in semi-shade as well as full sun, in exposed or polluted sites, but does not tolerate coastal conditions well.

It can take up to 20 years for this tree to produce seed. The seed is best sown outdoors or in a coldframe as soon as it is ripe. Do not allow seed to dry out, sow as soon as possible as viability is very short - stored dry seed will rarely germinate even if soaked. It is best to sow the seed with its 'scar' downwards. Move seedlings to their final positions in early summer.

## Chestnut (Sweet/Spanish)

Latin: Castenea sativa
Irish: Castán Eorpach. Welsh: Castanwydd. Breton: Kistin.
Not native to Ireland or Britain.

There is no Celtic myth or lore related to this tree but in France it was used for roofing as it was believed to protect the home from lightning. Native to southern Europe, it was spread by the Greeks and Romans. It is said to have been introduced to Britain by the Romans, although evidence suggests it might have been later. It was introduced to Ireland somewhat later still, probably no earlier than the Norman period.

## Uses

The seed can be eaten raw or cooked although it is somewhat bitter tasting raw. The flavour improves considerably when cooked and is delicious baked, having a floury texture and a taste similar to sweet potato. The seed is rich in carbohydrates, it can be dried and ground for use as flour in breads, puddings, as a thickener in soups and roasted as a coffee substitute. A sugar can also be extracted from the seed.

Tannin is obtained from the bark, wood, seed husks and leaves. The ground seed has been used as a source of starch and also for whitening linen cloth. Shampoo can be made from the leaves and the skins of the fruits. The wood is hard, strong, light and the young wood is durable although it becomes more prone to cracking when mature. It has been popular for carpentry, turnery, baskets, fence posts and also makes very good firewood.

Sweet chestnut leaves and bark are a good source of tannins and these have an astringent action useful in the treatment of bleeding and diarrhoea. The leaves (best harvested in early summer) and bark are anti-inflammatory, astringent, expectorant and tonic. A decoction from leaves makes a gargle for treating sore throats. An infusion of leaves has been used in the treatment of fevers and ague, convulsive coughs such as whooping cough and general respiratory system ailments. The leaves can also be used in the treatment of rheumatism, lower back pain and stiff muscles and joints. The plant is used in Bach flower remedies for despair and depression.

## Cultivation

This deciduous tree grows up to 30m and about half that in breadth at a medium rate. It is hardy and is not frost tender. It flowers in July and the seeds ripen in October. The species is monoecious (individual flowers are either male or female, but both sexes can be found on the same plant) and is pollinated by insects and is a benefit to wildlife. This species can live for well over a thousand years, sometimes regenerating from the root system for far longer still.

It does well in most soil types but prefers a well-draining soil. It grows best in acid soils, dislikes alkaline soil and prospers in a relatively dry climate, hence the quality of the fruit and seed is not excellent in Ireland and much of Britain. This tree does very badly in shade, it can tolerate drought and coastal regions well. It tolerates being cut and re-grows quickly, hence it was formerly coppiced extensively. This species is resistant to honey fungus.

If possible, sow the seed as soon as it is ripe in a coldframe where it is protected from mice and squirrels. The seed has a short viability and must not be allowed to dry out. It can be stored in a cool place, such as a fridge, for a few months if it is kept moist. The seed should germinate in late winter or early spring. If sown outdoors the plants should be left in situ for 1-2 years before planting out in permanent positions. Pot grown specimens should be planted in the ground in late summer or autumn but protected from frost during their first winter with horticultural fleece.

## Elder

Latin: Sambucus nigra
Irish: Ruis, Trom. Welsh: Ysgawen. Breton: Skav.
15th letter of the Ogham alphabet.

This small tree (also called Bore-tree) is rather scruffy and is often found in hedgerows, it is quite poisonous but produces attractive edible flowers and berries. It is regarded as the feminine fairy tree in Ireland and has associations with evil and witchcraft, although it also has protective powers and many medicinal uses.

It was widely regarded as an unlucky tree, regarded as bad-tempered and symbolic of the mischief of the *sídhe*. This is borne out by the triad 'Three signs of a cursed place – elder, nettle and corncrake' despite beneficial properties of all three. It was advisable not to bring parts of the plant (except berries) into the house and it was also considered dangerous to fall asleep under or next to an elder tree. Burning elder wood was likely to bring misfortune, evil or death upon the household, but a practical reason lies behind this – the nodules that trap moisture can cause branches to explode spraying boiling hot sap everywhere! Elder was thought especially hostile towards children – in the *Annals of the Four Masters* a vengeful spell on a king's pregnant mistress is created using elder rods. In Ireland and Scotland particularly, it also had a reputation as a powerful protection against magic, evil and to keep bad spirits away from milk. It is also associated with the Cailleach and the Greek goddess Hecate.

## Uses

The flowers are used to make a delicious cordial, tea or wine and the berries were widely used as a foodstuff and for elderberry wine. The fruits are not very tasty raw but taste better dried and are much more enjoyable cooked in pies, jams etc.

Any part of the plant but especially the flowers help to activate compost heaps and aid fermentation. The leaves make an effective insect repellent if rubbed on the skin, but be careful not to ingest any. As a decoction the leaves are effective as both insect repellent for plants and as an anti-fungal agent. It is common in hedging and is useful in coastal barriers. The berries produce a purple or blue dye and the bark and root is used to make a black dye. A green dye can be made from the leaves. The wood can be used for musical instruments and small carpentry but it has generally not been used for this in the British Isles due to its unlucky or evil reputation.

Elder has been widely used historically by herbalists and folk healers as it has many medicinal uses. The flowers are used as a stimulant, making a refreshing tonic, elder water from flowers is a mild astringent. An infusion is used for chest complaints. A poultice of flowers treats pain and inflammation. The dried flowers are diaphoretic, diuretic, expectorant and pectoral. The inner bark is diuretic, a strong purgative and in larger doses emetic. Elder can be used in the treatment of constipation and arthritic conditions. The dried leaves are highly purgative and can cause nausea, they are poisonous and should be used with extreme care. They are also diaphoretic, diuretic, expectorant and haemostatic. An ointment made from the leaves is used in the treatment of bruises, sprains, chilblains and wounds. The berry juice is said to be a good treatment for inflamed eyes. A tea from the berries is a treatment for colic and diarrhoea. The pith inside stems can be used for relieving burns. The root was effective against dropsy and is a very strong purgative. The fruit is believed to retain many of the medicinal properties of this tree.

*NOTE: all parts of this tree are highly poisonous except the flowers and fruit and should be used medicinally only under the advice of an expert.*

## Cultivation

This small tree grows up to 6m high and about the same in width, it is fast growing.

It is fairly hardy and early to come into leaf, in flower from June to July, and the seeds ripen around September. The species is hermaphrodite (has both male and female organs) and is pollinated by insects. It is very valuable to wildlife, especially birds and insects. This tree grows well in most soils but particularly alkaline soils. It can tolerate shade, pollution and exposure to coastal conditions. It also grows back vigorously if cut back although it is relatively short lived. It is easily propagated and colonizes new land as a pioneer species.

The seed is best sown as soon as it is ripe in the autumn in a coldframe, when it most likely will germinate in early spring. Stored seed can be sown in the spring in a coldframe but will probably germinate better if it is given two months each of warm and cold stratification. If there is sufficient growth, plants can be placed in their permanent positions during the summer, otherwise they can be grown on in pots in a sheltered position until the following late spring. Cuttings of half-ripe wood can be made in late summer about 7cm long, in a coldframe, protected from direct sunlight. Suckers can be divided and replanted during the winter.

## Elm

Latin: Ulmus glabra
Irish: Úr, Ura, Leamhán, Lem. Welsh: Llwyfen. Breton: Evlec'h.
18th letter of the Ogham alphabet (depending on interpretation of source material).

The Wych Elm is native to Britain and Ireland as well as much of Europe, although Dutch elm disease has wiped much of it out in western Europe. It is a symbol of endurance and durability as it is resistant to water and rotting, but it is also associated with fertility and protection from evil and fairies. In Scotland it was used to protect milk and butter from fairies. A folk cure in Ireland was to write the man's name on an elm wand and hit him with it! It is associated with holy wells and Irish saints, including St. Patrick. In Gaul there was an ancient tribe called the Lemovices, meaning 'people of the elm'.

### Uses

Its resistance to water makes elm wood useful and valuable. It has been used in bridges, shipbuilding (including masts) and building or fencing in damp locations. It has also been used for furniture, water vessels, water pipes, wheels and coffins. Because of its flexibility it was popular for making longbows. The inner bark can be used to make mats and ropes.

The leaves, preferably young, can be eaten raw or cooked. The small fruits can be eaten immature and have a refreshing aromatic flavour. Ground inner bark can be used to thicken soups or in bread.

Medicinally the bark is demulcent, astringent and diuretic. It is used both internally and externally in the treatment of diarrhoea, rheumatism, wounds, piles etc. and is also used as a mouthwash in the treatment of mouth ulcers. A decoction was used to treat ringworm and other skin conditions. It has also been used as an essiac cancer treatment. It is also said to be good for IBS and digestive problems. It can also be used for reflux, colic, bronchitis, colitis and urinary tract problems.

## *Cultivation*

This deciduous tree lives well over 100 years and can reach heights of up 30m, growing at a fast rate. It is hardy and not frost tender, flowering from February and seeds ripening in May or June. It is a beneficial tree to wildlife, including insects. The species is hermaphrodite (has both male and female organs) and is pollinated by the wind. It will grow well in most soils of variable pH, including heavy clay and peat bogs, being extremely water resistant, although it prefers a moist loamy soil. It can tolerate coastal exposure and atmospheric pollution as well as coppicing. This species is very vulnerable to Dutch elm disease but in recent years resistant hybrids have been introduced to replenish the dwindled stocks of this tree.

Seed should be sown in permanent positions in summer or in a coldframe, which are generally quick to germinate, and should be kept fairly damp but not waterlogged. Green seed can be taken and sown rather than waiting for it to dry out and fall, which gives the seedlings a head start. Stored seed does not stay viable long and should be sown in early spring. If not sown in its permanent position, seedlings should be kept in a coldframe or greenhouse over winter. Trees should be sown in permanent positions before they are two years old and they don't take well to be transferred by this time.

# Gorse

Latin: Ulex Europeaus
Irish: Gort, Aiteann. Welsh: Eithin. Breton: Lann.
12th letter of the Ogham alphabet (depending on interpretation of source material).

Often also referred to as Furze or just 'bushes' in Ireland, gorse is a small tree that blooms for much of the year. The Irish word *gort* means field but gorse was a sign of the fertility and wealth of the land. It is linked with many folk customs, especially relating to *Bealtaine* – eggs were dyed yellow with gorse flowers, blossoming bows were brought into the house and *Bealtaine* fires were often made of gorse. It was placed around milk and butter to protect them from the fairies and in Wales it was regarded as a general protection from them. In Ireland it was a tradition that if you wore a sprig of gorse you would never stumble and in Kerry it was said that the man-in-the-moon carried a furze bush on his back. The *Metrical Dindshenchus* links gorse with the goddess of the land of both Scotland and Ireland.

## *Uses*

The yellow flowers are edible and flower buds when pickled in vinegar can be used like capers. A tea can be made from the young shoots. A yellow dye is made from the flowers. The soaked seed is reputed to be an effective deterrent against fleas. The wood burns very well and it has often been used for kindling, heating ovens and small fires. The ashes from the burnt wood are rich in potassium and can be used in making soap if added to vegetable oil. The ash also makes a good fertilizer. It can be used as a windbreak hedge in the most exposed positions, especially near the sea and it also makes a barrier that is hard to penetrate due to its long thorns. Young tips of gorse were formerly used as fodder and for bedding, gorse regenerates fast so both young and older growth could be harvested frequently.

Medicinally the flowers have been used in the treatment of jaundice and as a treatment for scarlet fever in children. The seed is said to be astringent and has been used in the treatment of diarrhoea and gall or kidney stones. It is used in Bach flower remedies for feelings of desperation and hopelessness. It has alkaloid properties that has led it to be used in heart conditions but should only be done so by an expert practitioner.

## Cultivation

Gorse is very good for stabilizing roadside banks on poor soils especially. Gorse is an excellent pioneer species for poor soils and areas with maritime exposure. It is fast-growing and colonizes new ground. This species has a symbiotic relationship with soil bacteria, forming nodules on the roots and fixing atmospheric nitrogen which provides good conditions for woodland trees to become established. It reaches a height of about 2m and the same width. The species is hermaphrodite (has both male and female organs) and is pollinated by insects, being of particular benefit to bees, butterflies and as nesting sites for birds. It will grow in more or less any soil, including nutritionally poor soils so long as they are not highly alkaline. It can tolerate drought, coastal exposure and strong winds but it will not grow well in shade. Although it is easy to grow, gorse does not tolerate transplanting very well. It can survive harsh winters and drought and even fire, dying back but usually recovering.

The seeds germinate quickly and have high viability. To grow from seed, pre-soak them for 24 hours in hot water and sow in individual pots in a greenhouse or coldframe in late winter to early spring. Germination usually takes place within two weeks. Young plants are vulnerable to predators and should be kept protected for their first year. Plant them out into their permanent positions in late spring or early summer, after risk of frost has passed. It is best to plant them in final positions early as they don't like to be repotted or replanted. Cuttings can be made from half-ripe wood, kept in semi-shade, they can be replanted in final positions the following spring.

## Hawthorn

Latin: Crataegus monogyna
Irish: Huath, Sceach gheal, Scé. Welsh: Draenen wen.
Breton: Spern-Gwern.
6th letter of the Ogham alphabet.

Hawthorn is the male fairy tree, known as the Maybush or Whitethorn, it has much folklore associated with it and is especially associated with the Celtic festival of *Bealtaine*. The first flowering is when *Bealtaine* was traditionally celebrated, usually happening around the beginning of May. Both feared and respected the wood was rarely used, particularly in Ireland where it was considered very bad luck to kill or even damage one and the superstition still persists in some areas, particularly if growing on a *rath* or fairy fort. In England the hawthorn is particularly linked to Glastonbury and the legend that the Glastonbury Thorn sprung up after Joseph of Arimathea stuck his staff in the ground there, but the original tree was felled in the 1640s. Generally not living more than about 500 years, some trees such as in the churchyard of Saint Mars sur la Futaie, in Mayenne, France is reputed be about 1800 years old.

It is regarded as an unlucky tree and it was thought the flowers, which smell similar to that of a deceased person, should not be brought into a house as they were thought to bring death to the house. Despite its fearsome reputation it was thought to protect from lightning and evil. It is especially associated with holy places such as wells, where offerings (withies) were and still are tied to the tree. A strange form of satire called *Glam Dichenn* involved a fasting Druid being joined by six additional Druids or Bards on the lands of the person satirized, on a hilltop where a hawthorn tree could be found. Each uttered a verse of satire with their backs to the tree, whilst holding a holed stone (sometimes called hag stone) and a thorn; these would then be placed under the hawthorn tree to complete the process. If they were in the right, the recipient and immediate family would be swallowed up by the earth; if the Druids were in the wrong, they would be swallowed up by the earth instead.

## Uses

Hawthorn has been used mostly as a hedging plant as its thorns make a great barrier and it can tolerate repeated cutting, and windy and coastal locations. Although rarely used as firewood it gives a good heat and it is sometimes used for tool handles.

The fruit can be eaten raw or cooked but it is normally used for making jams and preserves. In hard times the fruit can be dried, ground and mixed with flour for making bread. The young shoots have a nutty flavour and were eaten raw, often referred to as 'bread and cheese' by children when eaten with flowers. The fresh leaves can be used in salads and a tea is made from the dried leaves. The roasted seeds can be used as a substitute for coffee. The flowers were used in syrups and sweet puddings as well as eaten raw. A heart-warming cordial can be made from the berries.

Hawthorn is a valuable medicinal plant, which is used mainly for treating disorders of the heart and circulation system, especially angina, hence it should be used by expert practitioners only.

Bioflavonoids in the berries are strongly antioxidant, and used by herbalists to increase blood flow to the heart and restore normal rhythm. The fruit is antispasmodic, cardiac, diuretic, sedative, tonic and vasodilator. The roots are thought to stimulate the arteries of the heart. The bark is astringent and has been used in the treatment of malaria and other fevers. Hawthorn is combined with ginkgo (Ginkgo biloba) to enhance poor memory, working by improving the blood supply to the brain.

## *Cultivation*

A small tree growing up to 6m high and about the same width, at a medium rate, it is hardy and is not frost tender. It is in flower from May to June, and the seeds ripen from September to November. It is an hermaphrodite species (has both male and female organs) and is pollinated by insects. It will grow in most soils including heavy clay and depleted soils and will tolerate both highly acid or alkaline soils. It grows better in moist soil in full sun but will tolerate both drought conditions and shade. It is also suitable for exposed, coastal or polluted conditions.

It is a very easily grown plant, as it will tolerate a wide range of conditions including harsh winters of down to -20°C. Although not fast growing, it can bear fruit after about 5 years. About 150 insects benefit from this tree - the smell of the flowers attracts midges, but they are also pollinated by other insects. The fruit is a good food source for birds and caterpillars. Although a very hardy tree it is susceptible to fireblight, which can only be cured by removal of limbs or complete removal of infected specimens.

The seed is best sown as soon as it is ripe in the autumn in a coldframe, some of the seed will germinate in the spring, though most will probably not until the following year. Stored seed can be unreliable, it should be warm stratified for three months at 15°C and then cold stratified for another three months. Stored seed can take up to two years to germinate although scarifying the seed before stratifying it may reduce this time as can fermenting the seed in its own fruit for a few days. The seed can also be sowed before it is fully ripe, leading to germination in spring.

Seedlings can be grown in pots for the first two years after which it is best if they are planted in permanent positions. Seeds should be protected from rodents in a coldframe if possible. Young plants should not be grown in shade, they only become tolerant of semi-shade or shade once they are well established.

# Hazel

Latin: Corylus avellana

Irish: Coll. Welsh: Cyll, Collen. Breton: Kelvz.

9th letter of the Ogham alphabet.

One of the most important trees in Celtic culture, it is linked with wisdom, fertility, sovereignty and poetic inspiration. The nine hazels of wisdom appear in various myths, either in otherworldy sources as a sacred well or at the source of major rivers, such as the Boyne in Ireland. The otherworldy well of the Tuatha Dé Danann lay beyond or under the sea, surrounded by hazels, with seven streams of wisdom that flowed from it. Connla's Well is also sometimes described as otherworldly (*Tír Fá Thonn*) but also as the source of the Shannon river, likewise the well of wisdom (*tobar segais*) is given as the source of the Boyne river. Depending on which version, one or nine hazel trees around the sacred well drop nuts into it, which the salmon (or five salmon) of wisdom/ knowledge (*bradán feasa*) feeds upon. The salmon is ingested by Fionn burning his thumb on and sucking it, obtaining its 'bright knowledge', paralleling the Welsh story of Taliesin who burns his thumb on three drops from Cerridwen's cauldron. Fionn's shield was made from hazel. After the 2nd battle of Moytura it is said that Balor's huge decapitated head was placed upon a forked branch of hazel. Manannán Mac Lir was said to have dug up the hazel from which Lucra made a shield which eventually passed to Fionn Mac Cumhaill.

Tuatha Dé Danann king Mac Cuill (son of hazel) was married to the land goddess Fodla, giving a clear link to the sovereignty of the land. The hazel tree is one of three things said to be valued by the Tuatha Dé Danann above all, the others being the sun and the plough. The hazel is also associated with various Christian saints in Ireland, Wales and Scotland.

Hazel was noted as a great protection against evil, hazel wands and sticks were used for this purpose. It was also regarded as a protection against fairies, and nuts joined together were regarded as a protection against witchcraft. Hazel was also a favourite of dowsers and diviners and is still used in this regard today. The nut is also often symbolic of the heart in folk tales.

## Uses

Shields were often made from hazel, for fencing and wickerwork as it is easily coppiced. It has an attractive wood that is used for furniture. It is still used for dowsing rods. Primarily it is used as a food source – the nuts can be eaten raw or roasted and used in breads, cakes, biscuits and desserts. Hazels nuts can be liquidized to make a milk substitute and an oil can be extracted from them which can be used on salads, in paints and cosmetics. Unshelled nuts can last for at least a year if stored in a cool and dry place. The bark and leaves are a source of tannin and small branches can be used to make high quality charcoal.

Medicinally it has been used for bronchitis and stimulation of the circulation and bile production. The bark, leaves, catkins and nuts can be used medicinally. They are astringent, diaphoretic, febrifuge, nutritive and odontalgic. The oil has been used to treat threadworm or pinworm infection in infants or young children. Magically, it is connected with the gaining of insight and wisdom.

## Cultivation

This deciduous tree grows to 6m and about half that in width, at a medium rate. Generally, they only live for about 80 years, but can reach up to 500 years, especially if coppiced. It is fairly hardy not frost tender. Flowering is from January to April and the seeds ripen from September to October. The species is monoecious (individual flowers are either male or female, but both sexes can be found on the same plant) and is wind pollinated. This tree is a valuable food source for squirrels and other small mammals. It will do well in most soils and can grow in very acid and very alkaline soils and in damp and windy locations. However, it cannot tolerate salty coastal conditions. It can grow in semi-shade or no shade and makes a good tree for under a woodland canopy.

Although it can tolerate freezing temperatures, the flowers, produced in late winter and early spring and can be damaged by heavy frost. There are many cultivars of the hazel that produce cob nuts or filberts (which are longer). It is often necessary to protect the nuts from squirrels and other rodents or even foraging pigs. It can be grown as a coppiced shrub especially for basket making as well as nuts. Hazel trees can be easily moved even when relatively large as they tolerate transplanting well. For good nut production they are best planted in a fertile soil that is not highly acidic or waterlogged.

The seed is best sown as soon as it is harvested in autumn in a coldframe. It usually germinates in late winter or in spring. Seeds (in the shell) can be stored for up to a year, but the seed (nut) should be pre-soaked in warm water for two days before two weeks warm stratification followed by three months of cold stratification. Depending on temperature, the seed will germinate in 1-6 months. Seedlings can be potted up when big enough to handle or left in a seedbed for their first year, preferably protected from severe weather (coldframe). They can be planted in permanent positions after the first year or even moved when much older. Hazel produces suckers, which can be divided and replanted in early spring into new permanent positions.

## Holly

Latin: Ilex aquifolium
Irish: Cuileann, Tinne. Welsh: Celyn. Breton: Kelenn.
8th letter of the Ogham alphabet.

The *ogham* name linked with holly is *tinne* which means fire in Irish but also molten metal, perhaps because of the bright red berries. This tree is symbolic of strength and championship as well as being linked with the winter solstice and the powers of winter. It features in traditions around Christmas in both Wales and Ireland (the Wren Boys). In Scotland, at New Year, boys beat each other with holly branches to gain a long life, through the drops of blood lost, and the houses were decorated with it to offer protection, from fairies in particular. Holly was believed to protect from witches, who supposedly hate it, and from malign influences on people or animals. Regarded as a warrior tree it is protective but has no fertility associations and indeed was regarded as unlucky, especially in relation to women remaining unmarried or childless.

In a Fianna tale, Fionn and his warriors are rendered helpless by three hags who use holly sticks to weave an enchanted yarn. A Breton tale tells of a man who is able to visit and return from the realm of the dead with the aid of a holly branch that had been dipped in holy water. It appears in many stories used as a spear, including the sea god Manannán Mac Lir who carries three blackened holly spears and Cú Chulainn who uses holly spears to hunt birds. In the Welsh tale *The Romance of Peredur*, Peredur throws darts of holly whilst in the forest and in *Sir Gawain and The Green Knight*, Gawain's opponent has a holly club. A story of the death of Fearghus Mac Róich tells how he was killed by a giant with holly darts, or in a later version a holly javelin.

### *Uses*

Traditionally it was used for chariot axles, spears, darts and poles. The young shoots were sometimes used as fodder and the berries to make a red dye. The heartwood was used for printing blocks and engraving. It makes an excellent hedging plant, tolerating hard clipping and maritime exposure and a strong deterrent to animals, although it takes a while to get established. The wood is very hard and is attractive when polished, making it popular for cabinets and furniture, although it must be well seasoned to avoid warping. The wood burns very well and can be burned green as well as when seasoned. The leaves have been used as a tea substitute and the roasted berries as a coffee substitute.

Holly is not widely used in modern herbalism but has been so in the past. The leaves are diaphoretic, expectorant, febrifuge and tonic. The juice of the fresh leaves has been used in the treatment of jaundice. The berries are purgative and emetic, especially if eaten fresh. Berries are used in the treatment of intermittent fevers, rheumatism, catarrh, pleurisy, dropsy and as a powder they have been used as an astringent to stop bleeding. The root has been used as a diuretic.

Holly can be used magically as a protection, water infused with holly was used to protect babies and promote good health. Despite it not having fertility associations and being unlucky it has been used in love and sexual magic as well as magical cures for insomnia. Holly is used in Bach flower remedies for negative emotions such as hatred and jealousy.

NOTE: *The berries are toxic, especially to children, and should not be used medicinally except under professional supervision.*

## Cultivation

Holly is an evergreen tree growing to about 9m and half that width at a slow rate. It is hardy but does not do well in prolonged extreme cold, below -15°C. It is in leaf all year, in flower from May to June, and the seeds ripen from November to March. The species is dioecious (individual flowers are either male or female, but only one sex is to be found on any one plant so both male and female plants must be grown if seed is required). Holly is not self-fertile, only the female produces berries and both sexes are required to produce seed, pollination is by insects.

It can tolerate a wide range of conditions including heavy clay soil, varied pH including very acidic, polluted areas, nutritionally depleted soils and exposed coastal areas.

It can survive in fairly waterlogged soils yet established

plants are fairly drought tolerant as well. It can also tolerate full sun as well as extensive shade. Although it tolerates cold, young growth in spring can be damaged by severe frosts. This tree is a benefit to wildlife, including bees, and is a valuable food source for birds during winter. It is resistant to fire and will often re-grow from the base, it is also resistant to honey fungus.

Holly berries are best sown as soon as they are ripe in the autumn in a coldframe. It can take 18 months to germinate. Scarification, followed by a warm stratification and then a cold stratification may speed up the germination time. Stored seed often needs two winters and a summer before it will germinate and should be sown as soon as possible in a coldframe. The seedlings, like the tree generally, are rather slow to grow. Sow them in individual pots, in slight shade in a coldframe if possible, for at least their first year. Holly does not transplant easily and should be grown in a permanent position if possible and preferably not transferred after it is two years old, in spring or summer. It can be grown from cuttings from ripening tips but should be kept in shade and not disturbed or repotted for at least a year. Interestingly, the leaf shape of the juvenile and mature tree is different – the well-known spikey leaf appears on younger trees, the older trees generally produce smoother leaves.

## Hornbeam

Latin: Carpinus betulus
Irish: Crann sleamhain. Welsh: Oestrwydd. Breton: Dudi.
Native to southern Britain and western Europe.

Now found throughout Britain and Ireland, it was introduced to Ireland by the English. The hornbeam has few mentions in myth and legend but is associated with clairvoyance, longevity, wisdom, healing and luck. In some myths it is said that the hornbeam is able to live forever, although they usually live for around 300 years.

## *Uses*

Often used for butchers' blocks. It was commonly used for charcoal and was coppiced for this purpose. The wood of the common hornbeam tree is very hard and is one of the hardest woods of all European trees. It has a creamy yellow colour and is heavy but with a beautiful grain. It has been used for the making of cabinets or furniture, musical instruments, in particular for making the hammers of pianos, pulleys, cogs, flooring, bowls, tool handles and for yokes worn by oxen.

Medicinally a tonic made from hornbeam was said to relieve tiredness and exhaustion, and its leaves were used to stop bleeding and heal wounds. The leaves are generally harvested in August and dried for later use. The leaves are haemostatic. A distillation made from the leaves is an effective eye lotion. It is used in Bach flower remedies for mental and physical exhaustion. It has no known edible uses.

## *Cultivation*

Hornbeam is a deciduous tree that grows up to 25m at a medium rate, they can be up to 20m wide but often grow in a more columnar habit. It is a hardy tree and is not frost tender. Flowering is from April to May, and the seeds ripen in November. Seed is produced after 10-20 years. The species is monoecious (individual flowers are either male or female, but both sexes can be found on the same tree). Like beech, a hornbeam hedge will keep its leaves all year round, providing shelter, roosting, nesting and foraging opportunities for birds and small mammals. Hornbeam is a good tree for caterpillars of a number of moth species, including the nut tree tussock. It is pollinated by wind. Birds and small mammals eat the seeds in autumn.

It can tolerate most soils including heavy clay and will grow in very acid or very alkaline soils but prefers a moist soil. This tree can tolerate full shade through to full sun, as well as extreme cold, which makes it suitable to grow almost anywhere, it is also highly tolerant of pollution.

Seed is best sown outdoors as soon as it is ripe, a coldframe is not necessary. Germination rates are high although it may take up 18 months to happen, but seed collected green and sown immediately should germinate in the following spring. Stored seed should be given one month warm and three months cold stratification before being sown outside. It is advisable to grow the trees for two years either in a seedbed or pot until 15cm or taller before transplanting to a permanent position during winter.

## Juniper

Latin: Juniperis communis
Irish: Aiteal, Samh, Crann Fir. Welsh: Merywen. Breton: Unknown.
23rd letter of the Ogham alphabet (depending on interpretation of source material).
Juniper is native to Ireland as well as all of Europe, it is associated with the *ogham* letter UI and description *uilen* which means elbow in Irish. Juniper was thought to possess protective powers, in Scotland particularly where it was put around cattle or on their tails to protect them against witchcraft and it was said that no house in which juniper was found would catch fire. Juniper rods were also placed over door lintels at *Bealtaine* and *Samhain* to protect the house against evil. The mature berries can be strung and hung in the house to attract love. In Wales it was thought that a person who cut down a juniper tree would be dead within a year of doing so. The wood and berries were burned for purification and protection in much of Europe. It is believed the berries were used with thyme in Druid and Grove incenses to promote sacred visions and it is often used with other herbs today as incense in ceremonies, although there is little to link it with Celtic mythology.

## *Uses*

Juniper is most famously used for making gin. The berries, raw or cooked, are edible. It is usually harvested in the autumn when fully ripe and is often dried for use later on. Berries are used to flavour sauerkraut, stuffings, paté and of course the main flavouring in gin. An essential oil is sometimes distilled from the berries which can be used as a flavouring and also in perfumes. The roasted seeds make a coffee substitute. A tea can be made by boiling the leaves and young stems, or from the berries. The wood is rarely used for anything other than burning it for fumigation or purification. The bark was used for cordage and as a tinder as were the branches on occasion. A decoction from the branches can used as an anti-dandruff shampoo. The resin 'Sandarac', collected via incisions in the trunk, is used in making a white varnish.

Juniper berries are useful in the treatment of digestive disorders plus kidney and bladder problems, although with expertise only. The ripe berries are strongly antiseptic, aromatic, carminative, diaphoretic and strongly diuretic. They are used in the treatment of cystitis, chronic arthritis, gout and rheumatic conditions. Externally, it is applied as a diluted essential oil, its gentle warming effect is thought to aid arthritis and elimination of toxins from the skin and tissues, it is used in aromatherapy for this purpose. When made into an ointment, it can be applied to exposed wounds to prevent irritation by insects.

*NOTE: The berries increase menstrual bleeding so should not be used by women with heavy periods or by pregnant women. Excessive ingestion can cause renal failure and severe diarrhoea.*

## *Cultivation*

Juniper is a small evergreen tree growing up to 9m and about half that in width at a slow rate, it is widely spread throughout Europe and beyond and has given rise to many species in the genus that are used ornamentally and for ground cover. Junipers can live a very long life and some (of the genus) have lived for over 2500 years. It is very hardy and is not frost tender. It flowers from May to June, and the seeds ripen in October. The species is dioecious (individual flowers are either male or female, but only one sex is to be found on any one plant so both male and female plants must be grown if seed is required). This tree is not self-fertile and it is pollinated by wind.

It is suitable for a wide variety of soils, including clay and depleted soils, but prefers well-drained soil. It can tolerate a wide pH range and grow in very acid and very alkaline soils. It can also grow in semi-shade as well as full sun and in exposed coastal conditions. Established plants are very tolerant of drought. This tree is usually very slow growing, often only adding just a few centimetres a year. The berries also take 2-3 years to ripen on the tree. This species is resistant to honey fungus but can be vulnerable to rust.

To germinate the seed requires a period of cold stratification, generally two periods of two or three months each. The seed has a hard seedcoat and can be very slow to germinate, but soaking the seed for 3-6 seconds in boiling water may speed up the germination process. Seed should be sown as soon as it is ripe in a coldframe in late autumn, some may germinate in the spring, although most will take another year. Seed harvested green, before the seedcoat has hardened, may well germinate more quickly. Dry seed, stored in a cool dry place, can remain viable for several years. Seedlings can be transferred to pots or planted out in early summer. Cuttings can be made from mature wood about 5cm or more, in mid-autumn, preferably in a coldframe.

# Lime/Linden

Latin: Juniperis communis
Irish: Crann teile. Welsh: Pisgwydd. Breton: Tilh.
Native to Britain and northern and western Europe.

The Lime tree was regarded as protective of the family and against lightning. Although there are no recorded mentions in Celtic myth it is thought that it was sacred to the Celts as well as the ancient Greeks, Slavs, Scythians and Germans. In Celtic and Germanic tradition, the Lime is thought to inspire fairness and justice resulting in the practice that evidence was heard beneath a lime tree.

## Uses

Fibre from the inner bark of semi-mature trees is used to make mats, shoes, baskets and ropes but can also be used to make cloth and paper. Obtaining the fibre is a complex process involving steaming of stems, and making paper or cloth involves further processing. The wood, which is soft, is useful for small carved items such as handles or wooden domestic tools. Charcoal from the wood is used by artists.

The young leaves can be eaten raw and make a good salad or sandwich filling. A chocolate substitute can be made from a paste of the ground-up flowers and immature fruit, which is very good although it goes off very quickly. A herbal tea can be made from the flowers and a syrup can be made from concentrated sap harvested in spring.

Medicinally a charcoal made from the wood is used in the treatment of gastric or dyspeptic complaints such as wind. The flowers are used for treatment of colds and other ailments where sweating is helpful. A tea made from the fresh or dried flowers is antispasmodic, diaphoretic, expectorant, hypotensive, laxative and sedative. The tea can also be used for treatment of indigestion, hypertension, hardening of the arteries, hysteria, nervous vomiting and palpitations. The flowers should be harvested when newly opened as they are thought to develop narcotic properties with age.

## *Cultivation*

Tilia cordata, the small-leafed lime, is deciduous and grows up to 30m and about a third of that in width, at a medium rate. It can be pollarded and lives particularly long – up to 2000 years. It is hardy and not frost tender. Its relative the large-leafed lime (Tilia platyphyllos) is less common, wider in growth habit and less tolerant of cold. The small-leafed lime is in flower from June to July, and the seeds ripen in October. The species is hermaphrodite (has both male and female organs) and is pollinated by insects, being beneficial to bees especially. Although suitable for many soil types, either acidic or alkaline, it prefers well-drained, moist soil. It does not prosper in extremely damp or extremely dry conditions. It can grow in semi-shade or full sun. It can tolerate windy positions but is not tolerant of salty coastal conditions. This tree can be transplanted quite easily, even when quite large - trees up to 60 years old have been successfully moved. This genus of trees is notably resistant to honey fungus but often suffers from attack by aphids.

This tree is not easy to grow from seed in colder countries such as Ireland and Britain. Seed grown in damp temperate countries can be unreliable so it is wise to cut open the fruit to check for seeds. If possible, take ripe fresh seed that has not yet developed a hard seed coat, this should be sown immediately in a coldframe. It may germinate in the following spring though it could take up to a year and a half to do so. Stored seed can take even longer to germinate, possibly eight years. To shorten germination time, stratify the seed for five months at high temperatures of up to 30°C followed by five months of cold stratification. Seedlings should be grown on in a coldframe or greenhouse for their first winter. Plant them out into their permanent positions in late spring or early summer. Suckers, although fairly rare, can be removed with as much root as possible during the winter and replanted in permanent positions immediately.

## Maple (Field/Hedge)

Latin: Acer campestre

Irish: Mailp. Welsh: Gwiniolen, Masarnen. Breton: Skav Gwrac'h.

Native to Britain and Europe.

There is little Celtic mythology and symbolism associated with the field maple, but in parts of Europe it was believed that maple branches hung around a doorway could prevent bats from entering the building and deter evil. It is said by some to be an important tree in Celtic culture and consecrated to the earth goddess Dana/Danu/Anu although there is little evidence to support this claim. Acer is a huge genus, common around the world, indeed the Sycamore and the Norway maple and Japanese maple are now common throughout the British Isles but are not native.

### *Uses*

The leaves are useful for preserving crops and were packed around apples and root crops for this purpose. It can be coppiced or pollarded and it makes an excellent hedge. The wood is fine-grained, tough, elastic, hard to split, takes a high polish and is resistant to insect damage. Not usually large enough for big items it was valued by cabinet makers despite its small size. The wood makes an excellent fuel and charcoal made from the wood is good quality.

The sap contains a decent amount of sugar and can either be used as a drink, or can be concentrated into a syrup by boiling off the water, although the sugar maple (Acer saccharum), found in North America is much more suitable for this application.

Medicinally the bark is astringent and slightly anti-cholesterolemic. The bark should be dried in the sun and then stored in a cool, dry place until needed. A decoction has been used to give relief to sore eyes.

## Cultivation

Field maple is a deciduous tree growing to around 15m at a fast rate. It is hardy and not frost tender. Flowering is from May to June, and the seeds ripen from September to October, it is pollinated by insects. The species is monoecious (individual flowers are either male or female, but both sexes can be found on the same plant). It will grow in most soils including highly alkaline soil and can grow in heavy clay soil. It is suitable for semi-shade and full sun although it prefers a moist soil. This tree can tolerate strong winds and polluted areas but not salty coastal conditions.

Like most acers it is fairly easy to grow from seed - best sown as soon as it is ripe in a coldframe, it usually germinates in the following spring. Stored dry seed should be soaked for 24 hours and then stratified for 2-4 months at just above freezing temperatures. The seed can be harvested 'green' and sown immediately and should germinate in late winter or early spring.

Seedlings can be grown in a seedbed or pots until around 1 foot (30cm) tall before planting them out in their permanent positions. Cuttings of young shoots (with two or three pairs of leaves) can be taken in June or July and grown in a shady position; protection for the first winter is advisable.

## Oak

Latin: Quercus robur, Quercus petraea
Irish: Duir, Dair. Welsh: Derwen. Breton: Derv.
7th letter of the Ogham alphabet.

There are approximately 600 species in the oak family (Quercus genus) but few of them are native to the British Isles or western Europe. A symbol of sovereignty, fertility and strength, it was sacred to the Celts and many other peoples of Europe. In Wales and Scotland, it was often used to start the bonfires at *Bealtaine* and at the summer solstice. The oak has associations with both magic and the otherworld. It was used (as a wand) to create a magic circle as protection against fairies and pieces of oak were used as a talisman for protection in Brittany. The word for oak in both old Irish and old Welsh has a double meaning – chief, highlighting its importance.

The oak is often regarded as the most sacred tree of the Druids because of its mentions in classical accounts, particularly Pliny who referred to the Druids of Gaul in relation to oak and mistletoe that sometimes grows on it. Other accounts link it with Taranis, Romano-Celtic Jupiter and Apollo Vindonnus, with the sun and lightning being associated with the oak tree. In Ireland the oak was thought to be sacred to Donn, often regarded as the otherworldly aspect of Dagda. While the oak was of obvious great importance to the Druids there is no evidence to prove that it was sacred above other highly revered trees such as hazel, ash or yew.

In myth Cú Chulainn writes (in *ogham*) upon a sapling of oak as a magical obstacle for queen Maedhbh and her army in the epic *Táin Bó Cúailnge*. Diarmuid in 'The Pursuit of Diarmuid and Gráinne' cuts seven doors from oak wood to provide a magical barrier against the Fianna. The chief god of the Tuatha Dé Danann, Dagda, possessed a magical harp named Oak of Two Meadows (*Daur Dá Bláo*), which he used to play joyful or sorrowful music that affected the mood of all listening. The mythological Oak of Mugna (in Co. Kildare) was linked with kingship, appearing visibly at the birth of king Conn Céadchathach, although it was planted much earlier by Fintan Mac Bóchna. This oak was said to be 135m tall (300 cubits), an incredible height, and magically bore three bountiful crops in a year – acorns, nuts and apples.

In Glastonbury, England, the two Oaks of Avalon, named Gog and Magog, are the remnants of an ancient avenue that approached Glastonbury Tor. Sadly, the avenue, which was thought to be over 2000 years old at the time, was cut down in 1906. Gog, which had already died, was accidentally set on fire by a candle in 2017 but was saved by the local fire brigade. Magog, standing next to Gog, is still alive and producing acorns.

## Uses

The wood is highly valued in building, barrels, shipbuilding and furniture and it is very durable, even under water. It makes a good fuel and high-quality charcoal. The wood is also a source of tar, creosote, quaiacol, acetic acid and tannin. Oaks can be coppiced to provide material for baskets or wickerwork. It was often coppiced or pollarded in the past for wood but over 50-year cycles. Tannin is extracted commercially from the bark and is also found in the leaves. An edible gum can also be obtained from the bark. An ink is made from the oak galls, mixed with iron salts and a black dye is made from the bark. A mulch of the old leaves repels slugs and grubs around plants. Dried oak bark is used in a compost activator with a powdered mixture of several herbs that can be added to a compost heap in order to speed up bacterial activity and thereby compost production.

The seed (acorns), when dried and powdered can be used to make a flour, as thickener in soups or stews. The roasted and ground seed can be used as a coffee substitute. Tannin in the seed can be removed by thorough washing in water for a few days before use. A traditional method of eliminating tannin from the seed was to bury it in boggy ground over winter.

Medicinally oak is anti-inflammatory, antiseptic, astringent, decongestant, haemostatic and tonic. The buds are used for chronic fatigue and for impotence or male libido problems. Bark is most commonly used in medicine - harvested from branches 5-12 years old and dried for later use. A decoction of the bark is used in the treatment of dysentery, chronic diarrhoea, fevers and haemorrhages. Externally, it is used to bathe wounds, skin eruptions, to relieve sweaty feet and piles. It also be used as a wash for throat and mouth infections and genital infections. A compress can be used for inflamed eyes. Oak galls are strongly astringent and can be used in the treatment of haemorrhages, chronic diarrhoea and dysentery. Oak is used in Bach flower remedies – for despair. A homeopathic remedy from the bark is used in the treatment of spleen and gall bladder disorders.

## Cultivation

Oak is a usually a deciduous tree growing to around 40m and at least half that width, but at a fairly slow rate. Quercus ilex ballota (Holm oak) is an evergreen oak that grows to about 25m and is now common in the British Isles although it is only native to mainland Europe, particularly the Mediterranean regions. It produces particularly small acorns.

Sessile oak is hardy and not frost tender. It is in flower from April to May, and the seeds ripen from September to October. The species is monoecious (individual flowers are either male or female, but both sexes can be found on the same plant) and is pollinated by the wind. It is particularly valuable for wildlife, especially squirrels and insects. It will grow in reasonably good loam or rich soil and can grow in heavy clay soil but not well in sandy or depleted soils. It will grow in acid, neutral and alkaline soils but it can also grow in very acid soils. It can tolerate semi-shade or full sun. It prefers a moist soil but can tolerate drought for a short period. This tree can tolerate strong winds but not coastal salty conditions, with the exception of the Holm oak that does well by the sea. Oaks are resistant to fire as they have a thick corky bark and young trees will often regenerate from the base if cut down or killed back by a fire. This species is notably resistant to honey fungus but is vulnerable to Phytophthora ramorum, discovered in 1995, which is known to cause the disease sudden oak death (SOD) now common throughout much of the world. *There is no cure and infected trees must be destroyed.*

The seed quickly loses viability if it is allowed to dry out and so should be sown while still fresh. It can be stored in a moist and cool place during winter but is best sown as soon as it is ripe in an outdoor seed bed or in pots. A coldframe is sensible as acorns are a favourite food of rodents and squirrels especially. Oaks produce a deep taproot and need to be planted out into their permanent positions as soon as possible, sowing in permanent positions generally gives the best results. Sapling trees should not be left in a bed or pots for more than two years if possible as they do not transplant well.

## Pine (Scots)

Latin: Pinus sylvestris
Irish: Giúis, Ochtach, Crann péine, Ailm. Welsh: Pinwydden.
Breton: Pin.
16th letter of the Ogham alphabet.

The Scots pine is associated with rebirth, renewal and eternal life and was used at May day and summer solstice ceremonies throughout Europe due to its symbolism. In Ireland, this species was native but became extinct about 2000 years ago due to over use, although recent research shows that a small number survived in Co. Clare. Bog pine were dug up and used as Christmas logs (*bloc Nollag*) in Munster particularly but also in

Scotland. The pine was re-introduced from Scotland in the 17th century and continued to be used for the *bloc Nollag* and other customs associated with Christmas. In Scotland, at Halloween, lit torches containing pine were carried sunwise through the fields to bless and protect them. In Wales pine is associated with *Gwynffd* (the white life), the upperworld of the gods in their Celtic tradition.

In legend Fionn Mac Cumhaill possessed a pine forest where the Fianna could always successfully hunt when there was nothing to be found elsewhere in Leinster. Pine, with its evergreen boughs, was a symbol of the eternal love between Deirdre and Naoise in the Irish story 'Deirdre Of The Sorrows'.

## *Uses*

Pine has a great many uses, which is perhaps why it was felled to near extinction in Ireland. This tree yields resin, pitch and turpentine and was often used for flaming torches. Rosin made from the resin has been used by players of bowed instruments, such as the violin, for centuries but is also used in making varnish and sealing wax. Pitch from the resin is used for waterproofing and as wood preservative. Essential oil obtained from the leaves is used in perfumery and medicinally. Fibre from the inner bark can be used to make ropes. The resinous roots burn well and can be used as a substitute for candles. The wood is light, soft, not strong, elastic, durable and is very popular for furniture, chopping boards and work surfaces as well as making paper. The fibrous material in the leaves (needles), if stripped out, can be used as packing for cushions and pillows. The wood burns well but can give off a lot of smoke due to the resin content. An orange/yellow dye is made from the cones. A tan or green dye is made from the needles. The needles contain a substance called terpene, which washed out with water, can be used as a weed preventer as it inhibits germination of many plants.

Pine has few edible uses - A vanilla like flavouring can be obtained from the pulpwood and the inner bark can be used in desperate times for making bread.

Scots pine has many medicinal uses, valued especially for its antiseptic qualities and benefits to the respiratory system. The turpentine obtained from the resin is antirheumatic, antiseptic, balsamic, diuretic and expectorant. It is used as a remedy in the treatment of kidney, bladder and rheumatic affections, and also in diseases of the mucous membranes and respiratory complaints. The leaves and young shoots are antiseptic, diuretic and expectorant. They can be added to the bath water for treating fatigue, nervous exhaustion, sleeplessness, skin irritations. The seeds are used in the treatment of bronchitis, tuberculosis and bladder infections. The essential oil from the leaves is used in the treatment of asthma, bronchitis and other respiratory infections, and also for digestive disorders as well as invigoration in aromatherapy. It is used in Bach flower remedies for feelings of guilt and despondency.

NOTE: *Pine should not be used by people who are prone to allergic skin reactions and the essential oil should not be ingested unless under professional supervision.*

## Cultivation

Scots pines are very long living, reaching 700 years, although some species of pine live as long as 5000 years – the world's oldest verified tree is a pine growing in California. It is an evergreen tree reaching around 25m and usually 10m width. It is very hardy and grows at a fast rate, despite its long lifespan. It is in flower in May, and the seeds ripen from March to June. The species is monoecious (individual flowers are either male or female, but both sexes can be found on the same plant) and is pollinated by the wind. The plant is not self-fertile. It will grow in most soil, including poor, sandy soils and both highly acidic or alkaline soil, but lives less long in chalky soil. It prefers a well-draining soil that is moist but it can also tolerate drought and extreme cold. It will grow in moderate shade or full sun. This tree does well in salty coastal conditions or in polluted areas. It is very vulnerable to forest fires and honey fungus. Very fast growing initially, it slows down considerably after 15m height. Cones take two seasons to ripen, which provide food to rodents. It is a good plant for butterflies and many species of insect.

Seed is best sown in individual pots as soon as it is ripe or otherwise in late winter, preferably in a coldframe. A short cold stratification of one month at just above freezing can improve the germination of stored seeds. Plant seedlings out into their permanent positions as soon as possible and protect them for their first winter or two if necessary, with horticultural fleece. Pines have a very sparse root system and the sooner that they are placed in their permanent positions the better. Moving larger trees is not recommended as they do not transplant well and may take years to recover and begin growing again, this also makes them more vulnerable to the wind. Cuttings can be made from young trees, of less than ten years. It is best to use only one or two leaves attached to a short stem, protected from full sun and wind and kept moist. It can take a couple of years for cuttings to get established.

## Poplar

Latin: Populus nigra
Irish: Poibleog. Welsh: Aethnen, Poplysen. Breton: Pupli.
17th letter of the Ogham alphabet (depending on interpretation of source material).
Not native to Ireland but native to Britain and Europe.

Often confused with Aspen, the common black poplar, it does not feature in Celtic folklore or myth extensively. Black poplar features in a well-known Greek mythological tale that tells of the sisters of the ill-fated Phaeton. Both the black and white poplar feature in Greek and Roman folklore and myth.

## Uses

The wood is very soft, very light, rather woolly in texture, and of low flammability. As it is not easy to work and as it is not durable it has limited uses. As it is fast growing it is often grown to form a windbreak. An extract of the shoots can be used as a rooting hormone for all types of cuttings. The bark has been used as a cork substitute. The inner bark is edible and can be used in flours but this is generally not a desirable use.

This tree is most useful medicinally. The leaf buds are covered with a resinous sap that has a strong turpentine odour and a bitter taste and also contains salicin, a glycoside that breaks down into salicylic acid; this is also found in the bark. The buds are antiscorbutic, antiseptic, balsamic, diaphoretic, diuretic, expectorant, febrifuge, salve, stimulant and tonic. A resin obtained from the buds is made into a salve and used in traditional medicine. They can be ingested in the treatment of bronchitis and upper respiratory tract infections, stomach and kidney disorders. Externally the buds are used to treat colds, sinusitis, arthritis, rheumatism, muscular pain and dry skin conditions. The buds can also be used as an inhalant for nasal congestion. The buds should be harvested in the spring before they open and are dried for later use.

Bark is harvested from side branches or from coppiced trees and dried. The stem bark is anodyne, anti-inflammatory, antiseptic, astringent, diuretic and tonic. It can be used internally in the treatment of rheumatism, arthritis, gout, lower back pains, urinary complaints, digestive and liver disorders, debility, anorexia and to relieve fevers or menstrual cramps. Externally, the bark is used to treat chilblains, haemorrhoids, infected wounds and sprains.

*NOTE: Poplar should not be prescribed to patients who are sensitive to salicylic acid (aspirin).*

## *Cultivation*

A deciduous tree growing up to 30m and about two thirds that in width, at a fast rate. It is very hardy and tolerates cold climates. Flowering is in April, and the seeds ripen in June. The species is dioecious (individual flowers are either male or female, but only one sex is to be found on any one plant so both male and female plants must be grown if seed is required). It is not self-fertile. It is wind pollinated. It will grow in most soils, including heavy clay and both acidic and alkaline soils. It does not tolerate shade well and prefers full sun, It is tolerant of strong winds but not salty coastal conditions.

Ideally seed should be sown as soon as it is ripe in early summer. The seed has an extremely short period of viability and needs to be sown within a few days of ripening. Sow on the surface of the ground or just lightly cover the seed, ideally in a coldframe. If there is not much growth leave seedlings in the coldframe for their first winter and replant in spring. If sufficient growth is made, they can be moved into their permanent positions in autumn. Most poplar species hybridize freely with each other, so the seed may not be true to type unless in an area where other types are absent. Cuttings can be made from the current season's growth, of about 20cm length in November/December these can be sown in a sheltered area or direct into their permanent positions if sheltered. Suckers are rare in this species but can be dug up and replanted in early spring.

## Rowan

Latin: Sorbus aucuparia
Irish: Caorthann. Welsh: Cerddinen, Criafolen. Breton: Kerzhin.
2nd letter of the Ogham alphabet.

Associated with the *ogham* letter *luis*, it is also called mountain ash, or quicken tree. Famed for its magical powers and protective ability, it is clearly linked with the Druids in Ireland particularly. Known as *Fid na nDruad* it was considered a tree of the Druids, associated with *Imbolc* and *Bealtaine* and the goddess Brighid. In Scotland and Ireland, it was particularly associated with protection from evil and it was hung in the house and in creameries to protect milk products and farmyards to protect livestock. In Wales it gave protection from evil, especially demons and was often found in churchyards. It was also used to ward off fairies and witches, especially in Ireland and Scotland, although it was also thought to have supernatural powers in Scandinavia and other parts of mainland Europe. In Irish tradition it is said that the first woman sprang from a rowan tree.

A magical rowan, guarded by a one-eyed giant, appears in 'The Pursuit of Diarmuid and Gráinne' whose berries nourish and protect from sickness and even had the power to restore youth to the elderly. In the story 'The Siege of Knocklong' Druids on opposing sides use the power of rowan to create magical fires to destroy each other. Druids also used rowan branches together with bull hides in order to perform a form of divination. In *Lebor Gabála Érenn* (The Book Of The Taking Of Ireland), the Philistines use rowan skewers to destroy demons created and sent by the Tuatha Dé Danann.

### Uses

A cosmetic face-mask is made from the berries and is used to prevent wrinkles. An oil can be pressed from the seed. A black dye can be made from young branches. This tree is very wind resistant and can be used in shelterbelts and at high altitudes. The wood is hard, fine grained, and flexible. It is widely used by wood turners and was also used to make hoops for barrels, cogs and smaller furniture.

The berries are edible raw or cooked but with the seeds removed. The fruit is very acid, containing hydrogen cyanide and large quantities of the raw fruit can cause stomach upsets and vomiting. It can be used to make jams and preserves usually in combination with more flavoursome fruit. The berries can also be dried and powdered to use in flours. The leaves and flowers can be used as a tea substitute. The seeds can be dried and ground up as a coffee substitute. The young leaves are edible but contain a cyanogenic glycoside so you should only be eaten in small quantities.

Medicinally it has several uses. The bark is astringent and it is used in the treatment of diarrhoea and for genital infections The berries are astringent and emetic if eaten in large quantities. It is used as a jam or an infusion to treat diarrhoea and haemorrhoids. An infusion of berries is used as a gargle for sore throats and as a wash to treat haemorrhoids. The seeds soaked in water form prussic acid, which is highly toxic. In small quantities this acts as a stimulant to the respiratory system but in larger doses can cause respiratory failure and even death. Both the flowers and the fruit are aperient, mildly diuretic; an infusion of which is used in the treatment of painful menstruation, constipation and kidney disorders.

*NOTE: the seeds can be highly toxic and should only be used by an expert practitioner.*

## *Cultivation*

Rowan is a small deciduous Tree growing up to 15m and half that width, at a medium rate. It is very hardy and is not frost tender. It is in flower from May to June, and the seeds ripen from August to September. The species is hermaphrodite (has both male and female organs) and is pollinated by insects. It will grow in most soil types, including clay, but prefers a well-draining soil and will grow fine in rocky, mountainous terrain. It can tolerate both acidic and alkaline soils, high winds, pollution and salty coastal conditions. It can also tolerate being coppiced. It will tolerate shade but prefers full sun, although it is not very tolerant of drought. It is valuable to wildlife, especially birds and insects. This tree is susceptible to fireblight and must be removed and destroyed if it becomes infected.

The seed is best sown as soon as it is ripe, ideally in a coldframe although it can be sown in an outdoor seedbed. Stored seed will germinate if given two weeks warm stratification followed by four months cold stratification. It is advisable to sow it in early winter after the warm stratification. Seedlings can be left in the seed bed or pots for the first year or two as they are very slow to put on top growth. It is good to plant them in their permanent positions in late spring of their second year, by which time they will have a good root system.

## Spindle

Latin: Euonymus europaeus
Irish: Feoras, Féorus. Welsh: Gwerthyd. Breton: Unknown.
22nd letter of the Ogham alphabet (depending on interpretation of source material).

Its attractive berries make it symbolic of the sun. There is little Celtic lore or mythology relating to this tree but it is mentioned in the *Metrical Dindshenchus* in a story concerning the king Cairpre Lifechair and his Druid Bicne. The Irish god Aoengus Mac Óg sent his four birds to bother Cairpre but eventually Bicne managed, after trying every other tree, to chant a successful incantation over a spindle tree that prevented the birds from following Cairpre further. Associated with the *ogham* letter **Ór** which means gold in Irish, probably on account of the flowers and berries.

### Uses

A yellow dye is made from the flesh around the seed, which becomes green with the addition of alum although neither are long lasting. All parts of the tree provide a volatile oil that is used in soap making, but the best source is probably the seed, although the oil from the seed may be chemically different from that of other parts. The roots provide a small amount of a rubbery substance called gutta-percha (if grown in a sunny spot), which can be used as an electrical insulation and for making natural plastics. The baked and powdered berries were used to remove lice in hair and also as an insecticide. The wood is very hard, easily split, fine-grained, but not durable. Traditionally it was used for spindles (hence the name), skewers, pegs, knitting needles and toothpicks. It was coppiced for making these useful items. A high-quality charcoal is made from the wood, used by artists. An edible food colouring comes from this tree: yellow dye from the fruit, pink from the fruit case and orange from the seed.

The bark is alterative, cholagogue, hepatic, laxative, stimulant and tonic. The root bark is the part most used, although bark from the stems is sometimes also used. In small doses it stimulates the appetite, in larger doses it irritates the intestines. The bark is especially useful in the treatment of liver disorders. The fresh leaves, and the dried fruit and seeds, are used externally to treat scabies, lice, ticks and other skin parasites. The seeds are strongly emetic and purgative and poisonous in large quantities.

## *Cultivation*

This is a deciduous small tree growing up to 6m and usually half that in width. It is hardy and not frost tender and can tolerate as low as -25°C. It flowers from May to June, and the seeds ripen from September to November. The species is hermaphrodite (has both male and female organs) and is pollinated by insects. It is suitable for most soils, including clay, although it prefers a well-draining soil. It can grow in acidic and alkaline soils including highly alkaline soil. It will grow well in semi-shade or full sun but does not prosper in very boggy ground. There are many species in this genus, many of which are valued for their ornamental foliage. It is a benefit to insects such as butterflies and aphids as well as some birds.

The seed is best sown as soon as it is ripe in a coldframe. Stored seed requires up to three months warm stratification followed by three or four months of cold stratification and can then be sown in a coldframe. Although spindle is hardy the young seedlings are more vulnerable and should be grown on in the coldframe or greenhouse for at least their first winter. Plant out in permanent positions in late spring or early summer once they are at least one year old. Cuttings can be made on half-ripe wood, about 5cm long, taken in July/August and grown in a coldframe, protected from full sun.

## Strawberry Tree

Latin: Arbutus unedo
Irish: Caithne. Welsh: Mefusbren. Breton: Unknown.
Native to Ireland and southern Europe.

This tree is common only in the south-west of Ireland although it has become more widespread in modern times. Some place names in Kerry are linked to this tree e.g. Ard na Caithne, but also a few examples are in Waterford, Mayo and Clare. It was included in the Lower divisions of the wood (*fodla fedo*) in the Irish medieval tree list. There are not many mentions of it in Celtic myth and legend but it was scared to Hermes - a strawberry tree stood in his sanctuary at Tanagra and it is said the infant god was nursed beneath a strawberry tree. It appears in the story 'The Pursuit of Diarmuid and Gráine' and it is said that the Tuatha Dé Danann brought arbutus berries with them when they arrived in Ireland.

### *Uses*

It is primarily grown as an ornamental tree. Tannin can be extracted from the bark especially, but also the leaves and fruits. The wood is used for turning and makes a good charcoal. The fruit can be eaten raw or cooked, it is round and its texture and colour is similar to a strawberry, but it tastes rather bland. The fruit has quite a high sugar content (20%) and can be used to make jams and preserves, although best mixed with other more interesting flavours. The ripe fruit tend to fall from the tree so should be harvested as soon as they ripen.

All parts of the plant contain ethyl gallate, a substance that has strong antibiotic activity against the mycobacterium bacteria, although it has no real history of traditional therapeutic use. The leaves, bark and root are astringent and diuretic and can be used for diarrhoea or dysentery. The leaves and bark are a renal antiseptic and can be used in the treatment of infections of the urinary system such as cystitis and urethritis. A gargle can be made from an infusion for sore throats.

## *Cultivation*

This is a small, evergreen tree growing to 9m and up to the same width, at a medium rate. It is not particularly hardy and can suffer in prolonged frost. Unusually this tree produces both white flowers and red/orange fruit at the same time. It is in flower from October to December, and the seeds ripen from October to December. The species is hermaphrodite (has both male and female organs) and is pollinated by insects. It is a self-fertile tree. This tree is suitable for sandy and loamy soils and prefers well-drained soil but it can grow in heavy clay soil so long as it is not water-logged. It can tolerate both acidic and alkaline soils and can grow in semi-shade or full sun. This tree can tolerate coastal conditions, cold as low as -20°C and atmospheric pollution but it can be vulnerable to extreme cold winds. It is sometimes used as a hedging plant. This tree does not tolerate root disturbance well and they are best placed in their permanent positions while young. The fruit take about a year to ripen; hence it is in flower and fruit at the same time.

The seed is best surface sown as soon as it is ripe in a coldframe. Stored seed should be soaked for up to a week in warm water and then surface sown in semi-shade in a coldframe or greenhouse, where the soil can be kept from drying out. Cold stratification for one and a half months can help encourage germination. The seed usually germinates in three months at 20°C. Seedlings are best grown in pots or transplanted to individual pots as soon as they are large enough to handle and should be kept well ventilated as they are prone to damping off. Grow in a greenhouse of coldframe for their first winter and then plant out in late. Cuttings can be made from mature wood of the current season's growth in winter, grown in a coldframe although the success rate is generally low.

## Whitebeam

Latin: Sorbus aria, Sorbus hibernica
Irish: Fioncholl, Findcholl. Welsh: Cerddinen wen.
Breton: Unknown.
25th letter of the Ogham alphabet (depending on interpretation of source material).

Although from a different genus, related to the rowan tree, whitebeam was considered to be a form of hazel by the ancient Irish, hence it is linked with *emancholl* 'twin of hazel' or 'double hazel' also referred to as white hazel (*fionncholl*).The leaves are similar to the hazel although white underneath and the reddish brown fruits look similar to hazelnuts at first glance. It was considered to be a symbol of kingship, true leadership and authority. In 'The Wooing of Étain' the king Elcmar possesses a whitebeam forked stick. In *Táin Bó Cúailnge* Mac Roth carries a whitebeam staff when he brings a message to Cú Chulainn. Elsewhere, messengers of the king carry a staff of whitebeam when visiting the Fianna and in later times St. Patrick.

In Scotland the sub-species Arran Whitebeam (Sorbus arranensis) now only exists on the Isle of Arran on the west coast. It was first identified as a separate species in 1897 and is now found nowhere else in the world. Hence it is Scotland's rarest native tree, and officially classed as dangerously close to extinction by the WWF.

## Uses

The wood is hard and white in colour and was used for staves and staffs historically as well as beams in construction. Its tolerance of windy coastal conditions makes it useful as a windbreak. The fruit can be eaten raw or cooked and used in jams but it is not especially tasty. The flavour can be improved if the raw fruit is 'bletted' which involves storing it until it is almost rotten. The fruit has a delicious taste, somewhat like a luscious tropical fruit. The fruit can also be dried and ground into a powder and mixed with flour.

Medicinal uses are few: the flowers and the fruit are mildly diuretic, laxative and promotes menstrual flow. An infusion can be used in the treatment of constipation, painful menstruation, and kidney disorders.

## Cultivation

It is a medium sized deciduous tree growing to 12m and about two thirds that in width. It is reasonably hardy and is not frost tender but is particularly tolerant of wind and coastal conditions. It is in flower from May to June, and the seed ripens from September to October. This species is hermaphrodite (has both male and female organs) and is pollinated by insects. It is suitable for most soils from light to heavy and will grow in heavy clay, although it prefers a well-drained soil. It will tolerate both highly acidic or highly alkaline soil, semi-shade or full sun. It can also tolerate polluted conditions. It is a good pioneer species, especially on chalky alkaline ground. It regenerates well if cut back and can be successfully coppiced. It is a benefit to wildlife, particularly insects and birds. This tree is susceptible to fireblight, infected trees should be removed and destroyed.

The seed is best sown as soon as it is ripe in a coldframe. If you have sufficient seed it can be sown in an outdoor seedbed. Stored seed germinates better if given two weeks warm then 14 - 16 weeks cold stratification, so sow it as early in the year as possible. Prick out the seedlings into individual pots when they are large enough to handle. Seedlings are very slow to put on top-growth for their first year or two, but they are busy building up a good root system. It is best to keep them in pots in a coldframe for their first winter and then plant them out into their permanent positions in late spring.

## Willow

Latin: Salix caprea, Salix cinerea
Irish: Saileach, Saille, Sail. Welsh: Helygen. Breton: Haleg.
4th letter of the Ogham alphabet.

Willow is a large genus with several species that are native to the British Isles and Europe. It is regarded as a symbol of fertility but the weeping willow is particularly linked with grief in more modern thinking, although in Irish folklore the opposite was true. Sally rods were placed by milk churns to ensure that good butter was produced. It was considered good luck to bring a willow rod or stick with you on a long journey. In Scotland white willow was used in ceremonies associated with Brighid (Bride) at *Imbolc*. It was also considered good luck to bring branches of willow into the house on May Day (*Bealtaine*).

In Irish tradition, harps were usually made of willow, the oldest know example (from the 14th century) is made entirely of willow and willow harps feature in several stories, including a tale of king Labhraidh Loingseach having horse's ears! Because of its links to water, milk and cattle it is thought to be associated with the cow/river goddess Bóinn and also held sacred to the Welsh goddess Cerridwen.

## Uses

The stems are very flexible and have been used in basket making and fencing since ancient times. The plant is usually coppiced annually when grown for this purpose or bi-annually if thicker poles are required. The bark is tough and flexible and has been used as a substitute for leather. A good quality charcoal is made from the wood. The inner bark is edible both raw or cooked as are the young shoots but neither could be described as tasty. The bark is used as natural hormone rooting solution.

The fresh bark of all members of this genus contains salicylic acid, the main component of aspirin. A decoction of the leaves is used in the treatment of fevers as is the bark. The ashes of the wood are useful in the treatment of haemoptysis A distillation of the flowers is aphrodisiac, cordial and a stimulant. It is used externally in the treatment of headaches and ophthalmia. The stems and the leaves are astringent. A gum and the sap are said to help improve eyesight. Magically it is used in divination (rods) and for protection in otherworldly journeying and it is closely linked to the moon, hence it is used in moon magic.

## Cultivation

Willow is a deciduous tree growing to around 10m and about the same width (depending on variety) at a fast rate. It is fairly hardy to zone and is not frost tender. It flowers from March to April, and the seeds ripen in May. The species is dioecious (individual flowers are either male or female, but only one sex is to be found on any one plant so both male and female plants must be grown if seed is required). Willow is not self-fertile. It is pollinated by insects and is a good early food sources for bees. It will grow in most soils including heavy clay soil and boggy ground, surviving in many damp locations where other trees cannot. It will grow in acidic or alkaline soil and in semi-shade or full sun. It prefers damp soil but due to an extensive root system can often survive in drought conditions. It can tolerate coastal conditions as well as polluted sites. Depending on conditions, they can live for up to 300 years although some varieties (weeping willow) may only live for 30 years.

This tree is notably fast growing and it can be used as a windbreak, hedge and shelterbelt. The seeds are very light and so can travel some distance in the wind. It makes a good pioneer species except in very wet soils, but will eventually be largely out-competed by other woodland trees. Trees of this genus are notably susceptible to honey fungus.

The seed must be surface sown as soon as it is ripe in late spring as it has a very short viability of around a week. They can be grown in a coldframe or straight into pots and planted into permanent positions as soon as the autumn. It is easy to grow from cuttings, taking half-ripe stems from June onwards and keeping in a coldframe with plenty of moisture. The cuttings can be moved to permanent positions the following year in late spring.

## Yew

Latin: Taxus baccata
Irish: Iúr, Ibar, Iubhar. Welsh: Ywen. Breton: Ivin.
20th letter of the Ogham alphabet.

The yew is associated with long life but also death, eternity and the afterlife. The Ballyconnell yew (Co, Cavan), estimated as between 2000 and 5000 years old, is the oldest tree in Ireland and is possibly the oldest tree in Europe. To this day, the tree is commonly found in graveyards and churchyards and in some cases the trees may pre-date the churches built close to them, having had a sacred value in pre-Christian times. It is associated with the last letter (proper) of the *ogham* alphabet given as *iodha* or *idho*. It was associated with the sacred grove of Druids (*fidnemed*) and was reputedly used by them for divination purposes in Gaul, in particular sticks on which *ogham* or rune type symbols were carved. In the story of Midhir and Étain the Druid Dallaán uses four yew sticks which he carves *ogham* letters on, in order to locate Étain.

Although it is highly poisonous it was used as a protection for milk and milk products and also as a deterrent to witches. It was considered fatal to go to sleep under a yew tree.

In myth the spear of Lugh (spear of Assail), which never missed its target (if its name, Iúr, was called out) was made from yew. His yew spear was one of the four treasures of the Tuatha Dé Danann. In the tale of Mad Sweeney, Sweeney shelters under a yew tree after fleeing the battlefield. Cúchulain was taught the arts of war in Scotland by the Druidess Scathach, associated with yew. Linked to the goddesses of the land, yew has protective powers over both the living and the dead despite its negative associations. One of the great trees of Ireland was *Eo Rossa*, the yew of Ross, which stood near the seat of the Kings of Leinster (in Co. Carlow), which was said to have been felled by St. Laserian, presumably because it was held sacred by Pagans.

### Uses

Yew was popular for weapons, in fact the oldest wooden object, dated as 150,000 years old is a yew spear founds in England. Yew was also used in construction. The Irish form Taxus baccata 'Fastigiata' was originally discovered in County Fermanagh in 1767, and it is thought to be a mutant form of the common yew and is widely cultivated as an ornamental tree throughout the world because of its upright columnar growth habit. Common yew makes an attractive, although slow growing hedge. A decoction of the leaves can be used as an insecticide. The wood is heavy, hard, durable, elastic, takes a good polish but requires long seasoning before it can be used for furniture etc. The wood is burnt as an incense as it is aromatic. The fruit is edible but not very tasty, however, the seed like all other parts of the tree is highly toxic and should not be ingested under any circumstances.

Yew been used medicinally mainly in the treatment of chest complaints. Taxol, in the shoots, has shown exciting potential as an anti-cancer drug, particularly in the treatment of ovarian cancers. All parts of the plant, except the fleshy fruit, are antispasmodic, cardiotonic, diaphoretic, emmenagogue, expectorant, narcotic and purgative. Externally, the leaves have been used in a steam bath as a treatment for rheumatism. The leaves have been used internally in the treatment of asthma, bronchitis, hiccup, indigestion, rheumatism and epilepsy. A homeopathic remedy is made from the young shoots and the berries used for cystitis, eruptions, headaches, heart and kidney problems and rheumatism.

NOTE: *yew is highly poisonous, the seeds can kill children and eating 50g of leaves could kill an adult. It should not be used medicinally except by an experienced, expert practitioner.*

## Cultivation

Yew is an evergreen tree growing to 15m height and about 10m wide at a slow rate, although the Irish yew is slenderer. It is very hardy down to -25°C and is not frost tender. It is in leaf all year and in flower from March to April, and the seeds ripen from September to November. The species is dioecious (individual flowers are either male or female, but only one sex is to be found on any one plant so both male and female plants must be grown if seed is required). Yew s pollinated by wind and is not self-fertile. It is suitable for: light through to heavy clay soil but prefers well-drained soil, it can grow in very acid and very alkaline soils. Yew can grow in full shade, semi-or full sun but grows more slowly in full shade. This tree can tolerate strong winds but not salty coastal exposure, it can also tolerate drought and atmospheric pollution. Because it is so versatile it is an easy tree to grow. Growth can be fairly quick in the first few years but slows thereafter, growing negligibly after the age of 100. The bark is fragile and trees can die if significant portions are damaged. Yew is susceptible to phytopthera root rot but highly resistant to honey fungus. This tree is beneficial to wildlife, especially birds.

The seed can be very slow to germinate, often taking two or more years but is viable for a long time. It is best sown as soon as it is ripe in the autumn and it should germinate about a year and a half later. Stored seed may take two years or more to germinate and needs four months of warm stratification followed by four months of cold stratification to help reduce the germination time. Harvesting the seed 'green' (when fully developed but before it has dried on the plant) and then sowing it immediately has not been found to reduce the germination Seeds can be sown in a seedbed or planted in pots in a coldframe. The seedlings are very slow-growing and will probably require at least two years before being large enough to plant out, which is best done in late spring or early summer. Cuttings of half-ripe terminal shoots, 5 - 8cm long, can be taken July/August and placed in a coldframe in shade. It may take a few months for roots to form and so should be kept moist and not moved until the following spring or summer.

## Chapter 9

# Shrubs & Herbaceous Plants

*"The first battle of Moytura was fought between them and the Fir Bolg; and the Fir Bolg were routed, and a hundred thousand of them were slain, including their king Eochaid son of Erc. In that battle, moreover, Nuada's hand was stricken off—it was Sreng son of Sengann that struck it off him— so Dian-cecht the leech put on him a hand of silver with the motion of every hand; and Credne the brazier was helping the leech...*

*... Now Nuada was in his sickness, and Dian-cecht put on him*

*a hand of silver with the motion of every hand therein. That seemed evil to his son Miach. He went to the hand which had been struck off Dian-cecht, and he said 'joint to joint of it and sinew to sinew,' and be healed Nuada in thrice three days and nights. The first seventy-two hours he put it over against his side, and it became covered with skin. The second seventy-two hours he put it on his breasts. The third seventy-two hours he would cast white [unknow] of black bulrushes when they were blackened in fire.*

*That cure seemed evil to Dian-cecht. He flung a sword on the crown of his son's head and cut the skin down to the flesh. The lad healed the wound by means of his skill. Dian-cecht smote him again and cut the flesh till he reached the bone. The lad healed this by the same means. He struck him the third blow and came to the membrane of his brain. The lad healed this also by the same means. Then he struck the fourth blow and cut out the brain, so that Miach died, and Dian-cecht said that the leech himself could not heal him of that blow.*

*Thereafter Miach was buried by Dian-cecht, and herbs three hundred and sixty-five, according to the number of his joints and sinews, grew through the grave. Then Airmed opened her mantle and separated those herbs according to their properties. But Dian-cecht came to her, and he confused the herbs, so that no one knows their proper cures unless the Holy Spirit should teach them afterwards. And Dian-cecht said 'If Miach be not, Airmed shall remain."*

From The 2nd Battle of Moytura (*Cath Maige Tuired*), translated by Whitely-Stokes

Shrubs and herbaceous plants also feature heavily in mythology and Celtic folklore, perhaps the most famous example connected to the Druids is the parasitic plant mistletoe, that grows on trees and was stated by Pliny to be revered by Druids. Since the beginning of civilization or earlier still humankind has been availing of plants for medicinal purposes – every culture has its cures based on plants (including trees) and this has formed the building blocks of what has become a worldwide pharmaceutical industry. Although a great many medicines are totally artificial or nature identical replications, natural ingredients are still used and indeed pharmaceutical companies continue to investigate the medicinal properties of previously unexploited plants such as the vast array of plants that grow in the, sadly shrinking, Amazon rainforest.

Shrubs can be broadly defined as 'woody perennials', being plants that live for more than two years (i.e. not annual or bi-annual). These, being woody plants that are not large enough to be classified as trees, are referred to as shrubs or bushes and represent a huge proportion of the plant kingdom.

Herbaceous plants, refer not only to what are often called 'herbs' but all plants that are 'soft' and that do not produce woody trunks or stems. To confuse matters, some woody perennials that are really shrubs are sometimes referred to as 'herbs' even though they are not, strictly speaking, because they have common medicinal, aromatic or culinary uses. Herbaceous plants are, by definition, non-woody and may vary enormously in longevity. Plants such as Hairy Bittercress are what is called 'ephemeral', meaning that they have an extremely short lifespan, in this particular case a matter of weeks between germination, setting seed and death. Such plants are extremely good at propagating themselves and can quite often become a menace to the conventional gardener, although in the case I used, it makes a great salad item, similar in taste to rocket. Some herbaceous plants are defined as annuals, meaning that they live for one year maximum, although generally that is less in practice. Other herbaceous plants may be bi-annuals, such as foxglove, which establishes itself in the first year and flowers and sets seed in its second year, before dying. Many herbaceous plants are perennials, for instance 'bulbs', many 'grasses' and a whole host of common plants. These will all live two or more years, sometimes decades and most of these will appear to die off in the winter time. In this case the above ground parts of the plant die back; with the energy they contain being absorbed by the root system in preparation for the following spring when favourable conditions return.

Grasses, a huge family of plants, which grow from simple one leaf embryos (monocotyledonous) are sometimes annual but often perennial and often do not die back at all in winter weather. Other types of plants such as lilies, asparaguses and alismatids are monocots. Most other plants, woody or herbaceous grow from double leaf embryos (dicotyledonous) and may live only a few weeks or a great many years and may or may not die back in winter time. Much of the care of shrubs, and to a lesser extent herbaceous plants, is the same as or very similar to that of trees, so please also refer to the beginning of chapter 8 for more details on general care.

## Sacred planting

As with trees (discussed in chapter 8), I like to say a short blessing in acknowledgement of gardening as sacred work. This can be adapted for other plants, e.g. those which may not have an upright growth habit at all and give good ground cover. As I stated before, the blessing doesn't need to be the one I offer or be long and complicated, but should convey your intentions effectively and should be said as you plant the seed or seedling to help it to make a good start. Again, other considerations such as the lunar cycle and Biodynamics may be of use to you and these can be more easily understood with the aid of a yearly *Biodynamic Sowing & Planting Calendar* or Ellen Sentier's *Gardening With The Moon & Stars*.

*May you be blessed by Earth and rain and wind and sun.*
*May you grow [insert appropriate qualities] and strong and true.*

## Growing From Seed

As with trees, planting of shrubs and herbs is an activity often filled with mishaps. Once again there are two ways to go about growing from seed, the first being the natural way and the second being to emulate natural conditions to precipitate germination.

In common with trees, shrub seeds are usually dispersed in late summer through to autumn and in most cases, germination will occur the following spring as the weather warms up. Depending on the type of shrub the seed will need to undergo dormancy of one or more types as discussed in chapter 8.

In the case of herbaceous plants stratification or scarification might also be required, but generally speaking, herbaceous plants will often need warmer temperatures in order to germinate than trees or woody perennials (shrubs) do. This can be left entirely to chance or one can create warmer conditions with the use of a heating mat under a seed tray (indoors) or the use of a coldframe or greenhouse. Where the plants are germinated away from total exposure to the elements it will also provide total or partial protection from frost, which can be especially damaging for herbaceous plants, often causing death.

If you plant herbaceous plants outside, with no protection, they can be vulnerable to late frosts that might wipe out an entire crop, although they can be equally vulnerable to unexpected torrential rain or extreme wind.

As with trees, if the seed is viable and conditions are favourable the seed planted in the ground or in a pot will germinate in spring and hopefully survive to become a healthy and mature plant. In both cases, it is wise to make sure the seed is not planted too deep, generally the larger the seed the deeper it can be planted. Please see the beginning of chapter 8 for more details on growing from seed as the same general principles apply, although with herbaceous plants they often require a higher level of care and protection.

## Cuttings

As with trees, many shrubs can be grown from cuttings or from suckers. Suckers are generally easy to manage, if transplanted in the dormant season (winter) but cuttings require far more care. Herbaceous plants often require more special care as it is not possible to make cuttings from mature or semi-ripe material and you cannot take cuttings during the dormant (winter) season, as is the case with shrubs such as roses. Most vital is that cuttings are kept in a moist growing medium and protected from strong sun and wind, particularly with the softer cuttings.

## Planting Seedlings

As with trees, both shrubs and herbaceous plants grow at widely varying rates. Shrub seedlings are likely to harden up far quicker than herbaceous plants, which never become woody. To a large extent, shrub seedlings can be treated in the same way as tree seedlings, of course, dependent on the particular species. In general, herbaceous seedlings need more care and will need to be protected from harsh sun, wind, torrential rain and possibly pests (such as slugs) for a longer period than shrub seedlings.

## Growing From plugs, rootballs and bulbs

Sometimes shrubs and herbaceous plants are sold as 'plugs', which are very small but reasonably well established, often these are available in early spring and can be grown on in pots or in the ground if they are not vulnerable to frost or severe winds where you live. The majority of shrubs and herbaceous plants are sold in pots, at different stages of development – obviously the larger they are the more expensive they are. Generally speaking, it is better to buy a young plant and plant it in its permanent home (either the ground or a large pot) sooner rather than later, where it will acclimatize to your local environment and have more room to grow. Some plants such as raspberry canes, blueberry bushes or rhubarb are sold in a loose bag as a form of rootball, but this is relatively rare for non-edible plants.

Bulbs are sold either loose, in packets or in pots. Bulbs that are not in pots are kept dry and away from sunlight, otherwise they are likely to either rot or begin trying to grow. They can survive in a dormant state for quite some time but it is important to plant them at the appropriate time to give them the best chance of getting established. With bought bulbs their roots have been trimmed back and need to re-establish from the base-plate of the bulb, by using the stored energy which is meant primarily for supplying energy for new growth above ground.

## Plants of the Druids

There are thousands of shrubs and herbaceous plants that could be mentioned that are beautiful or beneficial in some way, from all over the world, but (as with the trees) I will stick to the most important plants that are known to be used or familiar to the Druids of western Europe. As with trees, there are a huge number of non-native plants that have been introduced to all areas of the world and, in Europe at least, the vast majority of commercially available plants are not native. As a result of modern tastes and commercial considerations, a great many native and wild species are no-longer common or are under threat of extinction - a very sad and unhealthy situation for our flora and also for wildlife generally.

Knowledge of the native plants of Europe was certainly held among the Celts and the Druids particularly, however little has been recorded about what the Druids actually knew about plants and what plants they held in particularly high esteem. It is generally considered that there are seven sacred Druidic herbs, which are usually given by their common English names as Clover, Henbane, Mistletoe, Monkshood (Wolfsbane/Aconite), Pasque-flower, Primrose and Vervain. However, alternative versions might include Meadowsweet, St. John's Wort, Mint, Mugwort or Thyme. In truth, there were a huge number of plants known and used by the Druids, as was also the case with the ancient Greeks, Romans, Persians, Egyptians, Germans, Norse and many other ancient cultures. In our times the most available information derives from classical sources that had been rediscovered in the late medieval or renaissance periods and so it has become very difficult to discern what is Druidic and what is knowledge derived from somewhere else.

## Plant Names

One of the problems with all plants (including trees), particularly today with international connections, is that common names vary enormously. Within one country there can be several names for a single plant or the same name is attributed to several different plants, which causes great confusion. The situation is made worse by the fact that different countries suffer from the same problem and, apart from the difficulties of translation, the names often do not correspond with their equivalents elsewhere in the world.

This problem was addressed by Swedish scientist Carl Linnaeus with the publication of his *Systema Naturae* in 1735. He devised a system of classifying the three kingdoms of the natural world – animal, vegetable and mineral, dividing them into classes and various subdivisions. He was also responsible for the binomial nomenclature, or two-part naming system, that is used today by the horticulture industry, herbalists and gardeners all over the world. The system uses Latin and is generally two words – the genus (family) first, followed by the specific epithet (species), although a third word can be added for varieties or sub-species if needed. Every single known plant has a unique name so that any confusion regarding a particular plant can be eliminated by using the scientific Latin name.

Despite the invention of this wonderful system, common names persist as they are easier to remember and to spell, continuing the confusion when referring to or discussing plants.

For this reason, I have also given the scientific Latin names for all plants listed, which is particularly relevant for shrubs and herbaceous plants, as they tend to have more common names (or more multiple uses of the same name) than is the case for trees.

## Druidic Shrubs

The following are some shrubs that are native to Britain, Ireland or western Europe where the Druids would have lived. This is by no means an exhaustive list but includes at least most of the shrubs that are mentioned in relation to the Druids or Celtic peoples.

### Bracken (Fern)

Latin: Pteridium aquilinum, Pteris aquilina
Irish: Raith, Raithneach Mhór. Welsh: Rhedyn. Breton: Raden.
13th letter of the Ogham alphabet (depending on interpretation of source material).
Member of 'bushes of the wood' (losa fedo) in the Irish medieval tree list.

There is great confusion about this plant, which possibly relates to the 13th ogham letter NG or nGetal, although this is also interpreted as Fern (of which there are many), Broom, Reed (also many types) or Dwarf Elder. Although Bracken is a type of fern its growth habit is upright, with long stems, unlike most ferns, which have very short stems and are less tall. Bracken is tall enough to be regarded as a bush, while other types of European fern would not.

Other ferns that could be referenced in relation to folk medicine and ogham are Male Fern (Dryopteris filix-mas), Royal Fern (Osmunda regalis), Shield Fern (Aspidium spinulosum), Spleenwort (Asplenium ceterach), Polypody (Polypodim vulgare) although Bracken is the most obvious interpretation of ancient Irish references.

Bracken was often associated with magic and was regarded as a mysterious plant that reproduced via invisible seeds (actually spores). In both Britain and Ireland, it was believed that gathering minute Bracken seed (on St. John's Eve) would make one invisible and also that carrying fern seeds generally brought good luck. It was also associated with the fairies, but not always in a positive light. In Scotland bracken roots and stems were used in love charms. Many traditions relating to ferns and St. Johns Eve/Day survived across Europe, linked with finding gold or treasure. In England ferns were used as a protection of the house from lightning storms.

In legend, King Nechtan of Munster avoided paying tax on his *dun* cows by using a fire of fern and ash from flax seed to make them appear dark brown or black. In the Cattle Raid of Cooley (*Táin Bó Cúailnge*) Nera returns from the otherworld via a fairy mound bearing golden fern, primrose and garlic.

Viking excavations indicate that bracken was used as bedding and it known that the Norse used bracken in making beer. The first beer maker, Malaliach, mentioned in the 'Book of The Taking of Ireland' used bracken to make ale, although it could possibly have also been bog-myrtle.

## Uses

Bracken has been traditionally used for bedding. A brown or green dye can be made from the fronds. The fibrous parts of the roots make good tinder or kindling, the root can also be used with water as a soap. A shampoo can be made from a decoction of the root. The ash of the burned plant has several uses – potassium rich fertilizer, in glass manufacturing and for making vegetable-based soap. Being rich in potassium (potash), particularly in summer, it is a useful addition to compost. Dried leaves make a durable thatch, a packing material or a liner for baskets and boxes, especially for fruit as it helps to repel insects. They also make an effective mulch in the garden.

The root, which is rich in starch, can be cooked and powdered for use in baking and can be stored for a long time. The starch can also be extracted and used to make dumplings although eating large amounts can cause constipation. The young shoots can be eaten raw or cooked.

Ferns generally have many medicinal uses, but with Bracken particularly young shoots are diuretic, refrigerant and vermifuge. It has been regarded that the spores are implicated in causing stomach cancer, although shoots have been ingested as a treatment for cancer. A tea from roots can be used for stomach cramps, chest pains, internal bleeding, diarrhoea, colds and tapeworms. A decoction of leaves and stems was used in treating tuberculosis. A steam bath made with the leaves is used to relieve arthritis and a tincture of the root was used for rheumatism. A poultice made from fronds and leaves was used to promote healing of broken bones and for sores or burns.

NOTE: *parts of this plant are poisonous and should not be ingested without appropriate caution.*

## *Cultivation*

Bracken grows to around 1m but has been known to reach almost 2m in height and about the same in width. It does not produce flowers. It grows quickly. It is hardy and will grow throughout Europe including mountainous areas. It can grow in any type of soil, including heavy clay and will tolerate both alkaline and acidic soil, particularly highly acid soil. It grows well in semi-shade or full sun and will tolerate wind, including salty coastal conditions. Bracken produces rhizomes and is quite an invasive plant, regarded as a troublesome weed by some, although continual cutting back (three or more times in a year) will cause them to die.

This plant is particularly easy to grow, the seeds are extremely small (spores) and are easily dispersed over a wide area. The seeds, which ripen from July to August, should be surface sown and simply left to germinate. Young plants can be dug up and transferred, it is also possible to divide established plants and replant in permanent positions in autumn or early spring.

*NOTE: it is advisable to handle the spores with gloves as they are possibly carcinogenic.*

## Bilberry

Latin: Vaccinium myrtillus
Irish: Fraochán. Welsh: Lius. Breton: Lus.
Possible member of 'bushes of the wood' (*losa fedo*) in the Irish medieval tree list.

Bilberry is also referred to Whortleberry, Blaeberry or Fraughan in Ireland as well as a host of more local names. It is primarily associated with the festival of *Lúghnasadh* in August, which is when the berries are ripe. Since ancient times billberries played an important part in this celebration of first harvests and it was believed a good billberry crop was indicative a good general harvest to come. To drop or damage collected bilberries was considered a bad omen, it was also considered bad luck to collect them after 1st August, which were cursed by Crom Dubh, the ancient Pagan god associated with this time of year. Niall Mac Coitir suggests that this, along with heather (*fraoch*) may have been referred to in the Brehon law texts of Ireland, incurring a fine for unlawful clearing. Bilberries were given as an annual ritual gift at *Lúghnasadh*, to the king of Tara (Co. Meath).

## *Uses*

A valued food in summer until the 20th century. A green dye is made from the leaves and the fruit can be used to dye fabric blue or black. The fruit juice can be also used as an ink. A tea can be made from the leaves. The fruit can be eaten raw or cooked. The berries make an excellent jam but are sweet eaten raw, although somewhat acidic. The berries can be dried and used like currants or raisins.

The leaves, harvested in early autumn, have many medicinal uses, they are usually dried first. It is advisable not use the leaves for more than a three-week period due to the tannin content. Tea made from the dried leaves is strongly astringent, diuretic, tonic and antiseptic. It was used for urinary tract infections and also to treat diabetes or pre-diabetics. The leaves contain glucoquinones, which reduce the levels of sugar in the blood. A distillation of the leaves is an excellent eyewash for inflamed or sore eyes. A decoction of the leaves or bark can be used topically for treatment of ulcers and in ulceration of the mouth and throat. The fresh fruit can have a laxative effect if eaten in large quantities. Dried fruit was used in treatment of diarrhoea, having an astringent effect and it is also antibacterial. Anthocyanin in the fruit skins is used in treatment of hemeralopia. The fruit is also useful in treatment of varicose veins and haemorrhoids due to its dilating effect on blood vessels.

## *Cultivation*

Although rarely seen today billberries were a popular and vital fruit in Celtic countries up until the last century, they can still be found growing wild in many mountainous areas. It is a small deciduous Shrub growing up to 0.3m by around the same width. It is hardy and frost tolerant. Flowering is in April to June and the fruit ripens from July onwards. Billberry is hermaphrodite (has both male and female organs) and is pollinated by insects. It is self-fertile and a valuable plant for wildlife, especially bees, moths and butterflies.

It grows in well-drained soils mostly and prefers acid soils and will tolerate highly acidic ground, but struggles badly in alkaline soil. It will grow fine in semi-shade but prefers full sun. It will tolerate strong winds but is vulnerable to salty coastal conditions. Can be found in woodlands if the soil is acidic and often spreads via suckers, it is quick to regenerate after forest fires or after heavy grazing. This species is resistant to honey fungus.

Seed should be sown immediately when ripe or in late winter in a greenhouse or coldframe with the seed just covered, in acidic or neutral soil. Stored seed might require three months of cold stratification before sowing. Billberries dislike root disturbance, plants are best grown in pots or a seedbed until being planted out in their permanent positions. It's best to keep them protected for their first winter and planted out in early summer. Cuttings can be made from half-ripe wood in early autumn and suckers can be divided and replanted either in spring or the autumn after fruiting.

## Bog Myrtle

Latin: Myrica gale
Irish: Raideog, Rait. Welsh: Myrtwydden. Breton: Unknown.
Member of 'bushes of the wood' (*losa fedo*) in the Irish medieval tree list.
13th letter of the Ogham alphabet (depending on interpretation of source material).

In Irish folklore it was regarded as a blessed plant due to its pleasant fragrance and in the Christian era has been used on Palm Sunday celebrations. Conversely it is also regarded as a cursed bush, again in relation to Christian lore. It was believed that walking on bog-myrtle or striking cattle with it would bring bad luck.

Bog myrtle is possibly referred to in the 'Book Of The Taking Of Ireland' in relation to the first brewer Malaliach making ale, it is not entirely clear if the correct translation is fern or bog-myrtle. It was certainly used in Britain and Gaul (France) as a flavouring for ales. There is little mention of this shrub in mythology but it was clearly of value to the ancient Celts, especially in Ireland, hence its inclusion in the medieval tree list and possibly the *ogham* alphabet.

## Uses

A yellow or brown dye can be made from the tips of the stems and a yellow dye from the seeds or bark. This plant generally repels insects and was once widely used to deter midges in Scotland. A wax that coats the fruit and leaves can be extracted by immersion in boiling water and skimming off the wax. Pulped fruit can be boiled to extract more wax, which again can be skimmed off. The resulting wax can be used to make aromatic candles, but it's a time consuming and inefficient process. A fragrant oil is made from the fruits which can be used in soap as well as insect repellent as a topical parasiticide.

The berries and leaves are edible and both can be used fresh or dried to flavour sweet or savoury dishes. The berries can be used in beers to increase foam and add flavour. A tea can be made from the dried leaves.

Medicinally the leaves are aromatic and astringent and stimulate menstruation. It was also an effective inducer of miscarriages and hence should not be ingested by pregnant women unless intending to terminate a pregnancy. It was used for sore throats and kidney problems.

NOTE: Not to be ingested by pregnant women.

## Cultivation

This deciduous shrub can reach 2m but rarely grows to more than 1m in areas where it can be grazed. It flowers in spring, from March to May and seeds ripen in early Autumn. It is pollinated by the wind, very hardy and frost tolerant. This species is dioecious (individual flowers are either male or female, but only one sex is to be found on any one plant so both male and female plants must be grown if seed is needed). It is not self-fertile. This plant is occasionally monoecious and also can change sex from year to year. Many caterpillars feed on this plant but it is generally a good deterrent to insects. Deer, goats and sheep are known to feed on the leaves and berries.

It will grow in most soils, including highly acidic soils, depleted soils and bogs. It will do fine in either semi-shade or full sun but preferring a moist soil. This plant is known for suckering and will form thickets if left to its own devises, hence some consider it an invasive pest. It is a good nitrogen fixing plant due to the symbiotic relationship with soil micro-organisms. It can also do well in water-logged soils. This species is highly resistant to honey fungus.

It is best to sow the seed as soon as it is ripe in the autumn, preferably in a coldframe, the seed should be just covered over and kept damp. Seed viability is good but stored seed germinates better after three months of cold stratification before sowing. Seedlings can be transferred to pots but should remain under protection ideally for their first winter. Planting in permanent positions should take place in late spring or early summer. Cuttings can be made of half-ripe wood, about 5cm long in summer. Cuttings generally have a good success rate, leave until the following spring and protect from direct sunlight and strong winds. As these produce suckers frequently, division of suckers during winter is a handy way to propagate these plants, replanting them straight into their permanent positions.

## Blackberry/Bramble/Briar

Latin: Rubus fructicosus
Irish: Dris, Sceach, Driseog. Welsh: Mwyaren. Breton: Mouar.
Member of 'bushes of the wood' (*losa fedo*) in the Irish medieval tree list.
11th letter of the Ogham alphabet (depending on interpretation of source material).

Blackberries were highly valued as autumn food throughout the Celtic world but in both Ireland and Scotland it was considered bad luck to pick or eat them after *Samhain* (Halloween), various traditions exist that the *púca* (pooka) or the devil urinated or spat on them, making them unpalatable. Similar traditions exist in England and Brittany but around other dates. Blackberries often featured in *Samhain* foods such as pies, cakes and breads. A double headed bramble (forming an arch) was thought to possess malign powers associated with evil spirits or the devil but also to cure diseases such as whooping cough. Brambles were sometimes used in curses but it was also considered to have protective powers over houses, livestock and milk products. The Bride's Wand or *slachtan Bride*, associated with *Imbolc* was sometimes made from bramble/briar.

Blackberry appears in many legends including the tale of Mad Sweeney (*Suibhne Geilt*), although not in positive terms in this case. It also appears in the Lays of Fionn' in relation to Queen Maeadhbh's seven sons, and in *Táin Bó Cúailnge*, in relation to Cú Chulainn and in various stories or poems relating to the Fianna.

## *Uses*

A blue or purple dye is made from the fruits. The fibrous stems can be used to make twine. The roots of large specimens have been used for smoker's pipes. The primary use of blackberry is for food – the berries raw or cooked have excellent flavour and are used widely in desserts and jams, although not fully ripe fruit can cause stomach upsets. The roots can also be eaten cooked by boiling. A tea can be made from dried leaves, the young leaves are best for this. Young shoots, especially from suckers can be eaten in salads. The young roots of suckers also make an excellent natural rooting hormone solution – chopped up and steeped in water for a day.

There are several medicinal uses – the root bark and leaves are astringent, depurative, diuretic, tonic and vulnerary. It has been used as a traditional remedy for dysentery, diarrhoea, haemorrhoids and cystitis. A decoction of leaves can be used to treat ulcers, sore throats, thrush and gum inflammation. Berry juice was used to cure dropsy, the leaves to aid swelling, cuts, sore feet, burns, boils and spots. Magically the plant was used to cure whooping cough, hernia and rickets, It was also used in magic for binding spells, protection and for abundance.

## *Cultivation*

Blackberry is a deciduous shrub growing up to 3m height and is known to produce stems of over 10m long. It grows very rapidly; it is hardy and is not frost tender. Flowering is from May onwards and seed is produced from July until November. This species is hermaphrodite (has both male and female organs) and is pollinated by insects. This plant is self-fertile and is noted for attracting wildlife. It colonizes ground easily and although considered a troublesome weed by many, can offer protection to young trees from rabbits and other grazing animals. Thickets of it also provides good cover for animals, birds especially. It will grow in any soil, either acidic or alkaline, light or heavy, including heavy clay. It can grow in deep shade, semi-shade or full sun. This plant can grow almost anywhere and propagates easily hence the expression that it will 'grow in your ear' if you remained still long enough. It tolerates cold and wind although it does not tolerate salty windy conditions that well but will still survive, although somewhat stunted.

Much seed is produced by a non-sexual method (Apomixis) and is therefore genetically identical to the parent plant. Sexual reproduction has resulted in a vast number of sub-species. The plant is perennial but the stems are generally biennial (lasting two years).

This plant is very easy to grow from seed or from suckers. Seed usually requires cold stratification and should be sown in early autumn in a coldframe or outside. Stored seed needs four weeks stratification and should be sown in early spring. Plant seedlings out into their permanent positions in late spring of the following year. Cuttings can be made from half-ripe wood, in July or August. Suckers can be divided in early spring or in late autumn when the leaves fall off. This plant is so easily propagated that it can become a nuisance if not actively controlled.

## Dogwood

Latin: Cornus sanguinea
Irish: Conbhaiscne Welsh: Cwyrosyn, Cwyrialen, Pren Ci.
Breton: Unknown.
Native to Britain, Ireland and Europe.

There is not much to be found in the way of Celtic lore relating to Dogwood. It was reputed to have been the wood that cross Jesus of Nazareth was crucified on. Legend says that the Dogwood was huge like an Oak but after the crucifixion became stunted, with spindly, twisting branches and blossoms in the shape of a cross. Another legend is that it was the favorite tree of the biblical Adam and the Devil tried to destroy its flowers but failed in his attempt.

### *Uses*

The pericarp (ovary wall) and the seed is rich in an oil that can be used in lamps and also in the making of soap. A blue-green dye can be made from the fruit. The wood is hard and tough and is useful for tool handles and small turnery, but the young branches are flexible and are useful for baskets etc. often being coppiced for this purpose. It also makes a good charcoal and the wood burns well as a fuel.

The fruit is edible raw or cooked but has a bitter flavour. The refined oil from the seed is edible, although hardly worth the effort. Medicinally Dogwood is an emetic, astringent and febrifuge. The leaves are a good astringent especially applied externally. The fruit is especially emetic. Tinctures of the bark can be used as a substitute for quinine and a tincture of the berries aids alcoholics with stomach problems. Magically it offers protection and the four-petal flower is symbolic of the four directions and the elements of earth, air, fire and water.

## *Cultivation*

It is a deciduous shrub that grows to 3m and about the same in width. It is hardy and is not frost tender. Flowering is from June to July, and the seeds ripen in September. It is hermaphrodite (has both male and female organs) and is pollinated by insects. It is suitable for any type of soil, including heavy clay and will grow in both alkaline or acidic soil, including very alkaline soils. It prefers moist soil and will grow in semi-shade or full sun. Although it can tolerate extreme cold it does not like harsh cold winds. This plant produces suckers and can form thickets easily and tolerates coppicing. It is highly resistant to honey fungus.

The seed is best sown in autumn when ripe outdoors or in a coldframe. It is best to remove the fruit first as this inhibits germination. Stored seed should be cold stratified for up to four months and sown in early spring. Germination may be accelerated by scarification of the seed, although germination can often take well over a year. Seedlings can be potted up once easy to handle or planted in permanent positions in spring or summer. Cuttings can be made from half-ripe side growth in autumn, with a high chance of success. Suckers can be separated and replanted during the winter.

## Gooseberry

Latin: Ribes uva-crispa
Irish: Spinian, Tor spíonán. Welsh: Eirin Mair. Breton: Spezad.
24th letter of the Ogham alphabet (depending on interpretation of source material).

Opinions vary about the connection with the *ogham* letter *pín* and *spinan*, the name for Gooseberry in Irish. Scholars McManus, Kelly and Mac Coitir disagree on this but I tend to agree with Mac Coitir that Gooseberry is the right choice, although it is thought that this bush was not native but introduced from

Britain. With its sweet berries it is the most obvious choice and it was probably introduced to Ireland during the Celtic era.

There is little or no ancient folklore associated with this bush but in later times it is associated with being a chaperon for lovers (play gooseberry), although various theories exist about this, it is not clear from where this originates. It was also said in England that children were born under a gooseberry bush, perhaps a convenient way of avoiding a more truthful explanation. Today use of that phrase usually relates to implied foolishness or gullibility. In Britain 'Old Gooseberry' was a euphemism for the Devil.

## Uses

It has not many real uses apart from for food but the long thorns do make a significant barrier for animals so it could be used for hedging. Both the leaves and fruit are edible. The fruit can be rather tart when raw, also varying in size, depending on the variety. It can be cooked both ripe or under-ripe if sweetened. It is still popular for pies and jams. The young leaves can be eaten in salads but this is not common any more. A small amount of hydrogen cyanide is present in the leaves so it's advisable not to eat vast quantities. Medicinally the fruit can be used as a laxative, especially the unripe berries. The leaves have been used for treating kidney stones (gravel) and an infusion was used to aid menstruation and to help with childbirth. The leaves can also be used as an external astringent for fevers and wounds. A folk treatment for a sty in the eye was to prick it with a gooseberry thorn every morning or alternatively to point it at the sty while shouting 'away' three times. The juice of the berries was used to reduce inflammations. A jelly from the berries was considered good for lethargy and those suffering from bile reflux. Magically it is used in healing charms, especially the thorns. It can be used in healing spells for the eyes.

## *Cultivation*

This is a deciduous shrub growing to up to 3m high and up to 11m wide at a medium rate, although they are usually much smaller than this. It is hardy and not frost tender, tolerating as low as -20°C. Flowering is from March to May and the seeds ripen around July onwards. It is hermaphrodite (has both male and female organs) and is pollinated by insects. It is a self-fertile plant. It will grow in any soil type including heavy clay but prefers a well-drained soil. It will grow in either alkaline or acidic soil. It does best in full sun but will tolerate semi-shade.

Although it grows well anywhere it will need good quality soil and humus to produce good fruit and requires plenty of potassium, especially in alkaline soils. This is a good plant for birdlife and is also beneficial to insects. Fruiting is best on one- or two-year-old growth, so it is advisable to prune this bush annually if you are growing it for fruit. This plant is susceptible to honey fungus and white pine blister rust (that also affects pine trees).

The seed is best sown as soon as it is ripe in the autumn in a coldframe, removed from the fruit. Stored seed requires three months of cold stratification and should be sown in late winter. Seed can be viable for over 15 years if stored in a dry place. Seedlings should spend their first winter in the coldframe and be planted out the following spring. Cuttings can be made of half-ripe wood, about 10cm long, in early autumn.

## Heather

Latin: Calluna vulgaris, Erica cinerea
Irish: Fróech, Fraoch. Welsh: Grug Mêl. Breton: Brug.
18th letter of the Ogham alphabet (depending on interpretation of source material).
Member of 'bushes of the wood' (*losa fedo*) in the Irish medieval tree list.

This is the only plant mentioned in relation to the *ogham* letter úr but most commentators don't mention any plant at all. The Irish or Scots name *fraoch* means fury or anger and appears in myth as the name of the husband of Findabair, the daughter of queen Maebh and king Ailill. Heather was associated with poor land hence the phrase 'where there's heather there's poverty.' A folk story states that no plant wanted to cover the mountains at the creation of the world but heather did so and was rewarded by God with beautiful small flowers. It was considered lucky to wear a spring of heather, both in Ireland and Britain and it was common for Traveler women to sell heather sprigs to the public for luck, but in Scotland white heather was considered to be unlucky. Heather was associated with *Lúghnasadh* and the last Sunday of July (Garland Sunday) in Ireland. It was also associated with fairies in Ireland, Scotland and Wales and in Brittany it was revered as a symbol of St. Anne.

In legend it is associated with the story of Viking beer and how the last two Viking survivors from a battle in Ireland went to their graves rather than reveal how their heather beer was made. In Scotland the heather beer tradition is claimed to date back four thousand years and heather beer is still made there to this day. In 'The Pursuit of Diarmuid and Gráinne', they sleep on a bed made of heather. Also, heather mentioned in an 8th century Irish poem on the hermit Marbán. With its link to bees and honey it is also linked to the goddess Brighid.

## Uses

The flexible branches have been used for thatch, bedding and to stuff mattresses or cushions. It can also be used for baskets, ropes, broom heads and as an insulator. The dry branches burn well and make good kindling. A yellow dye can be made from the twigs, the bark is also a source of tannin. It can be used for ground cover and also as a low hedge. There are now a vast number of ornamental varieties and it has become a very popular garden plant. The dried flower stems are used in floral displays.

A tea can be made from the flowering stems but it is primarily used in beer. Heather honey is highly popular and is of high quality. They honey as well as the flowers is still used in making of mead. The young shoots were used in making beer and this is still used by some small breweries.

Medicinally it has often been used in folk medicine, particularly to treat urinary tract infections due to its antiseptic and diuretic properties. The flowering shoots have many uses, being astringent, causing sweating, purifying, expectorant, vasoconstrictive and slightly sedative. If pounded strongly it can be made into an ointment for rheumatism and arthritis or a poultice for chilblains. It was used for asthma and heart problems. An infusion of shoots is used for coughs and colds as well as kidney or bladder problems and gout. It is used Bach flower remedies for vanity and selfishness. A homeopathic use is for insomnia. Magically it can be used in connection with the *sídhe* or fairies or the divine feminine.

## Cultivation

Heather is an evergreen shrub that grows to just over 0.5m high and about the same width, although there are also dwarf varieties. It is hardy, frost and wind tolerant. It is in leaf all year and flowers July to October although some cultivated varieties (cultivars) flower in winter. The seeds ripen from October to November. This species is hermaphrodite (has both male and female organs) and is pollinated by both insects and the wind. It is highly valuable to wildlife, especially insects. It grows in most soils, including heavy clay but will grow in very depleted soils. It does not like alkaline soil but will grow in neutral to highly acidic soils. It can tolerate semi-shade or full sun as well as windy coastal conditions. It can tolerate extreme wet but not drought but can often survive wildfires. The seeds often germinate following a fire.

Seed should be sown as soon as it is ripe in early winter or in February in a coldframe, either surface sown or barely covered. Cold stratification of at least three months is need. It will germinate within one or two months if temperatures reach 20°C. Potted seedlings can be transferred to permanent positions in late spring and cuttings can be made of half-ripe wood of about 5cm in summer, with a high success rate so long as they are protected from drying out. Plants can be divided in spring – a trick to help with this is to dig up a plant and replant it deeper for about a year to encourage stems to produce roots.

## Honeysuckle

Latin: Lonicera periclymenum
Irish: Féithleann. Welsh: Gwyddfid, Llaeth y gaseg. Breton: Unknown.
23rd letter of the Ogham alphabet (depending on interpretation of source material).

Well known for its fragrance and bright flowers, it is a symbol of the summer and of beauty. Known also as woodbine, it is also a symbol of power due to its ability to strangle and choke the growth of the trees that play host to this parasitic climber. It was believed to protect from malign influence and a decoction drunk was used to negate the effects of the 'evil eye'. A multitude of beliefs in its protective powers exist is Ireland and Scotland especially, as well as the Isle of Man. In England it is more associated with romance. The well-known Irish song *Samhradh* refers to the honeysuckle as *bainne na ngamhna*.

Honeysuckle features in the tale 'The Death Of King Fergus' and in the epic *Tain Bo Cúailnge* as well as the Welsh *Cad Godeu* (Battle Of The Trees). Honeysuckle also appears in the tragic tale of Baile MacBuain and Aillinn, being symbolic of intertwining and love. It also appears as one of the 'lower division of the wood' in some later versions of the Irish medieval Brehon laws on trees.

## Uses

Apart from medicinal uses honeysuckle has no known use apart from as a natural substitute for twine or rope. The nectar from the flowers is edible and was once very popular with children.

Medicinally it has expectorant and laxative properties. A syrup made from the flowers has been used in the treatment of respiratory diseases whilst a decoction of the leaves is considered beneficial in treating diseases of the liver and spleen. In Ireland it was used as a gargle or ointment for mouth or throat infections. It was also used to treat tuberculosis (consumption) and the bark was used to treat jaundice. The flowers were also thought to be a preventative for fevers and it was also believed to cure toothache. It was thought to offer magical protection to milk and livestock.

## Cultivation

This deciduous climber grows to about 4.5m against a tree or high wall. It is hardy and is not frost tender surviving in as low as -20°C. Flowering is from June to August, and the seeds ripen from July to October. The species is hermaphrodite (has both male and female organs) and self-fertile and it is pollinated by insects. It grows in any soil, including heavy clay and will tolerate both highly alkaline or highly acidic soils. It will grow in heavy shade but just as happily in full sun as it is quite tolerant to drought, although it prefers its roots to be in shade. This plant is beneficial to wildlife but can be extremely damaging to host trees, causing their growth to be restricted by its tightly binding branches. The seed is best sown as soon as it is ripe in a coldframe. Stored seed requires about eight weeks of cold stratification and should be sown as soon as possible in a coldframe. Grow seedlings in individual pots and or prick out to grow them on in the greenhouse for their first winter. Planting in final positions is best done in late spring when frosts have passed. Ideally grown on a wall or against a dead tree – this way there is no damage to the host. Cuttings can be made of half-ripe wood, of around 7cm in late summer, kept in a frame. Cuttings have a high success rate.

## Ivy

Latin: Hedera helix
Irish: Eidhneán. Welsh: Eiddew, Iorwg. Breton: Iliav.
Member of 'bushes of the wood' (*losa fedo*) in the Irish medieval tree list.
12th letter of the Ogham alphabet (depending on interpretation of source material).

Ivy has a long history in Britain and Ireland, it is still commonly used in Christmas decorations and may well have been used for this purpose in the Pagan era too. It is a common belief that it is unlucky to have it in the house at any other time than Christmas. Ivy is linked with the custom of the 'Wren Boy's on St. Stephen's Day (26th December) which is still current in Dingle, Co. Kerry. Variously the wren is carried on a bush or platform of ivy or holly. This custom relates to a story of St. Stephen in which he hid in a tree covered with Ivy. It is thought to have powers of protection for the house and for animals, particularly in Scotland.

In legend Ivy is linked with the infant Fionn MacCumhaill and it is also mentioned favourably in the story of Mad Sweeney

(*Suibhne Geilt*) and the Welsh tale of Trystan and Esyllt. Ivy is perhaps more famous in classical mythology – being linked with the Roman god Bacchus, Egyptian Osiris and Greek gods Attis and Dionysus.

## Uses

The twigs are used to make a yellow dye. Leaves, as a decoction, can be used to restore black in faded black fabrics and also as a rinse to darken hair. Soap can be made by boiling the leaves with soda, which is suitable for clothes washing. The mature wood makes excellent firewood, it can also be used as a strop to sharpen knives. It is often used decoratively, on walls or fences to hide them.

Medicinally Ivy has many uses. It has been used extensively in folk remedies for rheumatism and for respiratory problems. It is often prescribed as a tincture for treatment of coughs and bronchitis. It can be applied externally for skin lesions, burns, cuts and for joint pains. Ivy leaves contain an amoebicidal alkaloid and triterpene saponins that have proven effective against internal parasites and fungal infections. An infusion from the twigs in an oil helps relieve sunburn. The leaves also have antibacterial, antirheumatic, antiseptic, antispasmodic, astringent, cathartic, diaphoretic, emetic, emmenagogue, stimulant, sudorific and vasoconstrictive properties. It should only be used under the supervision of a qualified herbalist. The leaves are harvested in spring and early summer, they are used fresh and can also be used. Dried. It was believed that cups made of ivy would neutralise bad or poisoned wine.

*Note: ivy is mildly toxic and can cause diarrhoea and vomiting in large does.*

## Cultivation

This evergreen climber grows up to 15m if given support, such as a tree or building, it can also reach about 5m in width. It is hardy and not sensitive to frost. It flowers from October to December and so is off great value to insects. Seeds ripen around June and are a valuable source of food to birds especially. It will grow in almost any soil, including heavy clay and very poor soil. It can tolerate both highly acidic and highly alkaline soils, strong winds, drought, full shade or full sun, atmospheric pollution and salty coastal conditions. As a result, it is extremely versatile but it does best in a fairly damp climate. It has become very popular as an ornamental garden plant with a great many cultivators being available commercially.

Opinions vary greatly on Ivy, with its aerial roots it is able to cling onto walls or large trees, effectively smothering them and constricting their growth if left unchecked. Some gardeners consider it to be a troublesome pest that damages trees, while others consider it to be harmless and a great benefit to wildlife. Personally, I agree with author Risteard Mulcahy, who believes it is extremely detrimental to trees, but that more research is required in this area. Although it takes no nutrients from trees, the roots compete with those of the host tree and the limbs can constrict trunk growth (fasciation) and the leaves and branches can shade out the leaves of the tree. In some cases, Ivy can reach the top of the tree and full extent of the branches, causing it to die. Ivy is generally not a problem on an already dead tree or on a building but it can cause huge problems in hedgerows and woodlands if not controlled.

To sow from seed, it is best to remove the flesh, which inhibits germination, and sow the seed in autumn or spring time in a coldframe. One month of cold stratification, if possible, will improve germination. One can prick the seedlings out into individual pots and grow them on in the coldframe for their first winter or otherwise sow directly into pots, germination rates are generally high. It is best to plant them out into their permanent positions in late spring or early summer. Cuttings can be made of half-ripe wood in July/August, kept in a shady position in a coldframe. Ivy often layers naturally and plants can be divided at any time apart from mid-summer to produce more plants. The mature plant has a different leaf shape from the juvenile plant – the well-known lobed leaf appears on younger trees; the older plants generally produce more oval leaves.

## Lavender

Latin: Lavandula angustifolia, Lavandula stoechas
Irish: Labhandar, Ulus Liath. Welsh: Lafant. Breton: Lavand.
Native to southern Europe, naturalised in Britain and Ireland.

Lavender was used by the ancient Egyptians in their funeral rites and as an aphrodisiac but it was also known by the ancient Greeks, Persians, Indians, Romans and Celts. It has long been used for medicine, fragrance and for magic. It is not native to Britain or Ireland but it grows in France and was probably introduced to Britain by the Romans, if not earlier. It was probably introduced to Ireland by the Normans but may have been imported earlier for its fragrance, medicinal and sleep-inducing properties. Lavender became very popular in medieval times onwards, used by all levels of society from monarchs downwards. It was thought to have protective properties, to attract benign fairies and induce love and pleasant moods. Although there is no real Celtic folklore about this plant, probably due to is late introduction to northern and extreme western Europe it has been a hugely popular herb since the late medieval period and remains popular the world over.

### Uses

The most common use is of the essential oil that has a wonderful fragrance. This oil has been utilized domestically and commercially for thousands of years and is widely found in cosmetics, soaps, perfumes, detergents, bath products, cleaning products, aromatherapy and massage oils. It also acts as an insect and rodent repellent, both fresh or dried. Dried flowers are used in pot pourri and in small bags or packets to freshen cupboards or clothes. It can also be used as incense and the fresh or dried flowers are used in flower displays. It is hugely popular as a garden plant both in formal and informal gardens as well as in herb gardens.

The leaves, petals and flowering tips can be eaten raw. It is used as a condiment in salads, soups, stews and has even been used in jams, vinegar, ice-cream or sweets and desserts. The flowers provide a very aromatic flavour and should be used sparingly if not the main flavouring. The essential oil can be used as a food flavouring. The fresh or dried flowers can be used as a tea.

Medicinally it is commonly used as a relaxant for nervous disorders or anxiety and is also used to help with insomnia. It is common for a lavender pillow or essential oil to be used at night time to promote a restful sleep. The oil is also used as an antiseptic, applied directly to the skin and helps with burns and minor wounds. The essential oil from the flowers is antihalitosis, powerfully antiseptic, antispasmodic, aromatic, carminative, cholagogue, diuretic, nervine, sedative, stimulant, stomachic and tonic. It can be rubbed on the head as a restorative and relaxant and to cure headaches. It is also very relaxing if used as an oil in the bath. It has great anti-bacterial properties as well as aromatherapy uses. Magically it has been used in love potions, to promote well-being and relaxation, to promote psychic ability, as an offering to the gods at the summer solstice and to attract the *sidhe* (fairies).

## *Cultivation*

Lavender is an evergreen shrub growing up to 1.2m by 1m although fairly slowly. It is inclined to become woody and straggly looking if not cut back on a regular basis. Many varieties exist, many of which are dwarf varieties. It is reasonably hardy but will struggle with prolonged freezing or rain. It is in flower from July to September, and the seeds ripen from August to October. This species is hermaphrodite (has both male and female organs) and is pollinated by bees, moths and butterflies.

It is suitable for light to medium soils although it can often survive in heavy clay if it is on a slope or area where water does not collect for long periods. It prefers a well-draining soil and hates to grow in waterlogged soil, which often leads to death. It can grow in both acidic and alkaline soils, particularly highly alkaline soil. It also tolerates very salty coastal conditions, drought and a fair bit of wind, although it cannot tolerate deep shade.

This plant is very popular in all types of gardens but does best in a sunny position. For best production of oil, it should be grown in poorer soil with plenty of sun, otherwise it will tend to be leafier. It generally does not live more than ten years unless kept in a fairly juvenile condition by annual pruning, best done in early spring. It is advisable not to prune Lavender in autumn as any late growth is unlikely to be frost hardy. It makes an excellent companion plant for cabbages especially.

To grow from seed, it is best to sow the seeds in spring in a greenhouse, polytunnel or coldframe and only just cover them with soil. It usually germinates in 1-3 months at temperatures of 15°C or more. Seedlings should be grown on in the greenhouse or coldframe for their first winter, planting them out in late spring after the last frosts. Cuttings can be made from half-ripe wood of about 10cm with a heel, best done in July/August in a frame but protected from heat and too much light. Quick to establish, cuttings have a high success rate if not allowed to dry out. Lavender generally does better if it has only moderate water levels, exposure to damp conditions for any prolonged period or waterlogging is likely to lead to rotting and death of part or all of the plant.

# Olive

Latin: Olea europaea
Irish: Crann Ológ. Welsh: Olewydden. Breton: Olivez.
Native to southern Europe, introduced in Britain and Ireland.

The Olive was particularly valued in south-eastern Europe, north Africa and the Middle East but it was of course also known to the Celts of northern Spain (Iberia) and France (Gaul). The mythology and folklore relating to the Olive tree comes mostly from Greece, Rome and the Middle Eastern empires, but it would no doubt have been a valued tree among the Iberian and Gaulish tribes. Olives were of great economic value in the ancient world both for their fruit and the oil extracted from them. Massalia (modern Marseille) in southern Gaul was a centre of Greek and Phocaean trade between Gaul and the whole Mediterranean region, remaining independent until the Roman siege on 49 BCE. The Olive branch is a traditional symbol representing peace to this day.

Homer is said to have referred to olive oil as liquid gold as it was a highly valuable commodity and Olive trees were grown in plantations throughout the Mediterranean but particularly in Iberia, which exported huge quantities of oil to Rome in amphora pots of approximately 60L volume.

Today the olive oil industry thrives in much the same regions as it always did, with many olive plantations being thousands of years old, especially in the Middle East. Olive trees have also become a popular ornamental plant, even in wet countries like Britain and Ireland where they do not produce usually fruit unless kept in a greenhouse or similar structure.

## *Uses*

The most common use is as a foodstuff – both fruit and oil but it has other uses too. The oil from the seed is used in soap making. Olive oil has traditionally been used for dandruff and also as a general hair tonic. The oil from both the fruit and the seed can be used as lighting oil and also as a lubricant. A purple die can be obtained from the ripe fruit of the black olive and a blue or black dye from the skins. The leaves can be used for a yellow or green dye and leaves also yield an oil that has medicinal benefits. Olive trees grow well in hilly, dry land and help to keep the soil together, giving stability to vulnerable areas that might otherwise be eroded by flooding. The wood is hard and has an excellent grain, making it popular for wood turning and cabinet making. The seeds are now used in eco-friendly coal – ground up seeds are combined with coal dust and fragments to make combustible nuggets for use in fires and stoves. Albumen can also be extracted from the seeds.

Medicinally olive oil helps with excess acidity by reducing production of gastric juices. The oil of the pericarp (wall of the ripe fruit) stimulates bile flow in the liver and also acts as a laxative and emollient. Olive oil is used as a laxative and also to relieve peptic ulcers and it can be used externally on the skin for burns and stings and in the hair for dandruff and cosmetically. The oil is also used a carrier oil for other therapeutic oils. The leaves are antiseptic, astringent, febrifuge and sedative. A decoction can be used in treating fevers, calming nervous tension and hypertension, as tea it is general tonic as is high in anti-oxidants. Extract of the leaves can reduce blood sugar levels by up to 20%. Extract from the bark can be used as an astringent and act as substitute for quinine in malaria treatment. Olive is used in Bach flower remedies for exhaustion and mental fatigue.

## Cultivation

The Olive is a slow growing evergreen tree, which can reach 10m high if allowed to grow in its natural habit, it can also reach about 8m in width. The species is hermaphrodite (has both male and female organs) and is pollinated by Wind. The plant is self-fertile. This tree grows best in a Mediterranean climate, in a light soil although it can survive in clay. It prefers a free-draining soil and will suffer or die in a very damp soil. Suitable for both acidic and alkaline soils, it will do fine in soil with low nutritional value and low rainfall as it is drought tolerant, but does need to be in a sunny location to prosper. It can tolerate cold, down to about -10°C.

This tree has become a popular ornamental plant in Britain and Ireland but they rarely produce significant edible fruit (olives) and generally do badly in areas with high rainfall and low sunlight levels. Although they are slow growing, they can produce a crop after just six years but generally commercial olive groves are much older. They can survive to immense ages – the tree S'Ozzastru (Sardinia) is estimated to be close to 4,000 years old, another in Greece is thought by some to be 5,000 years old.

To encourage fruit production branches are encouraged to grow in an arch shape or are weighted down to have the same effect. To grow from seed - sow late winter in a shady position in a greenhouse or polytunnel. Seed should be given a period of cold stratification first for at least eight weeks. Where possible, it is best to sow the seed as soon as it is ripe in autumn, preferably in a greenhouse, sunroom or polytunnel. Seedlings can be transferred to a permanent position when they are 2–3 years old, in late spring or early summer. They may need protecting from the cold in their first year after replanting (e.g. horticultural fleece). Cuttings can be made from half-ripe wood of at least 5cm in length, and put in a coldframe away from direct sunlight until root is established.

# Privet

Latin: Ligustrum vulgare
Irish: Pribhéad. Welsh: Tad. Breton: Unknown.
Native to Europe, including Britain and Ireland.

Although privet is a common plant, especially for hedging, there is little in the way of folklore relating to it. In the north of England, some considered it bad luck to bring the flowers into the house. The name is attributed to Roman writer and philosopher, Pliny The Elder in the 1st century CE.

## Uses

A yellow dye can be made from the leaves and the bark and a blue-green or black dye from the berries. The berries have also been used to make ink. The wood is useful for turning and small tools if sufficiently wide branches can be obtained. The wood makes a good quality charcoal and the young branches can be used to make baskets and hurdles. Privet is mostly used as a hedging plant.

There are no edible uses for privet as it is poisonous, causing vomiting although not likely to be fatal. The leaves are bitter, astringent and detergent and aids healing of wounds. It can be used externally safely but is best not ingested internally except the berries in order to induce vomiting.

## Cultivation

This evergreen shrub grows to around 3m high and about the same in width at a medium rate. It is hardy and not frost tender. Flowering is from June to July and the small white flowers attract insects that pollinate it. It is a beneficial plant for wildlife, especially butterflies and moths. The seeds ripen September to October. It grows in most soil types, including heavy clay and will tolerate both acidic and alkaline soils, including highly alkaline soil. It can grow well in both semi-shade and full sun.

It is fairly drought tolerant and will take coastal salty exposure well, as well as polluted areas. It does not tolerate water-logged soil well. This species is susceptible to honey fungus.

Seed should be sown in spring in a coldframe. Stored seed germinates better if it is cold stratified. It is best to remove any fruit flesh from around the seed before it is sown since this can prevent germination. Seedlings can be transferred to pots when large enough or planted in permanent positions in late spring the following year or left for up to four years before final planting. Cuttings can be made from half-ripe wood of about 5cm long in late summer. Mature cuttings can be made in winter of about 20cm length and grown in permanent positions if desired.

## Rose (Guelder)

Latin: Viburnum opulus
Irish: Unknown Welsh: Dolen. Breton: Unknown.
Native to Europe, including Britain.

This plant is rather confusingly named, as it is unrelated to the rose. There is no real folklore associated with the Celts, although it is an important plant in Slavic Paganism. The plant (called *kalyna* in Ukraine) was associated with the creation of the universe and the 'fire trinity' of sun, moon and star and also feminine beauty. The berries were said to symbolize the land, home, blood and ancestral roots.

### Uses

The berries can be used to make a red dye and an ink when the berries are dried. The wood is mostly used to make skewers. This plant is sometimes used for hedging. The fruit is edible although it can cause diarrhoea and vomiting if ingested excessively. The fruit is best cooked, making it more palatable. It can be used instead of cranberries in preserves and jellies.

Medicinally it is an antispasmodic (bark especially) that can be used for asthma, cramps, colic and painful menstruation. It also acts as a sedative and can be useful for nervous conditions. The bark is also astringent. A tea from the bark is used for menstrual pain and after childbirth. Bark, which is usually dried, is best harvested in late summer before the leaves turn or in spring before the leaves emerge. A homeopathic remedy for menstrual pain is made with the bark. The leaves and berries are emetic and laxative in large quantities.

## *Cultivation*

This deciduous tree/shrub grows up to 5m high and about the same in width at a medium rate. It is a hardy plant and not frost tender, coping with as low as -30°C. Flowering is from June to July and the fruit ripens around September. This species is hermaphrodite (has both male and female organs) and is pollinated by insects and it is self-fertile. It will grow in most soils including heavy clay and will tolerate acidic or very alkaline soils. It will do well in semi-shade or full sun but prefers a moist soil and is not drought tolerant. These can be coppiced as the plant regenerates quickly and can also produce suckers. It is a host for broad bean aphids and hence should be kept away from the vegetable garden.

The seed is best sown in a coldframe as soon as it is ripe. Germination can be slow, sometimes taking over a year and a half. If the seed is harvested and sown immediately in a coldframe, it should germinate in the following spring. Stored seed will require eight weeks warm and then 12 weeks cold stratification but can still take up to 18 months to germinate.

Seedlings can be pricked out and grown in pots or beds in a greenhouse or polytunnel when big enough to handle. They can go out into their permanent positions in late spring or early summer of the following year. Cuttings of soft-wood can be made in early summer in a frame. Cuttings of half-ripe wood, about 5cm long with a heel if possible, can be done around July.

All cuttings can be difficult to overwinter, so it is best to keep them in a greenhouse or coldframe until the following spring before planting them out in a permanent position. Suckers can be dug up in winter and relocated, usually getting established by late spring.

## Rose (Wild/Dog)

Latin: Rosa canina, Rosa rugosa,
Irish: Feirdhris, Spin, Rósóg, Róisín. Welsh: Draenen, Rhosyn gwylit. Breton: Roz-agroaz.
Member of 'bushes of the wood' (*Iosa fedo*) in the Irish medieval tree list.

Rosa canina is native to Europe, including Britain and Ireland. Rosa rugosa is non-native but naturalized in Britain and parts of Ireland.

The Rose has become a symbol of love in modern times and indeed the modern forms of rose are descendants of the Rosa canina/rugosa. In ancient times they were valued for their flowers and especially for their rose-hips (fruits) as a source of food. In Irish tradition, including many folk songs, the rose appears as a symbol of beauty and of love. In England the rose was a symbol of the rival houses in Wars of the Roses – red and white being the respective colours of the Lancastrian and Yorkist rivals. The Tudors took on the combined red and white rose as a symbol of the monarchy and it became a symbol of England. As well as a valuable foodstuff, rose-hips were used in children's games in Britain and Ireland. In myth the rose appears as a symbol of beauty, such as in the tale of Finn meeting Niamh from Tir na n-Óg. It also features in the tragic end of the story of Tristan and Isolt. The Romans used rose petals in celebrations and both bride and groom wore rose crowns. In both Greece and Rome, the rosette in graveyards was a symbol of life beyond death, which may have also been the case in Celtic lands. In ancient Irish legal texts rose-hips were defined as rough (*fiadan*) fruits as opposed to sweet, along with wild apples, acorns, sloes, haws and rowan-berry. As well as a food it may have been known to have medicinal value, the rose-hips are a great source of anti-oxidants and vitamin C.

## Uses

Roses are primarily an ornamental plant but they can also make a useful hedge that will deter animals, due to the sharp thorns and tangled branches. In the mature plant the branches become woody and have a distinctive grain that is valued by wood turners and cabinet makers.

In the past the fruit was prized as it remains edible on the bush long after many fruits (e.g. apple) have fallen and rotted. The fruits (or hips) are a fantastic source of vitamins C, A and E and can be used for jams and syrups. Rose-hip syrup is still used to this day as a health-giving tonic and a nutritional supplement particularly for babies and children. Depending on variety the hips can vary in size from 0.5cm to 3cm in diameter. Both the flower petals and the fruits can be used to make a tea, both can be added to other foodstuffs whole or ground up. Rose petals are often used in cosmetics and perfumes due to the wonderful scents from the flowers.

The petals and hips have medicinal qualities, being astringent and diuretic, slightly laxative and a general tonic. Rosehips are traditionally eaten for colds, flu scurvy and minor infections or they were ingested as a syrup. A similar syrup from the petals can be used as a mild laxative. Rose water is used as a mild astringent and cleanser for the skin and eye tonic. Rose hip jelly is used to treat coughs and a tea made from the skins (minus the hairs and seeds) is good for sore throats. Rose is used in Bach flower remedies for apathy and general lethargy. It is used in homeopathy for hay fever and for ear problems. Rose is used in some alternative cancer treatments – it is rich in flavonoids and essential fatty acids and ascorbic acid. Magically rose is linked with love spells and attracting a lover.

## Cultivation

It is thought that the cultivated roses we are familiar with today originated in Persia and were common in both ancient Greece and Rome, although thousands of new varieties have come into existence in the last two centuries.

Wild roses can grow up to 3m in height and 4m wide at a fast rate, however many cultivated varieties have a much slower and restricted growth habit. It is fairly hardy and can flower right up until heavy frosts occur. Flowering is from June onwards and can continue until winter, the fruit ripens from October onwards. The species is hermaphrodite (has both male and female organs), self-fertile and is pollinated by a large variety of insects. It is valuable to wildlife generally, including birds.

Wild roses can grow in most soils, including clay so long as it is not water-logged. They can tolerate both acidic and alkaline soils and will tolerate a limited amount of coastal exposure and can survive strong winds. Rose prefer a free-draining soil in a sunny position but they do not tolerate prolonged drought well. Some modern varieties are not so versatile and highly disease prone (black spot and honey fungus) and are vulnerable to aphids especially.

To grow from seed can take up to two years as both cold and warm scarification is often necessary to erode the seedcoat and enable germination. Manual scarifying the seed and placing it in a damp and warm location (e.g. a heated propagation tray) for two weeks will reduce the time required. Following this a period of about three months at a low temperature will then lead to germination. An alternative is to sow the seeds green, i.e. when ripe on the plant and this may lead to germination in late winter or early spring. Seedlings may need protection in a coldframe from severe weather and can be planted out in summer if they have grown enough (over 20cm), otherwise they should be grown on until next spring.

Growing from cuttings is very popular, both softwood and hardwood cuttings are highly successful, indeed most commercial roses are grown this way or grafted. Mature (hardwood) cuttings are taken in late autumn from the current or previous year, about the width of a little finger, at least 10cm long. They may take up to a year to get established. Cuttings of newer growth can be taken in summer and should be protected from sun and wind until strong enough (next spring). Roses can also be divided in winter with suckers being transplanted directly to a new permanent location.

## Rosemary

Latin: Rosmarins officinalis
Irish: Ros Mhuire. Welsh: Rhosmari. Breton: Unknown.
Native to Europe, but naturalized in Britain and Ireland.

This plant was originally native to the Mediterranean region, its name, translated from Latin means 'dew of the sea'. Roman Pagan priests used rosemary as an incense in religious ceremonies, and like many cultures considered it a herb to use as protection from evil spirits and malevolent witchcraft. In England, it was burned in the homes of those who had died from illness, and placed on coffins before the grave was filled with dirt. In Ireland it was used to clear the mind as well as protection and this is still used for that purpose in county Kerry.

Rosemary is also associated with Aphrodite, Greek artwork depicting this goddess of love sometimes includes a plant that appears to be rosemary. It was used by the ancient Greeks to relieve mental disorders, as they believed that would help alleviate confusion and increase focus. Scholars used to braid rosemary into their hair, and make garlands to wear on their heads as they thought it would lead their memory to be enhanced. Traditionally, the plant is a symbol of friendship and fidelity and a wreath of it would be worn by a bride to denote love and loyalty in some countries.

## *Uses*

Planted next to plants that suffer from insect attacks, it is said to deter their presence. Dried leaves in a packet or cloth bag were used to keep moths away from clothes as well as adding a fragrance. Rosemary is used in cosmetics and sanitary products such as shampoo, and combined with borax has been used effectively as a dandruff treatment. An essential oil from the leaves and flowering stems has multiple uses – soap, perfume, medicine, culinary. The burned leaves act as a fumigant, disinfectant and as incense. A bright yellow dye can be obtained from the leaves and flowers. The plant is most popular as a culinary herb, but also is ornamental. It can be used as a hedge and the prostrate variety 'Prostratus' makes very effective ground cover for large beds or sloping banks.

Rosemary is edible - the juvenile shoots, leaves and flowers are eaten raw or cooked. The leaves are quite bitter but the flowers are somewhat milder in taste. Flowers are used in small quantities as a flavouring in soups and stews, with vegetables such as peas and spinach, and in some sweet dishes or jams. As a herb it can be used fresh or dried and is popular served on some meats such as lamb. A fragrant tea is made from the fresh or dried leaves and can be used in combination with other plants such as tansy.

Medicinally rosemary has been grown in the herb garden as a common health remedy, used especially as a tonic and pick-me-up when feeling depressed, mentally tired, nervous or exhausted. Scientific research has shown that the plant is rich in volatile oils, flavonoids and phenolic acids, which are strongly antiseptic and anti-inflammatory. Rosmarinic acid has potential in the treatment of toxic shock syndrome and the flavonoid diosmin is thought to be effective in reducing capillary fragility. Rosmarol, an extract from the leaves, has shown remarkably high antioxidant properties. The whole plant is antiseptic, antispasmodic, aromatic, astringent, cardiac, carminative, cholagogue, diaphoretic, stimulant, stomachic and a great tonic. An infusion of the flowering stems made in a covered container is effective in treating headaches, colic, colds and nervous diseases. Flowers soaked in pure water is used as a soothing eyewash. An essential oil distilled from the stems and leaves is often used medicinally, that distilled from the flowering tops is best when available. The oil is applied externally to be rubbed in, added to liniments, rubbed into the temples to treat headaches and used internally as a stomachic and for nervousness. The essential oil is used in aromatherapy. Is also used for rheumatism, dyspeptic complaints and loss of appetite.

Magically Rosemary is associated with purification and mental faculties, together with juniper (dried berries particularly) it can be burned as protection from disease.

## *Cultivation*

Rosmarinus officinalis is an evergreen shrub growing to 1.5m and roughly the same in width, at a medium rate. It is hardy and is not frost tender and is usually in flower from March to October, and the seeds ripen from August to October. The species is hermaphrodite (has both male and female organs) and is pollinated by insects, bees in particular and is a benefit to wildlife generally. It prefers a light sandy soil but will survive in any soil, including clay, if it is free-draining. It will not tolerate excessive water for long and is likely to die in water-logged conditions. Rosemary is very drought tolerant and can also tolerate winds, including maritime exposure. It is suitable for any pH but does best in alkaline soils.

It is popular both as a herb and as an ornamental plant as well as for ground cover. It does best in a sunny position with free-draining soil, preferably alkaline. It can tolerate both high and low temperatures, surviving in conditions as low as -15°C. It is a highly aromatic plant and also a great benefit to bees in spring. The cultivar 'Corsican Blue' is one of the most aromatic varieties.

Rosemary can be pruned hard and will regenerate from old wood. It also makes a good companion plant for cabbages, legumes, root vegetables such as carrot and the herb sage. Although it can tolerate drought, it can suffer in prolonged periods of well over 30°C. To grow from seed, it should be sown in a greenhouse or coldframe and allowing several months for germination. It is advisable to leave seedlings in situ for the first winter and transfer to pots or permanent positions at the end of the following spring or in early summer. Cuttings can be taken from half ripe wood, using at least 10cm sections with a heel. Rooting is very easy and should take less than a month, so long as the soil is kept reasonably moist. Cuttings can also be made from new shoots in spring, again in a coldframe and rooting within three weeks. Cuttings definitely need protection for their first winter to be sure of their survival.

## Sage

Latin: Salvia officinalis
Irish: Sáiste. Welsh: Saets. Breton: Unknown.
Native to Europe, particularly the Mediterranean region,
naturalised in Britain and Ireland.

Sage is a widely known herb that grows all over the world, but there are hundreds of different varieties nowadays. It is famously used in cooking and also in spirituality for cleansing and purification. It also has a long history of medicinal use in ancient cultures including Greece, Rome and cultures on every continent.

It was most probably used by the Druids and most certainly was used by the ancient Norse. In Ireland Wood Sage (*Iúr*

*Sléibhe*) was used in medicine for wounds, scurvy and ulcers and also in brewing, but it is actually as completely different species (Teucrium scorodonia).

## *Uses*

Traditionally the leaves have been used as tooth cleaners by simply rub the top side of the leaf over the teeth and gums. The leaves have antiseptic properties and can aid the healing of diseased gums. The dried plant is burned as fumigant. Essential oil extracted from the leaves is used in perfume, hair shampoos (especially for dark hair) and also as a food flavouring, most notably in stuffing for roast dinners. It has been used to flavour toothpastes and is also an ingredient in 'bio-activating' cosmetic products. The dried flowers are one the ingredients in organic compost activators and speeds up bacterial activity. The growing or even dried plant is said to repel insects, and for this reason is often grown as a companion plant alongside cabbages and carrots. However, it dislikes growing with basil, rue or the cucumber and squash family. Both the leaves and flowers are edible, either raw or cooked, its strong taste and aroma makes it popular in flavouring in cooking. Sage is thought to be an aid to digestion hence it is often used with heavy, oily foods. The flowers can also be sprinkled on salads to add colour and fragrance. A herb tea is made from the fresh or dried leaves which is considered to be beneficial to the digestion. An essential oil obtained from the plant is used commercially to flavour ice cream, sweets and baked goods.

Sage has a very long history of effective medicinal use and is an important domestic herbal remedy for disorders of the digestive system. Its antiseptic qualities make it an effective gargle for the mouth as it can help heal sore throats and ulcers.

The pulverized leaves applied to toothache can provide some pain relief. The whole herb is antihydrotic, antiseptic, antispasmodic, astringent, carminative, stimulant, tonic and vasodilatory. Sage is also used extensively internally in the treatment of excessive lactation, night sweats, excessive salivation, excessive perspiration, anxiety, depression, female sterility and menopausal problems. The essential oil from the plant is used in small doses to remove heavy collections of mucous from the respiratory organs and mixed in embrocation for treating rheumatism. Externally, it is used to treat insect bites, skin, throat, mouth and gum infections and vaginal discharge. This plant is toxic in excess or when taken for extended periods - although the toxic dose is very high. In large doses Sage can cause epileptic fits, giddiness or fainting. If not used fresh, then the leaves should be harvested before the plant comes into flower and are dried for later use. etc. The essential oil is used in aromatherapy as a tonic.

NOTE: *This plant should not be prescribed to pregnant women or to people who have epileptic fits.*

## Cultivation

Salvia officinalis is an evergreen shrub growing to roughly half a metre high and wide, at a medium rate. It is hardy and is not frost tender. It is in leaf all year, in flower from June to August, and the seeds ripen from August to September. The species is hermaphrodite (has both male and female organs) and is pollinated by bees. It is fairly soft as a juvenile but the branches become increasingly woody with age. It will do well in sandy and medium (loamy) soils and prefers well-drained soil above all else. It will prosper in neutral and basic (alkaline) soils and can grow in very alkaline soils but does poorly in very acidic soil. It cannot grow in the shade but prefers light shade or full sun. It prefers dry soil to moist soil and can tolerate drought, it will not survive in waterlogged soil. It will also grow well in a rockery or close to the seashore.

There are a great many plants in this genus and a huge number of varieties of sage including purple (purpurea) which has tougher leaves. In order to prevent them becoming excessively woody and leggy they can be pruned in spring. If left unpruned they often degenerate after about five years and hence are often replaced around this time.

To grow from seed, it is best sown in mid spring in a greenhouse or coldframe. Germination is usually within two weeks and plants can be pricked out and placed in individual pots as soon as they are large enough to handle. In colder areas it is best to grow them on in a greenhouse over the first winter to help them get established and plant into permanent positions the following spring. Cuttings can be made from semi-mature branches with a heel around May and sown directly in the ground, cuttings can also be made from new growth, protected from wind and harsh sun and kept in a greenhouse or sunroom over winter. New plants can be made by burying lower branches in soil and removing them about six months or more later, by which time they should have developed some viable roots.

## Sea Buckthorn

Latin: Hippophae rhamnoides
Irish: Ramhdhraighean na mara. Welsh: Helygen y môr. Breton: Unknown.
Native to Europe, particularly the Mediterranean region, naturalised in Britain and Ireland.

Sea Buckthorn, despite its name is often found in mountainous areas and is known to have been valued by the ancients Greeks and the Chinese, amongst others. The legend of Pegasus is associated with this bush (hippophae means "shiny horse"), who is said to have eaten the berries and possibly was aided by them. It is also said that Genghis Khan used the berries as a stimulant and restorative in his conquest of much of the world.

## *Uses*

Very tolerant of maritime exposure, it can be used as a windbreak hedge. As it is very thorny plant, it quickly makes an impenetrable barrier, making a good hedge for animals. In areas prone to soil erosion it can be used to conserve the soil, especially in sandy areas as the extensive roots and suckering make it ideal for the purpose of colonising ground, especially as is it a nitrogen fixing plant. It is perfect for re-establishing woodland in difficult and exposed areas with poor soil.

An oil can be extracted from the seed. The flesh of the fruit is used in facial cosmetics and toothpastes and is very high in vitamins. A yellow dye can be made from the fruit, the stems, foliage and roots. A dark brown dye is made from young leaves and shoots. The wood is fine grained, hard and durable and is used in wood turning and for charcoal.

The fruit is edible raw or cooked and has many health benefits – recent analysis has come to discover its unusually dense nutritional content, a source of Omega-3, Omega-6, Omega-7, Omega-9, flavonoids, essential fatty acids, Vitamin A, several B Vitamins, Vitamin C, and Vitamin E. It has a bitter taste as is often enjoyed with other fruits which are tastier.

The twigs and leaves contain tannin and the young branches contain and oil that is highly bioactive which is useful for treating burns. Oil from the fruit is useful in treatment of cardiac disorders as well as healing eczema and burns or used internally for stomach and digestive problems. The fruit is a good general tonic and treatment for exhaustion. Recent research shows its potential for cancer prevention and for reducing or halting cancer growth. A decoction of the fruit is an effective face wash and also used for reducing spots and skin irritations.

## *Cultivation*

It is especially useful as a seashore hedge and for establishing woodland on poor land. It is a deciduous Shrub growing to 6m high and up to 3m wide at a medium rate. It is hardy is not frost tender, tolerating about -25°C, although it is also fairly heat tolerant. It is in flower in April, and the seeds ripen from September to October. The species is dioecious (individual flowers are either male or female, but only one sex is found on each plant so both male and female plants must be grown near each other if seed is to be produced, it is pollinated by wind.

It can grow in harsh maritime conditions, including on very poor sandy soil. It will grow in clay even but prefers a fairly free-draining soil and will tolerate drought well. This shrub requires full sun or semi-shade, it will not do well at all in shaded areas.

This plant is easy to propagate from suckers, but these will be the same sex as the parent plant. The sex of plants is impossible to distinguished before flowering, but on flowering plants the buds of male plants in winter are conical and highly visible whilst female buds are smaller and rounded.

To grow from seed sow in spring in a sunny position in a coldframe ideally. Germination is usually quick and but three months of cold stratification before planting may improve the germination rate. The seed can be sown in a coldframe as soon as it is ripe in the autumn, which may lead to immediate germination. Once the seeds are large enough to handle, they can be pricked out and kept in pots in the greenhouse/coldframe. Planting in permanent positions is best done in spring. Male and female saplings that are beginning to flower can be distinguished by the more prominent male buds. Cuttings can be made in summer from half-ripe wood but take with difficulty, it is much easier to divide suckers in winter and plant directly into new permanent positions.

# Thyme

Latin: Thymus vulgaris/serpyllum
Irish: Tím, Lus na mBrat, Mhic rí Breatan. Welsh: Gryw, Teim.
Breton: Tin, Munud-Braz.
Native to Europe, particularly the Mediterranean region, wild
species is native to Britain and Ireland.

In Scotland, the scent was meant to give strength and courage
and an infusion drunk at night was meant to prevent bad
dreams. In Britain, young women would wear thyme to attract
suitors as it was a symbol of love in folklore. In Roman society it
was used to treat melancholy as well as to increase courage. In
ancient Greece it was associated with sacrifice and death – being
a common plant to grow on graves. A similar custom relating
to thyme was found in Wales. Gypsies and Travelers in Britain
regard thyme to be an unlucky plant. Thyme has many medicinal
uses, in particularly beneficial for the respiratory system. It is
used to relieve phlegm and to treat whooping cough. It is also
helpful in regard to childbirth and recovery afterwards.

Magically it is used as a purifying incense and is used in
burial rituals – both on graves and drunk in communing with
the dead. It is also considered helpful for seeing otherworldly
beings and the *sidhe*.

## *Uses*

An essential oil from the leaves and flowering tops is used
in perfumery, soaps, medicinally etc. It has fungicidal and
disinfectant properties. The dried flowers were used to repel
moths from clothing. The growing plant is said to repel cabbage
root fly, hence should be planted with cabbages as a companion
plant. Leaves can be eaten raw in salads or added as a flavouring
to cooked foods. Thyme retains its flavour well in long slow
cooking, it is popular both fresh or dried as a culinary herb. If
the leaves are to be dried, the plants should be harvested in early

and late summer just before the flowers open and the leaves should be dried quickly. An aromatic tea is also made from the leaves.

Medicinally, wild thyme is a commonly used domestic remedy, being employed especially for its antiseptic properties and its beneficial effect on the digestive system. The whole plant is strongly antiseptic, antispasmodic, carminative, deodorant, diaphoretic, disinfectant, expectorant, sedative and tonic. It is taken internally in the treatment of bronchitis, catarrh, laryngitis, flatulent indigestion, painful menstruation, colic and hangovers. It is said to be effective in treating alcoholism.

## *Cultivation*

Thymus serpyllum is an evergreen shrub growing to 0.1m by 0.3m at a medium rate. It is hardy and is not frost tender and stays viable down to about -15°C. It is in leaf all year, in flower from July to August, and the seeds ripen from August to September. The species is hermaphrodite (has both male and female organs) and is pollinated by insects. It is noted for attracting wildlife. It prefers a light and well-drained soil and will struggle or die in boggy ground. It will tolerate a wide pH range, strong winds and drought but does not like salty coastal conditions much. If is inclined to get woody and straggly unless pruned on a regular basis. Grows well in a rockery and gives good ground cover as it matures. [200]. This species hybridizes freely with other members of the genus.

Seed is best sown spring in a coldframe. Seed can also be sown in autumn in a greenhouse or coldframe - surface sow or barely cover the seed. Germination can be erratic, sometimes very quickly but not always. When they are large enough to handle, prick the seedlings out into individual pots and grow them on in the greenhouse or coldframe for at least their first winter. Plant them out into their permanent positions in late spring or early summer, after the last expected frosts. Large plants can be divided in spring or autumn. Large sections can be planted out directly into permanent positions. Cuttings can be made from young shoots of about 5cm with a heel, best done in May/June in a coldframe. Cuttings of half-ripe wood, again 5cm can be made with a heel in July/August and placed in a coldframe but with some protection from harsh sun.

## Grape Vine

Latin: Vitis vinifera
Irish: Crann fíniúna. Welsh: Gwinwydden. Breton: Gwini.
Native to Europe, particularly the Mediterranean region, naturalised in Britain and Ireland.
11th letter of the Ogham alphabet (depending on interpretation of source material).

Grapevine is strongly associated with magic and religion. The grape harvest and wine produced from it has been associated with fertility gods such as Hathor in Egypt, the Roman Bacchus and his Greek equivalent Dionysus. In Sumer the goddess Siduri is associated with wine as well as beer and is mentioned in *The Epic of Gilgamesh*. In Africa, the goddess Yasigi was honoured as goddess of wine and alcohol by the people of Mali.

Grapevines are believed to have originated in or around Mesopotamia, and were cultivated as long as 6,000 years before the Romans introduced the plant to the British Isles in the late 1st century BCE, it is quite likely to be one of the first cultivated fruits. In Ireland it is mentioned in medieval *ogham* literature but is most probably confused with the small tree Buckthorn, which is native. Grapes are not suited to the Irish climate and would not have arrived until late medieval times – wine was imported from Europe.

The Vikings are said to have called North America 'Vinland' due to all the wild grapes they found there. In North America, native grapes (belonging to the genus Vitis) proliferated in the wild all across the continent, and were a part of the diet of many Native Americans. However, these varieties were considered to be unsuitable for wine, by the European colonists, arriving in the 16th century onwards.

## *Uses*

A yellow dye is obtained from the fresh or dried leaves and an oil from the grape seed can be used for lamps and as an ingredient in soaps and paints. Cream of tartar (potassium hydrogen tartrate or tartaric acid) is extracted from the residue of pressed grapes, is used in making fluxes for soldering as well as in cooking. The stems of very old vines can reach a good size and have been used as a very durable timber, although they seldom reach a decent size in more temperate climates like Ireland or Britain.

The fruit can be eaten raw or dried. The dried fruits are the raisins, sultanas and currants with different varieties producing the different types of dried fruit. A fully ripened fresh fruit is sweet and juicy but slightly acidic. The fruit juice can be concentrated and used as a sweetener as well as a drink. Grapes widely used in making wine. The leaves and young tendrils are also edible and can be cooked. Young leaves are wrapped around other foods and then baked, giving a pleasant flavour. An edible oil similar to sunflower oil can be obtained from the seed but it needs to be refined before it can be eaten. It is a polyunsaturated oil and is suitable for mayonnaise and cooking, especially frying, although it is expensive. The roasted seed can make an acceptable coffee substitute. The raw sap of the plant can be used as a drink, it has a sweet taste. The sap can be harvested in spring and early summer, though it should not be taken in large quantities as it will weaken the plant.

Medicinally grapes are a nourishing and slightly laxative fruit that can boost the body during illness, especially of the gastro-intestinal tract and liver. Because the nutrient content of grapes is close to that of blood plasma, grape fasts are recommended for detoxification as is the case for poor liver or bile duct function. The fresh fruit is antilithic, constructive, cooling and diuretic. The fruit is also helpful in the treatment of varicose veins, haemorrhoids and capillary fragility. The dried fruit is demulcent, cooling, mildly expectorant and laxative. The leaves, but especially red leaves, are anti-inflammatory and astringent, used for varicose veins, haemorrhoids and capillary fragility. A decoction is used in the treatment of fragile pregnancies, internal and external bleeding, cholera, dropsy, diarrhoea and nausea. It is also used as a wash for mouth ulcers and as douche for treating vaginal discharge. The leaves are harvested in early summer and used fresh or dried. The seed is anti-inflammatory and astringent. The sap of young branches is diuretic and it is used as a remedy for skin diseases and as an effective lotion for the eyes. The tendrils are astringent and a decoction is used in the treatment of diarrhoea. The plant is used in Bach flower remedies for overbearing and inflexible behaviour.

## Cultivation

Vitis vinifera is a deciduous climber growing up to 15m high at a fast rate, although it needs some form of support such as a wall or tree, it can live for over a hundred years. It is hardy and is not frost tender, tolerating temperatures down to about -20°C, however new growth can suffer in prolonged and severe late spring frosts. It is in flower from May to July, and the seeds ripen from September to October. The species is hermaphrodite (has both male and female organs) and is pollinated by insects.

It is suitable for most soils, including a moderate amount of clay, but prefers well-drained soil and will tolerate acid, neutral and alkaline soils. It grows best in a calcareous soil, but dislikes excessively chalky soils. It can grow in semi-shade but does better in full sun. In order to produce good fruit, it needs a sunny and warm environment, protected from strong winds. Britain and Ireland are at the northernmost limit of their range and tend to fruit poorly if not in a greenhouse or sunroom, due to the excessive rainfall, poor summer temperatures and low sunlight levels. It is quite common for the vine to be planted outside the greenhouse or sunroom and the above ground parts are to be found inside (usually via a hole or panel). Any pruning should be carried out in winter when the plants are dormant otherwise, they bleed profusely. The cultivated grape is thought to have been derived from Vitis vinifera sylvestris. Grapes grow well in the company of hyssop, chives, basil and charlock but grow badly with radishes, both the grapes and the radishes developing a poor flavour.

Grapes are very susceptible to attacks by phylloxera, this disease is especially prevalent in some areas of Europe and it almost destroyed the grape industry. However, American species of grapes that are resistant to phylloxera are now used as rootstocks and this allows grapes to be grown in areas where the disease is common. Plants in this genus are notably susceptible to honey fungus. It is also susceptible to the vine weevil that has been introduced across the world from North America, which eats the roots in the larval stage, and leaves as an adult.

Seed is best sown in a coldframe as soon as it is ripe. Six weeks cold stratification improves the germination rate, and so stored seed is best sown in a coldframe over the winter. Germination should take place in the first spring, but sometimes takes up to another year. Prick out the seedlings into individual pots when they are large enough to handle and grow them on in a coldframe or greenhouse for their first winter. Plant out in early summer. Cuttings of mature wood can be made from the current season's growth about December or January in a frame. These cuttings can be of at least 15cm long or they can be of short sections of the stem about 5cm long with just one bud at the top. If using short sections then a thin, narrow strip of the bark about 3cm long is removed from the bottom half of the side of the stem as this will encourage callusing and the formation of roots.

## Wayfaring tree

Latin: Viburnum lantana
Irish: Unknown. Welsh: Coeden yn ymdaith. Breton: Unknown.
Native to Europe and native in Britain.

Considered to be welcome sign that you're homeward bound, the wayfaring tree is so called because it grows close to paths, in hedges on the edges of woodland.

### Uses

The young stems can be used as a twine. In more recent times this species is used as a rootstock for all forms of viburnums that require grafting. There are no known medicinal uses. The fruit is edible, both raw or cooked. Regarded as a famine food, it is only used when all else fails. The oblong fruit is about 8mm long and contains a single large seed, it is not very tasty but has some nutritional value.

### Cultivation

This small tree is a deciduous shrub growing to 5m high by 4m wide at a medium rate. It is hardy and not frost sensitive. It is in flower from May to June, and the seeds ripen from July to September. The species is hermaphrodite (has both male and female organs) and is pollinated by insects. This plant is self-fertile and is easily propagated. It will grow in any soil type but prefers a free-draining soil, although it will survive in clay if not water-logged. It can tolerate almost any soil pH, including highly alkaline. It will grow well in full sun or in semi-shade, it does not do so well in full shade. It is intolerant of atmospheric pollution; hence it is not found much in large cities or industrial areas. It is reasonably drought tolerant, unlike most viburnums.

These plants can be pruned hard, which makes then suitable for hedges. It is popular as hedge, screen or as a specimen plant due to its pretty white flowers and cheerful red berries. Although it is self-fertile it is best to grow at least two genetically distinct specimens in order to ensure fruiting and viable seed.

To grow from seed, it is best sown in a coldframe as soon as the berries are ripe. Germination can be slow, sometimes taking a year and a half or longer. If the seed is harvested green and sown immediately in a coldframe, it should germinate in the spring. Seed that has been dried and stored seed require two months warm then three months cold stratification and yet can still take 18 months to germinate. Prick out the seedlings into individual pots when they are large enough to handle and grow them on in a coldframe or greenhouse. Planting out into their permanent positions should take place in late spring or early summer of the following year. Cuttings of soft-wood can be made in early summer in a frame. Once they start to root and they can be put into pots and planted in permanent positions in late spring or early summer of the following year. Cuttings of half-ripe wood, of at least 5cm long with a heel if possible are done in July/August in a frame, best to keep them in a greenhouse or coldframe until the following spring before planting them out. Cuttings of mature wood are done in winter in a frame. They should root in early spring - pot them up when large enough to handle and plant them out in summertime if there has been reasonable growth.

## *Druidic Herbacious Plants*

The following are some herbaceous plants that are native to Britain, Ireland or western Europe where the Druids would have lived. Once again, this is by no means an exhaustive list, (which would run into thousands of plants) but includes at least some of the herbaceous plants that are known in relation to the Druids or Celtic peoples.

Herbaceous plants can have an extremely short life and be barely 1cm in size or they can be metres in size and live for many years or everything in between. What distinguishes them most from trees and shrubs is that they are soft and far less tolerant of cold generally and many die back in the winter, remaining dormant until warmer and sunnier weather.

| Type | Lifespan | Size | Winter dieback |
|---|---|---|---|
| Ephemeral | 4-12 weeks | Small | No |
| Annual | Up to 1-year | Variable | No |
| Biannual | 2-year cycle | Variable | Often |
| Perennial | Several years | Variable | Not always |

## Agrimony

Latin: Agrimonia eupatoria
Irish: Airgeadán, Marbhdhraighean. Welsh: Maip.
Breton: Trenk Manac'h.
Native to Europe, common in Britain. PERENNIAL

The name Agrimony is from Argemone, a word from Greek for plants which were healing to the eyes, the name Eupatoria refers to Mithridates Eupator, a king who was a renowned herbalist. The magic power of Agrimony is mentioned in an old English medical manuscript:

*'If it be leyd under mann's heed, He shal sleepyn as he were deed;
He shal never drede ne wakyn, Till fro under his heed it be takyn.'*

Agrimony was one of the most famous vulnerary herbs, Germanic tribes believed that it would heal wounds, snake bites, warts, etc. It has been used for diarrhoea, sore throats, liver problems, as a tonic and astringent. It also makes a refreshing tea. Magically it is used for protection, to banish negativity and provide a psychic shield.

## *Cultivation*

It grows to just over half a meter and is not frost tender. It is in flower from June to August, and the seeds ripen from August to September. The species is hermaphrodite (has both male and female organs), is self-fertile and is pollinated by insects. It will grow in any soil type including highly alkaline soil. It can grow in semi-shade or full sun. To grow from seed sow in spring or autumn, either in pots or final position. It usually germinates in a minimum of two weeks at 13°C or more, though germination rates can be low, especially if the seed has been stored and sown in spring, however cold stratification help increase germination rates. Plants can be propagated by division in autumn, planted straight out into their new permanent positions.

## Angelica

Latin: Angelica archangelica
Irish: Ainglice. Welsh: Llysiau'r angel. Breton: Ael Dous.
Native to Europe, common in Britain and Ireland. BIENNIAL

Angelica is used as an incense when dried and can also be used as a tobacco substitute. It has a long history of use if traditional medicine for aiding digestion and to raise sweat in treating flus or colds. A decoction of the dried root is used to cure alcoholism, taken twice daily. A salve from the roots is helpful in easing rheumatism and increasing blood circulation. An essential oil from the root and seeds is used in perfumes, medicinally and as a food flavouring.

## *Cultivation*

It grows up to 1.5m and is not frost tender. It flowers around July and produces seed in autumn. It prefers a deep soil to allow room for its roots, but will grow in most soil types and will grow in semi-shade or full sun, it is also beneficial to insects.

The seed is best sown in a coldframe as soon as it is ripe as it has a short viability. Dried seed can also be sown in the spring, though germination rates will be lower. It requires light for germination and so should be sown on the soil surface. If sown in autumn they are best protected from the cold over winter for best results and placed out in late spring. Spring sown seed can be sown in permanent positions immediately.

*NOTE: excessive consumption can lead to respiratory, blood pressure, heart problems and photo-sensitivity.*

## Basil

Latin: Calamintha (genus), Clinopodium vulgare
Irish: Lus mic rí. Welsh: Brenhinllys. Breton: Basilik.
Native to Europe, common in Britain. PERENNIAL

Wild basil is common in Britain but relatively rare in Ireland. Used in food. Herbally it was used for menstrual and sciatica pain, to prevent conception. An infusion of the plant helps to overcome weak digestion. Magically it provides protection in conflict and deters thieves. It can be used for purification and to dispel bad energy. Most of what is known comes from Culpeper and later sources.

## *Cultivation*

Perennial, and not frost tender, flowers July to September. It is hermaphrodite (has both male and female organs) and is pollinated by insects. Grows in semi-shade and most soils. Sow in spring, will germinate at around 20°C within two weeks.

## Brookweed/Samolus

Latin: Samolus valerandi
Irish: Falcaire uisce Welsh: Claerlys. Breton: Sparfel.
Native to Europe, common in Britain and Ireland. PERENNIAL

Described by Pliny as dug up by the left hand of a Druid who had fasted for days. It grows wild in the British Isles and France; it was used as a cure for a variety of illnesses in cattle and pigs. The leaves are extremely bitter but were eaten to prevent scurvy but it was rarely used internally by humans due to the horrible taste. A poultice from it was used in Wales for sore eyes.

### *Cultivation*

It is hardy and not frost tender, growing to 0.3m high. It is in flower from June to August, and the seeds ripen from July to August. The species is hermaphrodite (has both male and female organs and is self-fertile. Grows in any soil and a wide pH range. It hates shade but can cope with very damp soil and even in water and will tolerate coastal conditions. Seed can be surface sow in a coldframe in the spring keep soil moist by standing the pot in about 2-3cm of water. Prick out the seedlings when they are large enough and plant in a bigger pot, again maintaining a high level of dampness. Plant out in the summer if there has been sufficient growth, otherwise plant out in late spring of the next year. Plants can be divided and replanted in spring.

## Butterbur

Latin: Petasites hybridus
Irish: Gallán Mór Welsh: Alan Mawr. Breton: Unknown.
Native to Europe, common in Britain and Ireland. PERENNIAL

The large leaves were used to wrap up butter pats and also as protection from the sun. The root can be used to help break a fever as it induces heavy sweating. It was also used for the treatment of rheumatism. Butterbur is widely considered to be an effective cough remedy and recent experiments have shown it to have remarkable antispasmodic and pain-relieving properties. A decoction is used as a remedy for various respiratory problems such as asthma, colds, bronchitis and whooping cough and also fevers and urinary problems.

## *Cultivation*

This plant reaches to 1m by 3m wide, growing at a fast rate. It is hardy and frost tolerant. It is in leaf from April to December and in flower from March to May. It is dioecious (individual flowers are either male or female, but only one sex is to be found on any one plant so both male and female plants must be grown if seed is required). It is pollinated by insects and the plant is not self-fertile, it is especially valuable to bees as a source of nectar. Grows in any type of soil and a wide pH range, it will also grow in deep shade or full sun. A very invasive plant, with roots that are very difficult to eradicate.

Sow when ripe in autumn in situ or use the dried seed in spring. Propagation by division can be done at almost any time of the year (not during frost) and grown on pots in semi-shade. Large plants can be divided and can be planted out directly into permanent positions.

## Buttercup

Latin: Ranunculus (genus)
Irish: Fearbán, Welsh: Blodyn Ymenyn. Breton: Unknown.
Native to Europe, common in Britain and Ireland. PERENNIAL

Associated with *Bealtaine* it was picked on May eve and also rubbed in cows' udders on May Day to protect them. Their fragrance was thought to induce madness yet if worn in a pouch around the neck they were thought to cure it. It is used in a popular children's game to see if you like butter by looking for reflected yellow colour (on a sunny day) if held under the chin. Medicinally their acrid juice is used to raise blisters and in rheumatism, relief of headaches, curing warts, jaundice, heartburn and kidney problems. A poultice of the chewed leaves has been used in the treatment of sores, muscular aches and rheumatic pains. The leaves are edible cooked and used as a pot-herb, it has a high level of toxicity, especially raw. The fresh juice can cause skin blistering.

## Cultivation

Growing barely 15cm high, it can spread more than 1m, it is not frost tender. It is in flower from May to August. The species is hermaphrodite (has both male and female organs) and is pollinated by insects. It is easily propagated and generally regarded as a weed, even fragments of root can regenerate into full plants in a few weeks.

## Centaury

Latin: Centaurium erythraea
Irish: Drímire Mhuire, Welsh: Canrhi Goch. Breton: Unknown.
Native to Europe, common in Britain and Ireland. BIENNIAL

Valued for its purifying properties and believed to be particularly powerful if picked on May Day. It was considered an excellent protection against magic. It was used by the ancients in wound healing. It is regarded as a blood purifier and effective against liver, kidney, stomach and rheumatic complaints. It was also used in Britain and some parts of Ireland for indigestion relief. The plant is used as a flavouring in bitter herbal liqueurs and is an ingredient of vermouth.

## *Cultivation*

Centaurium erythraea grows to 0.3m by 0.2m. It is in flower from June to October, and the seeds ripen from August to October. The flowers only open in fine weather and close at midday. The species is hermaphrodite (has both male and female organs) and is pollinated by insects and it is self-fertile. Suitable for light to medium soils and prefers well-drained soil and can survive in nutritionally poor soil and of a wide pH range. Does not grow well in wet soils. It can grow in semi-shade (light woodland) or no shade. To grow from seed sow February to May in situ or as soon as it is ripe in situ. Germination is usually rapid.

## Charlock

Latin: Sinapis arvensis.
Irish: Praiseach Bhuí, Welsh: Mwstard Gwyllt, Breton: Sezv.
Native to Europe, common in Britain and Ireland. ANNUAL

Also known as wild mustard. Formerly a common food, especially in times of famine, it came to be regarded as a nuisance weed in more recent centuries. However, during the Irish famine it kept many people alive, as well as being boiled like cabbage, its seeds were used to make a rough bread. It was also used to cure jaundice. The juice was also taken as a spring tonic. The seed can be ground into a powder and used as a food flavouring. It has a hot mustard flavour. An edible oil is obtained from the seed.

## *Cultivation*

Charlock is an annual growing to 0.8m high. It is hardy to zone and is not frost tender. It is in flower from May to July, and the seeds ripen from May to August. The species is hermaphrodite (has both male and female organs) and is pollinated by insects. Suitable for all soil types and grow in any pH including very alkaline soils. It cannot grow in the shade and prefers full sun although it prefers moist soil. The plant can tolerate strong winds but not salty maritime conditions. The seed can be sown in spring and autumn and germinates very easily. It should not really need much encouragement to grow and if found in the wild in abundance.

## Comfrey

Latin: Symphytum officinale
Irish: Meacan an chomparaí. Welsh: Llysiau'r cwlwm.
Breton: Unknown.
Native to Europe, common in Britain and Ireland. PERENNIAL

Comfrey is a commonly used herbal medicine with a long and proven history in the treatment of various complaints. The root and the leaves are used, the root being more active, and they can be taken internally or used externally as a poultice. It is referred to sometimes as 'knitbone' because of its healing effects of fractures and breaks. Comfrey is especially useful in the external treatment of cuts, bruises, sprains, sores, eczema, varicose veins, broken bones etc., internally it is used in the treatment of a wide range of pulmonary complaints and internal bleeding. The plant contains a substance called 'allantoin', a cell proliferant that speeds up the healing process. This substance is now synthesized in the pharmaceutical industry and used in healing creams. The root and leaves are anodyne, astringent (mild), demulcent, emollient, expectorant, haemostatic, refrigerant, vulnerary. Some caution is advised, however, especially in the internal use of the herb. External applications and internally taken teas or tinctures of the leaves are considered to be completely safe, but internal ingestion is dangerous as comfrey contains an alkaloid that can cause liver damage. The leaves are harvested in early summer before the plant flowers, the roots are harvested in the autumn. Both can be dried for use later on. A homeopathic remedy is made from the fresh root, harvested before the plant flowers.

It is edible but should not be ingested in large quantities - young leaves can be eaten raw or cooked. The leaf is rich in minerals but it is not pleasant tasting. It can be chopped up finely and added to salads, in this way the hairiness and acrid taste is not so obvious. The peeled roots are cut up and added to soups. A tea is made from the dried leaves and roots. The roasted roots are used with dandelion and chicory roots for making a coffee substitute.

## Cultivation

Comfrey is a perennial growing to 1.2m by 0.6m at a fast rate. It is hardy to zone and is not frost tender. It is in flower from May to June, and the seeds ripen from June to July. The species is hermaphrodite (has both male and female organs) and is pollinated by insects. It is suitable for all soil types including heavy clay and will grow in a wide pH range. It prefers a moist soil and grows in semi-shade or full sun. It is popular for ground cover and as a fodder plant, it also is used as a 'green manure', often grown specifically for that purpose.

Seed can be sown in spring or autumn in a coldframe or in situ. When they are large enough to handle, prick the seedlings out into individual pots and grow them on in the greenhouse for their first winter. Plant them out into their permanent positions in late spring or early summer, after the last expected frosts. Dividing plants succeeds at almost any time of the year. This plant is easy to grow and can be quite invasive.

## Crane's Bill/Herb Robert

Latin: Geranium pratense, Geranium robertianum
Irish: Crobh, Welsh: Mynawyd Y Bugail. Breton: Jeraniom.
Native to Europe, common in Britain and Ireland. PERENNIAL

Reputedly named after St. Robert (Herb-Robert) who used it for healing. Herb-robert is also thought to have gained its name from association with Robin Goodfellow, a house goblin from English folklore, also known as Puck. Herb-robert was traditionally carried to bring good luck and for fertility.

## Uses

Both plants were used to staunch bleeding, to cure kidney problems, treat coughs and sore throats and cure red-water fever in livestock. It is analgesic, anti-inflammatory and febrifuge, it is used in the treatment of fevers from influenza, inflammation of the lungs, pain and swellings of the limbs. A brown dye is obtained from the whole plant. Freshly picked leaves can be rubbed on the body to repel mosquitoes.

## Cultivation

Geranium pratense is a perennial growing to 1.2m at a fast rate. It is hardy to zone and not frost hardy. It is in flower from June to September. The species is hermaphrodite (has both male and female organs) and is pollinated by insects. Suitable for any kind of soil and a wide pH range. Cannot grow in shade and prefers a moist soil. Geranium robertianum is similar in appearance but grows to 0.4m, with smaller flowers and darker leaves, but the two plants are often confused.

To sow seed spring in a coldframe. When they are large enough to handle, prick the seedlings out into individual pots and plant them out in the summer. It can be divided in spring or autumn. Larger clumps can be replanted direct into their permanent positions, though it is best to pot up smaller clumps and grow them on in a coldframe until they are rooting well. Plant them out in the spring.

# Daisy

Latin: Bellis perenis/Leucanthemum vulgare.

Irish: Nóinín. Welsh: Llygad y dydd. Breton: Mararit.

Native to Europe, common in Britain and Ireland. PERENNIAL

Associated with the coming of spring and also childhood prophetic games as well as childhood daisy chains. The larger ox-eye daisy is associated with the summer solstice and several medicinal uses such as treatment of abscesses and boils. Daisies can be used to treat fresh wounds, liver inflammation, burns, sore eyes, ringworm, chilblains and as sedative (Chamomile). It is edible but not very tasty. An insect repellent spray can be made from an infusion of the leaves.

## *Cultivation*

Bellis perennis is an evergreen perennial growing to 0.1m at a medium rate, often regarded as a weed. It is hardy and is not frost tender. It is evergreen and in leaf all year, in flower all year, and the seeds ripen from May to October. The species is hermaphrodite (has both male and female organs) and is pollinated by insects and is self-fertile, valuable to bees especially.

Suitable for all soil types but prefers a well-drained soil, growing in semi-shade or full sun. It can tolerate drought fairly well. There are several commercial ornamental varieties available. Ox-eye daisies are a different genus and grow much larger (0.6m), liking similar conditions and having very similar flowers.

Seed - sow as soon as the seed is ripe in June, or in spring with ox-eye daisy. When they are large enough to handle, prick the seedlings out into individual pots and plant them out in late summer. They can be divided after flowering, for either type. Very easy, it can be done at almost any time of the year, although spring and early summer are generally best.

# Dandelion

Latin: Taraxacum officinale

Irish: Caisearbhán. Welsh: Dant y llew. Breton: Unknown.

Native to Europe, common in Britain and Ireland. PERENNIAL

Associated with *Imbolc* and the goddess Brighid it was one of several plants used to protect milk from malign influence. It is famously diuretic but also was used in magical healing of warts and chickenpox. It was also used for coughs and colds, as a blood tonic, cure for jaundice, liver and stomach upsets, rheumatism and tuberculosis, cuts, swelling, styes, sore throats and parasitic worms. In ancient Ireland 'Diancecht's Porridge' containing Dandelion was used for fourteen types of stomach disorder. The plant has an antibacterial action, inhibiting the growth of Staphylococcus aureus, Pneumococci, Meningococci, Bacillus dysenteriae, B. typhi, C. diphtheriae, Proteus etc. The latex contained in the plant sap can be used to remove corns, warts and verrucae.

## *Cultivation*

Dandelion grows up to 0.3m by 0.3m at a fast rate, although sizes vary hugely depending on conditions, also each leaf is totally unique as the shape is non-uniform. It is hardy, evergreen and is not frost tender. It is in flower from March - October, and the seeds ripen from April/May onwards. The species is hermaphrodite (has both male and female organs) and is pollinated by insects, to which it is of great benefit. It is apomictic (reproduces by seeds formed without sexual fusion and the plant is self-fertile, hence it is a highly prolific weed. It is noted for attracting wildlife, especially bees. It is suitable for any soil and pH but prefers well-drained soil. It can grow in semi-shade or full sun. The plant can tolerate maritime exposure and extreme drought due to its long tap root. There is little need to propagate this plant, seed germinate easily and plants can also be divided easily.

# Devil's Bit Scabious

Latin: Succusa pratensis

Irish: Odhrach Bhallach. Welsh: Tamaid Y Cythraul. Breton:
Bleun Koukoug.

Native to Europe, common in Britain and Ireland. PERENNIAL

Considered beneficial to cows' milk, and good to have on one's
land, it appears in folklore often in association with the 'evil eye'.
It was used in a magical potion to cure this and also as part of an
incantation to summon the aid of fairies in the household. It was
thought to have great healing powers, being used for plague,
fevers, anti-poisoning, swellings, wounds, bites, bruised, blood
clots, spots, coughs, inflammation, scurf, dandruff and sores. The
young shoots are edible. A green dye is made from the leaves.

## *Cultivation*

A perennial growing to 0.4m dying back in winter. It is hardy to
zone (UK) 5. It is in flower from July to October, and the seeds
ripen from August to October. The species is hermaphrodite (has
both male and female organs) and is pollinated by insects and
is noted for attracting wildlife. Suitable for all soils and a wide
range of pH, plus it can grow by the sea in salty soil. It prefers a
moist soil and grows best in full or partial shade.

To grow from seed sow in April in a coldframe. Germination
is usually rapid, but the seedlings are prone to damp off
so make sure they have good airflow. Prick them out into
individual pots once they are large enough to handle and plant
them out in the summer in permanent positions. Plants can be
divided in spring and placed straight out into their permanent
positions.

# Dock

Latin: Rumex (genus)
Irish: Copóg, Welsh: Suran. Breton: Unknown.
Native to Europe, common in Britain and Ireland. PERENNIAL

Well known to ease nettle stings, it was also used to wrap up items such as butter and was even used as impromptu toilet paper. It was associated with good quality land despite being a troublesome weed. It was used to staunch bleeding and was a cure for bronchitis, colds and coughs, liver troubles including jaundice, to cure boils, rheumatism, diarrhoea and skin complaints. The leaves are edible, best eaten cooked (removing the oxalic acid) and preferably fairly young. The seeds can be used to make flour.

## *Cultivation*

Rumex obtusifolius is a perennial growing to 1m and about 0.4m wide. It is hardy and not frost tender. It is in flower from June to October, and the seeds ripen from July to October. The species is hermaphrodite (has both male and female organs) and is pollinated by the wind. It is noted for attracting wildlife. It will grow in any soil and any pH range, in semi-shade or full sun, it is drought tolerant due to the tap root. Often regarded as a weed - sow spring in situ, divide plants in spring.

## Figwort

Latin: Scrophularia nodosa
Irish: Fothrom. Welsh: Gwenynddail. Breton: Unknown.
Native to Europe, common in Britain and Ireland. PERENNIAL

Said to have been used by Gaulish Druids in their midsummer fires, it was considered an important medicinal plant. In Ireland it was the 'queen of Irish herbs' and strongly linked with fairies, hence it was regarded with some trepidation and great respect.

It was commonly found under Elder trees, from which it was thought to gain power and was collected with due ceremony and care. It was used for treating fits, sore throats, bronchitis, sprains, swellings, wounds, liver complaints, as a blood tonic and for piles. Not really suitable as food although it is edible in emergencies.

## *Cultivation*

Scrophularia nodosa is a perennial growing to 1m by 0.3m. It is hardy and is not frost tender, tolerating down to -15 °C. It is in flower from June to September, and the seeds ripen from July to September. The species is hermaphrodite (has both male and female organs) and is pollinated by insects. Suitable for most soils so long as there is sufficient water, tolerates most pHs and will grow in sem-shade or full sun.

To grow from seed sow spring or autumn in a coldframe. When they are large enough to handle, prick the seedlings out into individual pots and plant them out in the summer. You can also in situ in the autumn or the spring. Plants can be divided in spring.

## Flag Iris

Latin: Iris pseudacorus.
Irish: Feileastram. Welsh: Gellhesgen. Breton: Elestr.
Native to Europe, common in Britain and Ireland. PERENNIAL

A symbol of beauty, purity and wisdom, it is associated with *Bealtaine*, being placed on windows or doorsteps and hung on the May bush. It is mentioned in Celtic myth and poetry in association with beauty. The leaves were used for bedding and thatch and a black dye was made from the root. Medicinally it was used to treat diarrhoea, toothache, colds, sore throats and jaundice. It was also used as a mild purgative. The seed is said to make an excellent coffee substitute as long as it is well roasted, but should not be consumed massive quantities. A yellow dye is obtained from the flowers. A black dye is obtained from the root if it is mixed with iron sulphate, otherwise it is brown. The root is a source of tannin and has been used in making ink. A delicately scented essential oil is obtained from the roots.

## *Cultivation*

It is a perennial growing to 1.5m by 2m at a medium rate. It is hardy and is not frost tender. It is in flower from May to July. The species is hermaphrodite (has both male and female organs) and is pollinated by insects. The plant is self-fertile. Suitable for any soil that is not too heavy and damp and can tolerate a variety of pH. It can grow in semi-shade or full sun. Suitable for: light (sandy) and medium (loamy) soils. Suitable pH: acid, neutral and basic (alkaline) soils. It can grow in semi-shade (light woodland) or no shade. It prefers moist or wet soil and can grow in water. The plant can tolerate strong winds but not maritime exposure. Prefers a humus rich and damp soil but grows in water up to 15cm deep. Seed is best sown as soon as it is ripe in a coldframe. Stored seed should be sown as early in the year as possible in a coldframe. A period of cold stratification improves germination time and rates. Prick out the seedlings into individual pots when they are large enough to handle and grow them on in the greenhouse or coldframe for their first year. Plant out into their permanent positions in late spring or early summer. Division in March or October. Early autumn is best. Very easy, larger clumps can be replanted direct into their permanent positions, though it is best to pot up smaller clumps and grow them on in a coldframe until they are rooting well. Plant them out in the spring.

## Forget-Me-Not

Latin: Myosotis (genus)

Irish: Ceotharnach. Welsh: Nâd-fi'n angof. Breton: Daoulagad Ar Werc'hez.

Native to Europe, common in Britain and Ireland. PERENNIAL

A symbol of love and constancy throughout Europe, it however has few uses. A decoction of the juice was said to harden steel and a syrup from the flowers was used for pulmonary (lung) complaints. Related plants such as Speedwell were used to provide protection on journeys and against ill luck, it was also used to relieve breast-feeding soreness, colds and jaundice.

### *Cultivation*

Forget-Me-Not is an evergreen perennial growing to 0.2m by 0.6m at a fast rate. It is hardy and not frost tender down to about -20°C. It is in leaf all year, in flower from May to September, and the seeds ripen from July to September. The species is hermaphrodite (has both male and female organs) and is pollinated by insects. It will grow in any soil including heavy clay and will tolerate a wide pH range. It can grow in light shade or full sun and prefers a damp soil, even a bog or shallow water.

To grow seed from sow outdoors in situ in late spring or early summer. Germination usually takes place within 2-4 weeks at 15°C+. It germinates easily and can pop up all over the garden. It can be divided in spring and large divisions can be planted out directly into their permanent positions. Cuttings of young shoots can be made in summer in a shady border, although this is seldom necessary as this plant spreads easily.

# Foxglove

Latin: Digitalis purpurea

rishL Lus Mór. Welsh: Bysedd y llwynog. Breton: Brulu.

Native to Europe, common in Britain and Ireland. BIENNIAL

Believed to be a fairy plant, its effect on the heart could revive listless patients hence it was used on children under the 'fairy stroke', but equally it could kill if administered carelessly. It was collected around the summer solstice, the most auspicious time and believed to offer powerful magical protection from fairies (*sídhe*) and appears in otherworldly mythology. Medicinally is can calm the heart but also raises blood pressure hence is potentially dangerous. It was also used to cure colds, fevers, sore throats, skin problems, wounds, swellings and burns. It was also used as a diuretic. Not edible. An infusion of the plant prolongs the life of cut flowers and a green dye can be made from the flowers.

## *Cultivation*

Digitalis purpurea is a biennial growing to 1.2m by 0.4m at a medium rate. It is hardy and is not frost tender. It is in flower from June to September in its second year, and the seeds ripen from August to October. The species is hermaphrodite (has both male and female organs) and is pollinated by insects and it is noted for attracting wildlife. It will grow in most soils and in a wide pH range. It prefers full sun but will grow in semi-shade.

To grow from seed, surface sow in early spring in a coldframe or in situ. The seed usually germinates in 2-4 weeks at 15°C+. When they are large enough to handle, prick the seedlings out into individual pots and plant them out in the summer. If you have sufficient seed it can be sown outdoors in situ in the spring or autumn.

# Fungi

Latin: Fungi (division).
Irish: Fungais, Welsh: Ffwng. Breton: Kabellou Touseg.
Native to Europe, common in Britain and Ireland. PERENNIAL

Strongly associated with fairies, they often grow in gradually expanding rings, which it was believed the fairies used to dance in. Various folk beliefs of ill luck or harm are associated with fungi rings. The field mushroom was eaten and but many other types have hallucinogenic or poisonous properties. Puffball spores were used to staunch bleeding, mushrooms to treat jaundice and the fly agaric to kill flies. Various types of mushrooms and toadstools were used due to their psychoactive properties – such as Psilocybe semilanceata or Amanita muscaria are associated with Druidic or Shamanic use and also associated with fairies, gnomes and pixies in childhood stories. These are very often poisonous and strongly hallucinogenic and hence are potentially highly dangerous or even deadly.

## *Cultivation*

This is an entire division of organisms and there are a huge multitude of fungi – fungus, mould, mushrooms and toadstools. Many of these are edible or have other uses but many are also deadly poison. It is best to obtain a specialist guide on fungi if you wish to pick or grow them and there are serious risks involved if you wrongly identify species.

# Grass

Latin: Gramineae (family).
Irish: Féara. Welsh: Glaswellt. Breton: Louzou.
Native to Europe, common in Britain and Ireland. ANNUAL,
PERENNIAL

Grass seeds provide a huge variety of foods and the plants provide fodder. In folk custom hungry grass is associated with illness and fainting and in Ireland with famine victims. Grasses were used for ropes, thatch, mats, baskets and bedding as well as food. Medicinally it could be used to cure boils, urinary or genital infections, kidney problems and poisoning in dogs.

## *Cultivation*

This family is enormous, containing the majority of monocotyledonous plants. This includes the grass we see on our lawns and cereals that we eat such as barley or wheat. Most of them are pollinated by the wind and are easy to grow, germinating fairly easily – which is why grasses are so widespread.

## Great Mullein

Latin: Verbascum Thapsus.
Irish: Coinnle Muire. Welsh: Pannog felen.
Breton: Molenez Braz.
Native to Europe, common in Britain and Ireland. BIENNIAL

Believed to protect against magic and also against sickness at certain times of year. It was used by women to condition their hair; the stalks were used to make torches and the leaves as padding for shoes. Medicinally it was used to treat tuberculosis, cure toothache, colds, coughs, bronchitis, asthma and to treat bee stings. An aromatic, slightly bitter tea can be made by infusing the dried leaves in boiling water for five or more minutes. A sweeter tea can be made by infusing the fresh or dried flowers. A yellow dye is obtained from the flowers by boiling them in water

## *Cultivation*

Great Mullein is a biennial growing to 1.8m at a fast rate. It is hardy and is not frost tender. It is in flower from June to August, and the seeds ripen from August to September. The species is hermaphrodite (has both male and female organs) and is pollinated by insects. This plant is self-fertile. It grows in any soil so long as it is reasonably well-drained. It can tolerate strong winds but cannot tolerate shade or maritime exposure. To grow from seed sow late spring to early summer in a coldframe and only just cover the seed. Germination usually takes place within two weeks. When they are large enough to handle, prick out the seedlings into individual pots and plant them out in late summer. The seed has a long viability and can be stored dry for a long time.

## Hemlock

Latin: Conium maculatum
Irish: Moing Mhear. Welsh: Cegiden. Breton: Unknown.
Native to Europe, common in Britain and Ireland. BIENNIAL

Part of the Umbellifers family, this famous poison was used to dispatch Socrates some two and a half thousand years ago. It often grows alongside brooklime and watercress and hence care was required not to pick it accidentally. However, despite its poison, it was used in poultices to cure swellings and sores and also used as a cure for rheumatism. It is a narcotic plant that sedates and relieves pain in small quantities. The plant contains coniine, an extremely toxic substance that can also cause congenital defects in children. It is a traditional folk treatment for cancer and was formerly widely used internally in very small doses to treat a variety of complaints including tumours, epilepsy, whooping cough, rabies and as an antidote to strychnine poisoning. Extremely dangerous and non-edible plant as it is highly poisonous.

## *Cultivation*

Hemlock is a biennial growing to 2m by 1m wide. It is hardy and is not frost tender. It is in flower from June to July. The species is hermaphrodite (has both male and female organs) and is pollinated by Insects. This plant is self-fertile. Grows in any soil and a wide pH range, but prefers shade or semi-shade. Seed is best sown in situ as soon as it is ripe in the late summer. It usually germinates in the autumn and is a very common weed.

## Henbane

Latin: Hyoscyamus niger
Irish: Gafann. Welsh: Llewyg Yr Iar. Breton: Unknown.
Native to Europe, common in Britain and Ireland. ANNUAL/
BIENNIAL

Another highly poisonous herb, it is also highly hallucinogenic, hence its reputation as a magical plant. The Celts were fearful of its power, especially towards children, it was also used in charms such as to banish hares or ward off evil spirits. The Gaulish Druids used belinimica in their rites to medicinal god Rectenus, this being a species of Henbane according to Moloney's *Irish Ethno-botany*. It was used (in small doses) as a sedative, painkiller, toothache cure, for whooping cough, gout, arthritis and nervous disorders. It is used extensively as a sedative and pain killer and is specifically used for pain affecting the urinary tract, especially when due to kidney stones. Its sedative and antispasmodic effect makes it a valuable treatment for the symptoms of Parkinson's disease. The biennial form is far more beneficial medically. The leaves scattered about a house will drive away or deter mice.

## *Cultivation*

Henbane grows to 1m by up to 1m wide. It is hardy and is not frost tender. It is in flower from June to August, and the seeds ripen from August to September. The species is hermaphrodite (has both male and female organs) and is pollinated by insects. Suitable for most soil types but prefers well-drained soil and tolerates a wide pH range, although preferring alkaline soil. It cannot grow in the shade but can tolerate maritime exposure and dry soils. Older plants do not transplant well due to the brittleness of the taproot. The flowers emit a rather fishy smell. Sow seed in summer in a coldframe and pot on as soon as possible before the taproot is too long for the pot.

## Hogweed

Latin: Heracleum sphondylium
Irish: Feabhrán. Welsh: Efwr. Breton: Unknown.
Native to Europe, common in Britain and Ireland. BIENNIAL/ PERENNIAL

Used to feed pigs as the name suggests, also called cow parsnip, its hollow stems were also used by children as peashooters. The seeds were burnt and breathed in to relieve lethargy and revive from coma. In Scotland, it was believed that it could break the power of fairies holding a child in their grasp or suffering from the 'fairy stroke'. The stem and young shoots can be eaten raw or cooked. It was used as a green vegetable, harvested just as they are sprouting from the ground, they are somewhat like asparagus in flavour. The peduncles, before flowering, can be eaten as a vegetable or added to soups, Roots can be eaten cooked, it is usually boiled. Not to be consumed in large quantities as it contains furanocoumarins. These have carcinogenic, mutagenic and phototoxic properties.

## Cultivation

It is a biennial or perennial growing to 1.8m high. It is hardy and is not frost tender. It is in flower from June to September, and the seeds ripen from July to October. The species is hermaphrodite (has both male and female organs) and is pollinated by insects. This plant is self-fertile and is noted for attracting wildlife. It is suitable for any soil and pH range and can prosper in deep shade through to full sun. If prefers a moist soil but is also drought tolerant due to the long tap roots. The root pattern is a tap root similar to a carrot going directly down [1-2]. Seed is sown mid to late spring or early autumn in situ. Plants can be divided in autumn, although this plant is often regarded as troublesome weed.

## Houseleek

Latin: Sempervivum tectorum
Irish: Lus an Tóiteáin. Welsh: LLysiau Pen Tai.
Breton: Unknown.
Native to Europe, common in Britain and Ireland. PERENNIAL

Believed to protect against lightning and fires, plants were attached to thatch roofs to protect the house, similar beliefs existed in Roman and Greek culture. It was used medicinally to cure ulcers, burns and inflammation, corns, warts and chilblains. It was also used to relieve sore eyes, cure headaches and also to induce premature birth (abortion). The young leaves and shoots can be eaten raw, often in salads. The juice of the leaves is used to make a refreshing drink.

## Cultivation

Houseleek is an evergreen perennial growing to 0.2m by 0.2m at a medium rate. It is hardy and is not frost tender. It is in leaf all year, in flower from June to July, and the seeds ripen from July to August. The species is hermaphrodite (has both male and female organs) and is pollinated by insects. It is suitable for light to medium soils and prefers well-drained soil, popular as a rockery plant. Suitable for a wide pH range but it cannot grow in the shade and can tolerate drought.

Seed is best surface sown in early spring in a coldframe. It usually germinates in 6 weeks at 10°C+. Prick out the seedlings into individual pots when they are large enough to handle and grow them on in the greenhouse for their first winter. Plant them out into their permanent positions in the summer if they have made sufficient growth. Division of plants can take place in spring or early summer and larger divisions can be planted out direct into their permanent positions. Stem cuttings can also be made from spring to autumn, protected from the elements preferably.

## Lady's Mantle

Latin: Alchemilla (genus)
Irish: Dearna Mhuire. Welsh: Mantell Fair. Breton: Unknown.
Native to Europe, common in Britain and Ireland. PERENNIAL

It was believed that the dew that collected in the leaves had magical properties. It was used against the evil eye in Scotland and Ireland. Alchemists also used the dew in their attempts to turn base metals to gold. It was also used for women's problems and particularly to encourage conception and also believed to cure sagging breasts and restore faded beauty! Medicinally the plant was used in treating wounds and staunching bleeding, to reduce inflammation, treat burns and kidney problems. Young leaves and the root can be eaten raw or cooked. Leaves can be mixed with the leaves of Polygonum bistorta and Polygonum persicaria then used in making a bitter herb pudding called 'Easter ledger' which was eaten during Lent.

## *Cultivation*

Alchemilla is a perennial growing to 0.3m by 0.3m. It is hardy and is not frost tender. It is in flower from June to September, and the seeds ripen from August to October. The species is hermaphrodite (has both male and female organs) and is pollinated by apomictic action (reproduce by seeds formed without sexual fusion). It is self-fertile. It is suitable for any soil so long as it is not water-logged and will tolerate a wide pH range but prefers alkaline soil. It can grow in semi-shade or full sun.

Seed should be sown in spring in a coldframe. The seed usually germinates in 3- 4 weeks at 15°C+. When large enough to handle, prick the seedlings out into individual pots and grow them on a coldframe for their first winter, planting out in late spring or early summer. Plants can be divided in spring or autumn. The divisions can be planted out direct into their permanent positions, though we find it best to pot them up and keep them in a sheltered position until they are growing away well. This plant spreads well by itself and can be quite invasive.

## Lords and Ladies

Latin: Arum Maculatum
Irish: Cluas Chaoin. Welsh: Pidyn Y Gog Breton: Frond Gwez.
Native to Europe, common in Britain and Ireland. PERENNIAL

Regarded as an aphrodisiac due to the phallic shape of the spadix. The berries are in fact highly poisonous and it was believed that both snakes and bears ate the berries. A starch was obtained from the plant to keep collars and ruffs stiff. Medicinally it was used to cure tuberculosis, spots, blemishes and freckles. The root was used to cure worms in children. The root can be eaten if it is dried and then cooked, however this plant is very poisonous, eating it is not advisable. This plant contains calcium oxalate crystals. Eating any part causes an extremely unpleasant sensation similar to needles being stuck into the mouth and tongue if they are eaten raw.

## *Cultivation*

Lords and Ladies is a perennial growing to 0.4m by 0.5m wide, it often dies back in winter, leaving just the spadix (bearing the fruit). It is hardy to zone and is not frost tender. It is in flower from April to May, producing bright red fruit in late summer. The species is monoecious (individual flowers are either male or female, but both sexes can be found on the same plant) and is pollinated by insects. It will grow in any soil type and a wide range of pH. It will grow in full shade but can also survive in full sun. This plant is now quite rare in many parts of Britain and Ireland.

Seed is best sown in a greenhouse or coldframe as soon as it is ripe. The seed usually germinates in a few months at 15°C+. Stored seed should be sown in the spring in a greenhouse and can be slow to germinate, sometimes taking over a year, although period of cold stratification can help to speed up the process. Plants can be divided in late autumn when dormant by separating corms (bulbotubers) and replanting in pots or new positions in the garden.

## Madder

Latin: Rubia tinctorum
Irish: Garbhlus na Boirne. Welsh: Cochwraidd Gwyllt.
Breton: Unknown.
Native to Europe, common in Britain and Ireland. PERENNIAL

Common to Britain and Europe, it was used to make a dye for wool, giving various shades of red. The root was used to treat urinary tract infections, bleeding, inflammations, diarrhoea, fevers, liver conditions, jaundice, skin problems and to speed healing of bones. The leaves and stem are prickly, the whorls of leaves having spines along the midrib on the underside, which made them useful for polishing metalwork.

## Cultivation

Madder is an evergreen perennial growing to 1m by about 1m wide at a medium rate. It is hardy and not frost tender. It is in leaf all year, in flower in June, and the seeds ripen in September. The species is hermaphrodite (has both male and female organs). It grows in light to medium soils and prefers well-drained soil. It can tolerate a wide pH range and grows in semi-shade or full sun and also succeeds in coastal salty conditions.

Seed is best sown as soon as it is ripe in a coldframe as stored seed can be very slow to germinate. Prick out the seedlings when they are large enough to handle and grow them on in light shade in the greenhouse for the first year. Plant them out into their permanent positions in early summer. Dividing can take place in spring or at any time in the growing season if the divisions are kept well-watered until established.

## Mallow

Latin: Malva sylvestris
Irish: Hocas Fiáin. Welsh: Hocysen. Breton: Mouk.
Native to Europe, common in Britain and Ireland. BIENNIAL/PERENNIAL

In Irish tradition one of seven herbs that were immune to natural or supernatural influence. It was picked at midday on a sunny day, close to or on the full moon. Travelers struck by the mallow were said to be protected from illness or fairies. It was used as food but also medicinally by the Celts, Greeks and Romans. The root was made into a paste used in sweets, giving its name to marshmallows, although sugar and artificial flavours are now used. It relieves aches and pains, sore throats, coughs, sores, cuts, bruises, ulcers and inflammation. It was also used for sprains, urinary complaints and as a general tonic. It was used as a sedative; its calming effect also made it an anti-aphrodisiac. Cream, yellow and green dyes can be obtained from the plant and the seed heads. A fibre from the stems is used for cordage, textiles and paper making.

## Cultivation

Mallow has a biennial and perennial form growing to 0.5m and about the same width at a fast rate. It is hardy to about -20°C and is not frost tender. It is in flower from June to September, and the seeds ripen from July to October. The species is hermaphrodite (has both male and female organs) and is pollinated by insects and it is self-fertile. It will grow in any soil but prefers a soil that is not overly dry. It will tolerate a wide pH range and grows in semi-shade or full sun. It prefers a reasonably well-drained and moderately fertile soil in a sunny position. Seed should be sown in early spring in situ. Germination should take place within two weeks.

## Mandrake

Latin: Mandragora (genus)
Irish: Mandrác. Welsh: Mandarogau. Breton: Unknown.
Native to South-eastern Europe. PERENNIAL

Well known throughout the ancient world, it is native to southern Europe but not the British Isles. It was widely used in magic and was known to the Gaulish Druids if not those of further west. It can be used to induce a trance state. It was also considered an aphrodisiac and cure for impotency and sterility, protection against demons and repeller of disease. The root often divides into two and is vaguely suggestive of the human body. In the past it was frequently made into amulets, which were believed to bring good fortune and cure sterility. There is a superstition that if a person pulls up this root they will be condemned to hell, which is why in the past people tied the plant to the bodies of animals and then used these animals in order to pull the roots out of the soil.

Medicinally it is a purgative and anaesthetic and strongly soporific. It was used for ulcers, pain and insomnia. Fruit can be eaten raw or cooked and is considered a delicacy. The fruit is about the size of a small apple, with a strong apple-like scent – extreme caution should be taken as this plant is poisonous, including the fruit if consumed in quantity.

## *Cultivation*

Mandrake grows to 0.1m by 0.3m at a medium rate. It is hardy and is not frost tender. It is in leaf from March to July, in flower from March to April, and the seeds ripen from July to August. The species is hermaphrodite (has both male and female organs) and is pollinated by insects, it is self-fertile. Suitable for most soils but it dislikes highly alkaline soils or gravelly soil. Prefers a deep humus-rich light soil that is not overly wet and a sheltered position in full sun, but tolerates some shade.

Seed is best sown in a coldframe in the autumn. The seed can also be sown in spring in a coldframe. When they are large enough to handle, prick the seedlings out into individual pots and grow them on in the greenhouse for at least their first winter. Plant them out into their permanent positions in late spring or early summer. Root cuttings can be made in winter or plants can be divided at this time. This plant does not like root disturbance, so cuttings and division need to be done with care and as quickly as possible, with minimum disruption.

# Marsh Marigold

Latin: Caltha palustris
Irish: Lus Buí Bealtaine. Welsh: Gold Y Gors.
Breton: Preder Dour.
Native to Europe, common in Britain and Ireland. PERENNIAL

A symbol of May and linked to *Bealtaine* it protects against evil and particularly against the *sídhe*. Bouquets of Mayflower were hung in the house or left on windows and doorsteps on May Eve. Medicinally it was used to cure fitting, relieve heart ailments and reduce boils. Its uses were limited though as it is strongly irritant. A yellow dye is obtained from the flowers, which makes a good saffron substitute

## *Cultivation*

Marsh Marigold grows to 0.3m by 0.3m. It is hardy and is in flower from March to July. The species is hermaphrodite (has both male and female organs) and is pollinated by insects. It is also noted for attracting wildlife. It can grow in virtually any soil, but does best in a damp soil, in bogs, beside water or even in shallow water. It can tolerate a wide pH range but prefers alkaline soil. It prefers full sun but will tolerate shade. It is nutrient hungry and can impede plants grow near it, legumes in particular. This polymorphic plant is perhaps the most primitive form of flora in the British Isles.

Seed is best sown as soon as it is ripe in a coldframe in late summer. Pots should be stood in 2-3cm of water to keep the soil wet. The seed usually germinates in a month or more at 15°C+. When they are large enough to handle, prick the seedlings out into individual pots and grow them on bigger pots until they are at least 15cm tall. Plant them out into their permanent positions in the summer. Larger plants can be divided in early spring or autumn. Very easy to divide, sections can be replanted direct into their permanent positions.

# Meadowsweet

Latin: Filipendula ulmaria
Irish: Airgead luachra. Welsh: Erwain. Breton: Unknown.
Native to Europe, common in Britain and Ireland. PERENNIAL

A sweet-smelling flower that was used to flavour beer and fragrance rooms, it was also considered dangerous as it was thought to send people into a deep and sometimes fatal sleep. It was used for cleaning milk vessels and to make a black dye. It was used magically to cure those believed to be wasting due to fairy magic. It was considered one of the three most sacred herbs to the Druids. Medicinally it was used to prevent diarrhoea and dysentery and to cure fevers, colds, sore throats, dropsy, kidney problems and as a nerve tonic. The root can be eaten cooked and the young leaves are cooked as a flavouring in soups. Young leaves, flowers and roots can be brewed into a tea. The dried leaves are used as a flavouring, especially as a sweetener in teas. The flowers are used as a flavouring in various alcoholic beverages and in stewed fruits. Adding flowers to wine or beer is said to improve the brew, they are also made into a syrup which can be used in drinks and fruit salads. A black dye is obtained from the roots and a yellow dye is obtained from the plant tops. An essential oil obtained from the flower buds is used in perfumery.

## *Cultivation*

Meadowsweet is a perennial growing to 1.2m by 0.4m at a medium rate. It is hardy and is not frost tender. It is in flower from June to August, and the seeds ripen from August to September. The species is hermaphrodite (has both male and female organs) and is pollinated by insects, valuable to wildlife and it is self-fertile. It can grow in most soils and can grow in heavy clay soil, preferring neutral and alkaline pH. It can grow in semi-shade and full sun and it prefers moist or wet soil. It generaly requires a humus-rich moist soil and succeeds in full sun only if the soil is reliably moist throughout the growing season. Dislikes dry or acid soils and has low tolerance to drought.

Seed is best sown in the autumn in a coldframe. The seed can also be sown in a coldframe in spring, germinating best at a temperature of 10°C+. When they are large enough to handle, prick the seedlings out into individual pots and plant them out in the summer if they have grown enough, otherwise plant them out in late spring the following year. Plants can be divided in autumn or winter with ease, larger clumps can be replanted directly into their permanent positions.

## Mint

Latin: Mentha (genus)
Irish: Mismín. Welsh: Mintys, Bathdy. Breton: Ment.
Native to Europe, common in Britain and Ireland. PERENNIAL

Mint is common throughout Europe, water-mint was considered one of three most sacred herbs of the Druids; it was also well used by the Greeks and Romans. It was used in love charms, in protection from the evil eye and to dispel stomach diseases and infections. It was used to deter fleas, flies and moths and to keep away mice in corn. Water-mint was used for coughs, colds indigestion and stomach disorders. It was also used in Ireland to cure deafness, jaundice, measles and as an antidote to nettle stings. Leaves are edible raw or cooked. It has very strong peppermint-like aroma, it is used as a flavouring in salads, cooked foods, desserts, sweets and liqueurs. A herb tea is made from the leaves and a popular sauce served with roast lamb. An essential oil with a strong peppermint scent is can be extracted from the whole plant. Spiders, Rats and mice intensely dislike the smell of mint and is acts as an effective deterrent.

## *Cultivation*

Mint is a perennial growing to 0.1m by 0.5m. It is hardy and is not frost tender. It is in flower from July to August. The species is hermaphrodite (has both male and female organs) and is pollinated by insects and is noted for attracting wildlife. It will grow in any soil, including heavy clay and in a wide pH range. It will do well in semi-shade or full sun but prefers a moist soil. Although it struggles with hard frost, the plant usually self-sows even when the parent plant is killed by frost as it can spread under the ground. The root pattern is rhizomatous with underground stems sending roots and shoots along their length and forms a mat under the soil. It is very invasive and for this reason is often grown in large pots or a separate bed from other plants.

Seed is best sown in spring in a coldframe. Germination is usually fairly quick. Prick out the seedlings into individual pots when they are large enough to handle and plant them out in the summer. Mentha species are very prone to hybridisation and so the seed cannot be relied on to breed true. Division can be easily carried out at almost any time of the year, although it is probably best done in the spring or autumn to allow the plant to establish more quickly. Virtually any part of the root is capable of growing into a new plant.

## Mistletoe

Latin: Viscum album
Irish: Drualus. Welsh: Uchelwydd. Breton: Uhelvarr.
Native to Europe, found in Britain but not native in Ireland.
PERENNIAL

Perhaps most famously associated with Druids thanks to Pliny, its Irish name means Druid's herb although it is not native to Ireland. It was considered a symbol of fertility and regeneration, growing parasitically on trees (usually apple and hawthorn, rarely oak) although appearing to grow without any source of nutrients, with unusual growth habits and producing flowers and fruit at late winter and early winter respectively. Folk customs still survive today and it is strongly associated with Christmas. It has been found in Celtic graves in Britain and was also connected with the god Baldur in Norse myth. Medicinally it was considered a 'heal-all' despite the fact that it is poisonous if over-prescribed. It was used to cure nervous disorders such as St. Vitus's dance and epilepsy. It was used for heart palpitations, nervousness, hysteria, and also in salves and washes for cuts and wounds. This whole plant is highly toxic, ingestion is not recommended, even the berries are poisonous.

## *Cultivation*

Mistletoe is an evergreen perennial growing to 1m by 1m. It is hardy and not frost tender. It is in leaf all year, in flower from February to April, and the seeds ripen from November to December. The species is dioecious (individual flowers are either male or female, but only one sex is to be found on any one plant so both male and female plants must be grown if seed is required), hence the plant is not self-fertile. It does not grow on soil; it can grow in heavy shade through to full sun. It is parasitic plant (epiphyte), growing on the branches of several deciduous species of trees such as oak or apple. It is not usually found on coniferous trees, though the subspecies V. album abietis is found on conifers such as pine and larix. The host tree must be at least 20 years old for the Mistletoe to survive. Although the host branch might eventually succumb to death, the host tree is rarely killed. To grow it you need to obtain berries and squash them onto the branches of suitable host trees in late autumn and early winter. This is best done on the lower side of the branch. It is then simply a matter of waiting and hoping that the seed will germinate.

## Monkshood/Wolfsbane/Aconite

*Latin*: Aconitum napellus/vulparia/lycoctonum

Irish: Acainít, Dáthabha dubh. Welsh: Cwcwll Y Mynach.

Breton: Unknown.

Native to Europe, including Britain and Ireland. PERENNIAL

Wolfsbane gets its name from the fact that it was once used to kills wolves as a poison. It is said that it was used to poison arrows for wolf hunting by the ancient Greeks. It was also used to poison meat left out by farmers for wolves or foxes. Wolfsbane has been used historically as a treatment for lycanthropy (werewolf-ism) and as an antidote to other poisons. In Greek mythology, Medea attempted to poison Theseus by putting wolfsbane in his wine. Wolfsbane has traditionally been used to protect homes from werewolves, vampires and can be used to prevent shapeshifting. It was often used in flying ointments. Aconite was used in funereal incense to honour the angel of death and recognize that the cycle of life also includes death as necessary for new life to be possible. It is also sometimes planted on graves for similar reasons. Bundles of wolfsbane were used around barns and pastures to protect livestock from predators, making sure that the livestock have no access to it. Because of its baneful nature, it could be used in sympathetic magic to bring harm to another.

### *Cultivation*

Monkshood is a perennial growing to 1.5m high by 0.3m. It is hardy and is not frost tender. It is in leaf from February to October, in flower from July to August, and the seeds ripen from June to July. The species is hermaphrodite (has both male and female organs) and is pollinated by insects. It will grow in most soils, including heavy clay and does best in acidic to neutral soil. It grows well in semi-shade or full sun, but prefers a fairly moist soil, especially if growing in a sunny spot. Plants take 2-3 years to flower when grown from seed. It is a greedy plant, inhibiting the growth of nearby species, especially legumes.

Seed is best sown as soon as it is ripe in a coldframe. The seed can be stratified (stored in soil) and sown in spring but will then be slow to germinate. When large enough to handle, prick the seedlings out into individual pots and grow them on in a coldframe for their first winter. Plant them out in late spring or early summer. Plants can be divided and this is best done in spring but it can also be done in autumn too. Be careful handling this plant!

*Note: It is extremely toxic and should not be used except by experts!*

## Mugwort

Latin: Artemisia vulgaris
Irish: Mongach Meisce, Welsh: Beidiog lwyd. Breton: Unknown.
Native to Europe, common in Britain and Ireland. PERENNIAL

Valued throughout Europe for women's problems and nervous disorders, it was also believed, by the Celts, to offer protection against evil. It is associated with the summer solstice and St. John's Eve, often being hung on doors or windowsills or worn throughout the British Isles. It was also thought to magically protect against sunstroke, tiredness and wild animals. Medicinally it was used to restore menstruation, ease childbirth and cleanse the womb. It was also a popular divinatory plant due to its narcotic properties that can induce a trance state. It was used to treat epilepsy and other nervous disorders, to fumigate patients' rooms and the smoke from burning it was inhaled by the sick as a general remedy.

The fresh or the dried plant repels insects, it can be mixed with water to make an anti-insect spray, but also inhibits plant growth, so use with care. An essential oil from the plant kills insect larvae. The leaves can be raw or cooked, it has a strong smell and tastes quite bitter. Mugwort aids the digestion and so is often used in small quantities as a flavouring, especially with fatty foods. In Japan the young leaves are used as a potherb. The dried leaves and flowering tops are steeped to make a tea. It has also been used as a flavouring in beer, although hops are now more common.

## Cultivation

Mugwort is a perennial growing to 1.2m by 0.7m at a fast rate. It is hardy and is not frost tender. It is in flower from July to September. The species is hermaphrodite (has both male and female organs) and is pollinated by the wind. It is also noted for attracting wildlife. Suitable for any soil type and a wide pH range, including highly alkaline soil. It will do well in semi-shade or full sun and is drought tolerant.

Surface sow seed from late winter to early summer in a greenhouse and do not allow the compost to dry out. When plants are large enough to handle, prick out the seedlings into individual pots. If growth is sufficient, they can be planted out into their permanent positions in the summer, otherwise grow them on in a coldframe for their first winter. Plants can be divided in spring or autumn. Basal cuttings (shoots from the stem) can be made in late spring. Harvest the young shoots when about 10 cm long, pot up in a lightly shaded position in a greenhouse or coldframe and plant them out when well rooted in late summer or early autumn.

## Nettle

Latin: Urtica (genus)
Irish: Neantóg. Welsh: Danadl poethion. Breton: Linad.
Native to Europe, common in Britain and Ireland. ANNUAL/ PERENNIAL

A potent symbol of desolation it does though have many uses as food, cloth and herbal medicine. In both Ireland, and South West England May Eve had a tradition of children stinging each other and passersby with nettles. The sting was considered effective against rheumatism, inflammation and also purified the blood. Nettle was used as a food — cúl *faiche* or 'field cabbage' and fertiliser was made from soaking them in water. Nettle juice was used to make a green dye. Medicinally it was used to treat skin problems, measles, poor circulation, bleeding, swollen limbs and the bite of a mad dog. A strong flax-like fibre is made from the stems which is used for making string and cloth, it also makes a good quality paper. The plant matter left over after the fibres have been extracted are a good source of biomass and have also been used in the manufacture of sugar, starch, protein and ethyl alcohol.

## Cultivation

Urtica dioica and most other Urtia species are perennial growing to 1.2m by 1m at a fast rate. Urtica urens is annual and does not sting so severely. It is hardy and is not frost tender. It is in leaf from March to November, in flower from May to October, and the seeds ripen from June to October. The species is dioecious (individual flowers are either male or female, but only one sex is to be found on any one plant so both male and female plants must be grown if seed is required). It is pollinated by wind and it is not self-fertile. It is noted for attracting wildlife, particularly insects. It will grow in most soils, including heavy clay, but prefers a rich soil. It will grow in a wide pH range, in semi-shade or full sun and I able to tolerate strong wind and moderate maritime exposure. Prefers a soil rich in phosphates and nitrogen. Plants must be grown in a deep rich soil if good quality fibre is required, plus they will be of better medical and nutritional value. Nettles are one of the most undervalued of economic and medicinal plants.

To grow from seed sow in spring in a coldframe, only just covering the seed. Prick out the seedlings into individual pots when they are large enough to handle, and plant them out in the summer. Division succeeds at almost any time in the growing season. Very easy to grow plant them straight out into their permanent positions. Often regarded as a weed, they are quite hard to eliminate from the garden as fragments of root can regenerate.

## Orchid

Latin: Orchis (genus)
Irish: Magairlín. Welsh: Tegeirian. Breton: Unknown.
Native to Europe, fairly rare in Britain and Ireland.
PERENNIAL

A symbol of fertility, its phallic shape led to its use as an aphrodisiac and as a love charm. Women would use the new tuber (root) to make a man fall in love with them; it was believed that to give the old (dying) tuber would send them mad. In Scotland, they were also used for love divination as well as for love charms. Much of their use relates to magic, including eating the root to strengthen the genitals, aid conception and to select the sex of the child. Medicinally they were used to treat tuberculosis and diarrhoea, in Scotland Salep (a drink made from the tubers) was used to sooth stomach and bowel problems.

The pyramidal and bee orchid is common in Europe, unlike exotic orchids, which are epiphytes (growing in trees) they grow in the soil. The tuber can be cooked. It is a source of 'salep', a fine white to yellowish-white powder that is obtained by drying the tuber and grinding it into a powder. It is said to be very nutritious and is made into a drink or can be added to cereals and used in making bread etc., one ounce of salep is said to be enough to sustain a person for a day.

### *Cultivation*

A perennial growing to 0.3m, and the bee orchid to 0.5m. It is hardy and not frost tender. It is in flower from April to June, and the seeds ripen in July. The species is hermaphrodite (has both male and female organs) and is pollinated by insects. The bee orchid is self-fertile. Both prefer full sun and will grow in most soils, but prefer alkaline soil. Orchids are, in general, shallow-rooting plants of well-drained low-fertility soils. Their symbiotic relationship with a fungus in the soil allows them to obtain sufficient nutrients and be able to compete successfully with other plants.

Seed is best surface sown, preferably as soon as it is ripe, in the greenhouse and do not allow the (organic) compost to dry out. The seed of this species is extremely simple, it has a minute embryo surrounded by a single layer of protective cells. It contains very little food reserves and depends upon a symbiotic relationship with a species of soil-dwelling fungus. Plants can be divided during the dormant season.

## Pasque-flower

Latin: Pulsatilla vulgaris
Irish: Lus na Cásca. Welsh: Blodyn Y Pasg. Breton: Bleun Pasik.
Native to Europe, rare in Britain and Ireland. PERENNIAL

Supposedly created from drops of Adonis' blood, it is associated with Adonis, Venus, Aphrodite, Anemos, and also the four winds when he was gored by a wild boar on Mount Lebanon. This plant is long association with the fairies, the flower being a resting place for them at night. Despite being a healing plant the Chinese, called it the flower of death and planted it on graves, while the Egyptians associated it with ill health.

Pasque flower is considered by herbalists to be of highly valuable modern. This plant contains the glycoside ranunculin, this is converted to anemonine when the plant is dried and is the main medicinal active ingredient. It is alterative, antispasmodic, diaphoretic, diuretic, emmenagogue, expectorant, nervine and sedative]. It is taken internally in the treatment of pre-menstrual syndrome, inflammations of the reproductive organs, tension headaches, neuralgia, insomnia, hyperactivity, bacterial skin infections, septicaemia, spasmodic coughs in asthma, whooping cough and bronchitis. Externally, it is used to treat eye conditions such as diseases of the retina, senile cataract and glaucoa. This remedy should be used with caution internally as excessive doses cause diarrhoea and vomiting. It should not be prescribed to patients with colds.

The plant is harvested soon after flowering, it is more poisonous when fresh and so should be preserved by drying. It should not be stored for longer than 12 months before being used. In homeopathy, the plant is used as a treatment of measles. It is also used for treating nettle rash, toothache, earache and bilious indigestion. A green dye is made from the flowers.

## *Cultivation*

Pasque flower is a perennial growing to 0.2m by 0.3m. It is hardy to -20°C and is not frost tender. It is in flower from April to May, and the seeds ripen from June to July. The species is hermaphrodite (has both male and female organs) and is pollinated by insects and this plant is self-fertile. It is suitable for light to medium soils and does not like clay or boggy soil, although it can grow in a wide pH range but prefers alkaline soil. It prefers full sun and is drought tolerant. Due to habitat loss (hedgerows mainly) it has become quite rare. This plant consumes all available nutrients, inhibiting the growth of nearby plants, especially legumes.

Seed is best sown as soon as it is ripe in early summer in a coldframe. The seed usually germinates in about 2-3 weeks. Sow stored seed in late winter in a coldframe. Germination takes anything up to 6 months at 15°C+. When they are large enough to handle, prick the seedlings out into individual pots and grow them on in the greenhouse for at least their first winter. Plant them out into their permanent positions in the spring. Root cuttings of about 4cm long taken can be in early winter, potted up in a mixture of peat and sand. Do this care as the plant dislike root disturbance.

## Pignut

Latin: Conopodium majus
Irish: Cúlarán. Welsh: Cneuen Ddaear. Breton: Unknown.
Native to Europe, common in Britain and Ireland. PERENNIAL

Well-liked by pigs, hence the name, it was also popular with children who roasted them, in recent centuries calling them 'fairy potatoes.' In Ireland, it was regarded as a fairy plant. Medicinally it was used as a blood cleanser.

The tubers can be eaten raw or cooked -tasty, with a flavour between a sweet potato and hazelnuts, with an aftertaste of radish. There is only one tuber on each plant, as this is rather small and difficult to harvest, it is not as practical as the potato.

### Cultivation

A perennial growing to 0.3m high. It is hardy and is not frost tender. It is in flower from May to June, and the seeds ripen from July to August. The species is hermaphrodite (has both male and female organs) and is pollinated by insects and it is self-fertile. It will grow in most soil types but not in alkaline soil. It does better in full sun or semi-shade and prefers a fairly moist soil.

Seed should be sown spring in a coldframe. Germination is usually quick and has a high success rate. Prick out the seedlings into individual pots as soon as they are large enough to handle and plant them out when in early summer or you can sow in situ, although this requires a lot more seed to produce the same amount of plants. Plants can be divided in late summer as the plant dies down.

# Plantain

Latin: Plantago (genus)

Irish: Slánus. Welsh: Llyriad. Breton: Unknown.

Native to Europe, common in Britain and Ireland. PERENNIAL

Believed to have great healing properties, in Ireland it was even thought to be able to revive the dead. It was considered dangerous to pick as a change in the wind could cause the collector to go mad. In Ireland and parts of Britain the flower heads were used to play 'fighting cocks' or 'soldiers' (similar to modern conkers), this game was still played when I was a child. Greater plantain is associated with St. Patrick, often used to heal wounds, although like many items attributed to this and other saints, it was probably used by Druids in the pre-Christian era. Plantain was especially valued for treatment of bleeding and wounds but also used for skin problems, corns, warts, headaches, coughs and jaundice. It is also especially beneficial for people with lung conditions and helps with colds. The seed can be ground into a meal and mixed with flour. It is very rich in vitamin B1.

## *Cultivation*

Plantain is a perennial growing to 0.1m by 0.1m at a medium rate. It is hardy and is not frost tender. It is in flower from May to September, and the seeds ripen from July to October. The species is hermaphrodite (has both male and female organs) and is pollinated by the wind and it is self-fertile. It is noted for attracting wildlife, especially caterpillars and butterflies. Suitable for any soil type as long as it reasonably well-drained. It will also tolerate a wide pH range and coastal conditions. It prefers a sunny position.

Suitable for: light (sandy), medium (loamy) and heavy (clay) soils and prefers well-drained soil. Suitable pH: acid, neutral and basic (alkaline) soils. It cannot grow in the shade. It prefers moist soil. The plant can tolerate maritime exposure.

Seed is best sown in spring in a coldframe. When they are large enough to handle, prick the seedlings out into individual pots and plant them out in early summer. It can also be sown outdoors in situ in mid to late spring if you have enough seeds.

## Poppy

Latin: Papaver rhoeas, Meconopsis cambria
Irish: Poipín. Welsh: Llygad y bwgan. Breton: Roz Aer.
Native to Europe, common in Britain and Ireland. ANNUAL

In Britain and Ireland, it was believed that staring at them caused headaches or that children could lose their sight. In Ireland, young women had a fear of touching them, although it is not clear why. In Britain and parts of Europe it is linked with thunder and lightning. It was well known to the Egyptians, Greeks and Romans, linked with fertility of the land. The western poppy varieties are narcotic but not half so much as the opium poppy that grows in Asia. The European poppy was used as a painkiller, especially for ear or toothaches, it was also used for coughs, sore eyes and neuralgia. Unlike many other poppies, it is not a source of opiates, but is slightly toxic.

Seeds can be eaten raw or cooked, often used as a flavouring in cakes, bread, fruit salads etc., it imparts a very nice nutty flavour. The seeds are rather small, but they are contained in fairly large seed pods and so are easy to harvest. The seeds are perfectly safe to eat, containing none of the alkaloids associated with other parts of the plant. Leaves can be like spinach or as a flavouring in soups and salads, however, leaves should not be used after the flower buds have formed. An edible oil is obtained from the seed, it can be used in salad dressings or for cooking. A red dye from the red petals is used as a food flavouring, especially in wine.

## Cultivation

This European poppy is an annual growing to 0.6m by 0.2m (0ft 8in) at a fast rate. It is hardy and is not frost tender. It is in flower from June to August, and the seeds ripen from August to September. The species is hermaphrodite (has both male and female organs) and is pollinated by insects and the plant is self-fertile. It is noted for attracting wildlife. It will grow in any soil so long as it is not water-logged, it will also tolerate a wide pH range. It will not grow in the shade. Seed is best sown in spring or autumn in situ, it is easy to germinate.

## Primrose

Latin: Primula vulgaris
Irish: Sabhaircín. Welsh: Briallen. Breton: Boked-Laezh.
Native to Europe, common in Britain and Ireland. PERENNIAL

In its wild form, it was considered a symbol of vitality of spring and of otherworldy beauty. It was also a powerful protection against malign influence. It is linked with *Imbolc*, Easter (vernal equinox) and *Bealtaine*, being widely used at these times for decoration or protection. They were often put around the outside of houses on May Eve in Ireland and the Isle of Man. Primrose appears in several myths in each case linked with fairies or otherworldly events. Medicinally it was used to relieve nervous disorders, insomnia, induce relaxation, treat toothache, burns, jaundice, tuberculosis and coughs in horses. Young leaves can be eaten raw or cooked as a potherb, added to soups etc., it has a mild flavour, although the texture is a rough.

## Cultivation

Primrose is a perennial growing to 0.2m by 0.3m at a medium rate. It is hardy and is not frost tender, Plants are hardy to about -25°C. It is in flower from December to May, and the seeds ripen from April to August. The species is hermaphrodite (has both male and female organs) and is pollinated by insects and it is self-fertile. It is suitable for any soil, including heavy clay and it will tolerate a wide pH range. It can tolerate coastal conditions and damp soils, although it is not particularly drought tolerant.

Seed is best sown as soon as it is ripe in a coldframe. Sow stored seed in early spring, also in a coldframe. Germination is inhibited by temperatures above 20°C so summer sowing in not advisable. When they are large enough to handle, prick the seedlings out into individual pots and plant them out in the summer. Larger plants can be divided in autumn. This is best done every other year to allow for regrowth.

## Ragwort

Latin: Senecio (genus)
Irish: Buachalán, Welsh: Gingroen, Benfelen. Breton: Unknown.
Native to Europe, common in Britain and Ireland. PERENNIAL

Although widely hated by farmers it had several uses. It was regarded as a vehicle for fairies, especially at *Samhain*, several stories relate to fairies riding them like horses and even abducting people whilst doing so. Ragwort is the national emblem of Yn Ellan Shiant — the 'Fairy Isle' or Isle of Man. It was stored with grains to deter mice and brooms and brushes were often made of Ragwort. Medicinally it was used to cure cuts, sores, burns, boils and ulcers. It was also used for jaundice, coughs, colds, sore joints and rheumatism. A green dye is obtained from the leaves, though it is not permanent.

### Cultivation

Ragwort a perennial growing to 1m by 0.5m. It is hardy and is not frost tender. It is in flower from June to October, and the seeds ripen from July to October. The species is hermaphrodite (has both male and female organs) and is pollinated by insects and the plant is self-fertile. It is noted for attracting wildlife. It is suitable for any soil but will prosper on the worst of soils, it can also tolerate a wide pH range. It prefers full sun but will grow in semi-shade. It can tolerate maritime exposure. It is regarded as a noxious weed in Britain, Ireland and many other countries spreading freely by seed. Ragwort can be eradicated by pulling it up just before it comes into flower, or by cutting it down as the flowers begin to open, although this may need to be repeated about six weeks later. Ragwort is a good food plant for the caterpillars of many butterfly and moth species but it is toxic to many mammals, hence it is prohibited on farmland. Easily propagates itself without any help from man.

## Rushes

Latin: Juncus (genus)
Irish: Luachra. Welsh: Brwyn. Breton: Broen.
Native to Europe, common in Britain and Ireland. PERENNIAL

Used for thatching and floor coverings, they are also used for the Crois Bride or St. Brigid's Cross. They symbolise hospitality, protection and also the purity and cleanliness of water, they are strongly associated with *Imbolc* and Brighid/St. Brigid. They appear in folklore in relation to Brighid and also to holy wells, by which they could often be found growing. As well as thatch, they were used for candles, mats, toys and ropes. Medicinally their uses were few but they were used for jaundice, ringworm and shingles and magically to cure a crick in the neck. The pith of the stem is antiphlogistic, depurative, discutient, diuretic, febrifuge, lenitive, lithontripic, pectoral and sedative.

### *Cultivation*

Juncus effusus is a perennial growing to 1.5m by 0.5m. It is hardy to zone (UK) 4. It is in flower from June to August. The species is hermaphrodite (has both male and female organs) and is pollinated by the wind. The plant can tolerate strong winds but not maritime exposure. Rushes will grow in most soils, including heavy clay and boggy ground. Rushes prefer moist or wet soil and can grow in water. Easily grown in a moist soil, bog garden or shallow water. Seed is best surface sow in pots in a coldframe in early spring and the compost must be kept moist. When they are large enough to handle, prick the seedlings out into individual pots and plant them out in the summer if they have grown sufficiently, otherwise in late spring of the following year. Plants are best divided in spring, larger clumps can be replanted direct into their permanent positions, though it is best to pot up smaller clumps until they are rooting well. Plant them out in final positions in the spring.

## Selago/Savine

Latin: Juniperus sabina/Lycopodium selago
Irish: Uilen. Welsh: Merywen or Cnwpfwsogl Mawr
(Lycopodium). Breton: Unknown.
Native to Europe, common in Britain and Ireland. PERENNIAL

Another herb referred to by Pliny. Often mistaken for Lycopodium selago, which is not native to Western Europe, Selago is in fact a diminutive member of the juniper family. It was used to purify and drive away malign influence. Common juniper has many practical and medicinal uses, savin juniper most probably shares many its attributes. The young shoots can induce abortions if ingested. This plant is diuretic, emetic, powerfully emmenagogue and irritant. Externally it is useful as an ointment and dressing to blisters to promote discharge of infection. The powdered leaves are also used in the treatment of warts. The shoots are harvested in spring and dried for later use. The leaves can be used as an insect repellent, a decoction of them is used against lice.

*NOTE: Juniperus sabina is poisonous and can produce abortions and should never be used during pregnancy. Lycopodium selago is also poisonous.*

## *Cultivation*

Lycopodium selago is a perennial fern growing to 0.3m, it is fairly hardy. The plant is an active narcotic poison and should not be ingested.

Juniperus sabina is an evergreen perennial growing to 3m at a slow rate, the young plant looks similar to Lycopodium selago. It is hardy and it is in leaf all year, in flower in April, and the seeds ripen in October. The species is dioecious (individual flowers are either male or female, but only one sex is to be found on any one plant so both male and female plants must be grown if seed is required). and is pollinated by wind, it is not self-fertile. It will grow in most soils but prefers a well-drained soil, it tolerates a wide pH range and grows best in full or partial shade.

The seed requires a period of cold stratification. The seed has a hard seedcoat and can be very slow to germinate, requiring a cold period followed by a warm period and then another cold spell, each of 2-3 months. Soaking the seed for 3-6 seconds in boiling water may speed up the germination process, as can scarification with a knife. The seed is best sown as soon as it is ripe in a coldframe. Some seeds could germinate in the following spring, although most will take over a year. Sowing the seed 'green' when ripe may result in faster germination. The seedlings can be potted up into individual pots when they are large enough to handle. Grow on in pots until large enough, then plant out in late spring or early summer. Cuttings can be made of mature wood, at least 5cm with a heel in September/October and kept in a coldframe.

## Scarlet Pimpernel

Latin: Anagallis arvensis
Irish: Falcaire Fiáin. Welsh: Llysiau'r Cryman.
Breton: Mervel Ruz.
Native to Europe, common in Britain and Ireland. ANNUAL

Thought to be a source of magical power, it was said to give clairvoyance and clairaudience to a person holding it. It was also believed to give the ability to understand the 'speech' of animals and birds. It was also thought to enable the bearer to see through illusions, a property similar to the shamrock. Medicinally it was used as an antidote for snake and dog bites and was also used for depression, liver problems, eye diseases, jaundice, dropsy, kidney problems, rheumatism and toothache. The leaves are edible raw or cooked, used raw in salads and as a spinach alternative. The tender shoots are cooked as a vegetable. It is best not to eat these leaves in large quantities due to the toxicity. It is insecticidal, or at least is repellent to some insects. The flowers open only in daylight and the flowers are also said to foretell wet weather if they close early

### *Cultivation*

It is an annual growing to 0.1m by 0.4m. It is hardy and is not frost tender. It is in flower from June to August, and the seeds ripen from July to September. The species is hermaphrodite (has both male and female organs) and is pollinated by insects, itis self-fertile. It will grow in most soils and will tolerate a wide pH range. It prefers sun and will not succeed in full shade. It does well in any soil that is not water-logged but prefers a light soil. Seed should be sown in spring, in situ – the seeds are poisonous to some mammals.

## Searack/Seaweed

Latin: Fusus (genus)
Irish: Feamainn. Welsh: Gwymon Codog. Breton: Bezhin.
Native to Europe, common in Britain and Ireland. PERENNIAL

Seaweed was a valuable fertilizer in Britain and Ireland, even well into the twentieth century. St. Brigid's Day/*Imbolc* was a traditional time for collecting it and also shellfish in Ireland. In the Scottish Highlands an annual sacrifice of ale was given at *Samhain* to the sea (Shony) to secure a good harvest of seaweed next year, this may well be Norse in origin in connection with Sjoni the god of the sea. Seaweed was eaten as food and used medicinally for rheumatism, bruising, pains and for coughs and colds: Carrigeen moss — a cure still in use today that I can personally testify is most unpleasant although effective.

### *Cultivation*

It grows in the sea, so cannot be cultivated as such. The key here is to take a reasonable amount and not destroy colonies by over harvesting!

## Selfheal

Latin: Prunella vulgaris
Irish: Duán Ceannchosach. Welsh: Craith Unnos. Breton: Irin.
Native to Europe, common in Britain and Ireland. PERENNIAL

Gains its name from its reputation as a healer of wounds. It is suggested that the Druids gathered it at a dark moon at the rise of the Dog Star in a similar manner to vervain. It was used in magical healing, a particular example being 'fairy struck' children that were wasting away. Medicinally it was used for heart conditions, strokes, fever, worms and tuberculosis. Self-heal has a long history of folk use, especially in the treatment of wounds, ulcers, sores etc. It was also taken internally as a tea in the treatment of fevers, diarrhoea, sore mouth, internal bleeding The leaves are edible raw or cooked. They can be used in salads, soups, stews etc. Tannin in the leaves can be removed by washing the leaves thoroughly or cooking. A cold-water infusion of the freshly chopped or dried and powdered leaves is used as a refreshing tea. An olive-green dye is obtained from the flowers and stems.

## Cultivation

Selfheal growing to 0.2m by 0.3m. It is hardy and is not frost tender. It is in flower from July to September, and the seeds ripen from August to September. The species is hermaphrodite (has both male and female organs) and is pollinated by insects. It prospers in any kind of soil that is not too dry and can tolerate a wide pH range. It does well in semi-shade or full sun. Seed should be sown in mid spring in a coldframe. When they are large enough to handle, prick the seedlings out into individual pots and plant them out in the summer. If you have sufficient seed then it can be sown outdoors in situ in mid to late spring. Plants can be divided in spring or autumn with ease. Larger divisions can be planted out direct into their permanent positions, while smaller divisions should be grown on in pots, in semi-shade until the following spring.

## Shamrock/Clover

Latin: Trifolium (genus)
Irish: Seamair/Seamróg. Welsh: Meillionen. Breton: Melchon.
Native to Europe, common in Britain and Ireland. PERENNIAL

Famously connected with Ireland, it was valued throughout the Celtic world. Shamrock is a small variety of the many forms of clover that exist. It is commonly associated with St. Patrick but its value probably dates to long before his time. Usually three leafed, the four-leaf shamrock or *seamróg nagCeithre* was considered fortuitous in Ireland and Scotland and also a bestower of supernatural powers such as seeing through illusions/deceptions and being immune to witchcraft or fairy sight. Similar beliefs relating to clover persisted throughout the British Isles even in my childhood and my friends and I spent many hours searching for four or more leafed clovers. Shamrock or clover appears in Irish and Welsh myth in connection with fertility or the supernatural. Clover is valuable as fodder and enriches the soil hence it is valued by farmers. Medicinally it was used to cure coughs, liver complaints, to cure cancer and to relieve bee stings. A tincture of the leaves is applied as an ointment for gout. An infusion of the flowers has been used as an eyewash.

Leaves can be used raw or cooked as a potherb. The young leaves are best harvested before the plant comes into flower and are used in salads, soups. It can also be used as a vegetable, cooked like spinach. Flowers and seed pods can be dried, ground into powder and used as a flour or sprinkled on cooked foods such as boiled rice to add flavour and nutrition. The dried leaves can be used to give a vanilla flavour to cakes. Dried flowering heads make a fair tea substitute.

## *Cultivation*

Trifolium repens is an evergreen perennial growing to 0.1m by 1m at a medium rate.

It is hardy and is not frost tender. It is in leaf all year, in flower from June to September, and the seeds ripen from July to October. The species is hermaphrodite (has both male and female organs) and is pollinated insects, of particular value to bees. It will grow in most soil including heavy clay and poor light soils. It will tolerate a wide pH range including highly alkaline soils. It does better in a fairly moist soil but prefers to be in full sun. This species has a symbiotic relationship with certain soil bacteria, these bacteria form nodules on the roots and fix atmospheric nitrogen. Some of this nitrogen is utilized by the growing plant but some can also be used by other plants growing nearby. It is useful as a green manure. To grow from seed, it is best to pre-soak the seed for 12 hours in warm water and then sow in spring in situ. When plants are large enough to handle, prick the seedlings out into individual pots and plant them out in late spring. Plants can be divided in spring and put into permanent positions.

## Spurge

Latin: Euphorbia (genus)
Irish: Spuirse. Welsh: Llaethlys. Breton: Euforb.
Native to Europe, common in Britain. ANNUAL/PERENNIAL

It was used magically in Ireland to rescue women from fairy abduction if collected at the appropriate phase of the moon during August. It was used as a quick method of catching fish in rivers and ponds as it poisons them. Medicinally it was used for warts and skin blemishes and as a general purgative, especially for diarrhoea. It makes good foraging for sheep and goats, but is not edible for humans except for the seed - the seed has been used as a substitute for capers. The leaves and the sap (latex) is a severe irritant, especially to the eyes.

### Cultivation

Euphorbia an annual or biennial growing to 1m. It is hardy to zone and not frost tender. It is in flower from May to June, and the seeds ripen from July to August. The species is monoecious (individual flowers are either male or female, but both sexes can be found on the same plant) and is pollinated by insects. Prefers a light well-drained soil in an open position, tolerates a wide pH range. Suitable for any soil but prefers a dry soil but grows almost anywhere. Members of this genus are rarely if ever troubled by browsing deer or rabbits. This genus has been singled out as a potential source of latex (for making rubber) in temperate countries. Often self-sows freely. Seed is best sown in spring in situ. Germination usually takes place within 2-3 weeks at 15°C+.

## St. John's Wort

Latin: Hypericum perforatum
Irish: Beathnua. Welsh: Eirunllys. Breton: Unknown.
Native to Europe, common in Britain and Ireland. PERENNIAL

Linked with the summer solstice and the Feast of St. John, this was an important magical and medicinal herb throughout the British Isles, still used today. Believed to provide great protection against evil, expel demons and bring abundance to the bearer. It was cast into midsummer fires and dried and smoked over them too. On St. John's Eve, children were given it to ward off sickness and it was also worn to protect against evil. It was also placed on windowsill and over doors of the home as protection from malign influences. In Scotland, it was said to be especially valued by St. Colmcille (Columba) and was valued as powerful protection from harm, placed under the armpit. At midsummer, it was used by girls in love divination and also in the making of love charms. In Wales, it was used to predict life expectancy. Medicinally it was used for lung and bladder problems, dysentery, jaundice, diarrhoea, sore eyes, cuts and scratches. Its primary modern usage is as an antidepressant, although it has fulfilled this function in ancient times under the guise of hysteria, melancholia, cure for the evil eye, evil spirits and general 'insanity'. The herb and the fruit are sometimes used as a tea substitute. The flowers can be used in making mead. Yellow, gold and brown dyes are obtained from the flowers and leaves. A red dye is obtained from the whole plant when infused in oil or alcohol.

## *Cultivation*

St. John's Wort is a perennial growing to 0.9m by 0.6m but at a slow rate. It is hardy and reasonably frost tolerant. It is in flower from May to August, and the seeds ripen from July to September. The species is hermaphrodite (has both male and female organs) and is pollinated by insects and is self-fertile. It will grow in most soils including heavy clay if it is not water-logged. It will tolerate a wide pH range and can grow in semi-shade, although it prefers full sun. It was a common weed but has become relatively rare except in truly wild areas. The whole plant, especially when in bloom, gives off a most unpleasant smell when handled.

Seed should be sown in a greenhouse or coldframe as soon as it is ripe in the autumn or in the spring. It normally germinates in 1-3 months at 10°C+. Prick out the seedlings into individual pots when they are large enough to handle and plant them out into their permanent positions in the summer. Larger plants can be divided in spring or autumn, with ease. Larger clumps can be replanted direct into their permanent positions, although it is best to pot up smaller clumps and grow them on in a coldframe until they are rooting well.

## Thistle

Latin: Cirsium (genus)
Irish: Feochadán. Welsh: Ysgallen. Breton: Askol.
Native to Europe, common in Britain and Ireland. PERENNIAL

The Scottish national emblem, credited with saving Scotland from a Viking invasion although it is probably only known for this from the Middle Ages onwards. In Ireland, it was a symbol of good land despite being a troublesome weed. It appears in *Tain bo Cuailgne* when Cailidín's children create an enchanted army from thistles and puffballs. It was used as fodder for livestock and poultry. The flowers of spear thistle were said to be able to curdle milk. Medicinally it was used for kidney infections, wounds and (in a tea) as a cure for depression. The root can be cooked and has a taste somewhat like a Jerusalem artichoke. It has a rather bland flavour, hence the root is best used mixed with other vegetables. The root can be dried and stored for later use. A fibre obtained from the inner bark can be used in making paper.

## *Cultivation*

Cirsium vulgare is a biennial growing to 2m at a fast rate, other wild thistles are annuals. Cultivated ornamental thistles are generally perennial. It is hardy and is not frost tender. The species is hermaphrodite (has both male and female organs) and is pollinated by insects and the plant is self-fertile. It will grow in any soil and tolerates a wide pH range and also drought conditions. It does not grow well in shade. The common thistle is a pernicious weed that spreads freely by means of its seeds, which can be dispersed by the wind over a huge area. The seedlings are capable of establishing themselves in grassland as well as open ground. This plant should not be encouraged unless a wild meadow for insects.

## Vervain

Latin: Verbena officinalis
Irish: Beirbhéine. Welsh: Ferfain, Hudlys. Breton: Unknown.
Native to Europe, common in Britain and Ireland. PERENNIAL

Recorded as used by the Druids of Gaul, it was widely used throughout the ancient world. It had the reputation of being powerful protection against evil and enchantments and also being able to amplify beneficial influences. The Gauls picked it in July/August at the rising of the Dog Star (Sirius) after first making an offering of fruit and honey to the earth. It is native to Western Europe, except Ireland, becoming naturalised in Ireland at an unknown date hence it does not feature much in early Irish legend or folk cures. It is said the Druids used it in religious ceremonies, in ratifying vows and treaties and for divination. Vervain is one of three herbs held to be most sacred to the Druids. At *Bealtaine* it was used to protect farms from evil influence, and especially to protect cattle by tying it to the horns or tail. It was sown into babies' clothes to protect them from fairies and it was often carried by travellers and fishermen for luck and protection. It was used magically to heal the 'evil eye', the 'fairy stroke', cure headaches and scrofula. It was thought to cure poisons, prevent disease, cure fevers and spread a convivial atmosphere where scattered or burned. Medicinally it was used for gout, swellings, sores, skin problems, jaundice, whooping cough, mastitis, edema, lymphatic disorders, rheumatism and ear infections. The leaves are edible parboiled and seasoned, they are also used as a tea substitute.

## *Cultivation*

Vervain is a perennial growing to 0.6m by 0.5m. It is hardy and is not frost tender. It is in leaf from April to October, in flower from July to September, and the seeds ripen from August to September. The species is hermaphrodite (has both male and female organs) and is pollinated by insects. This plant is self-fertile and it is noted for attracting wildlife. It will grow in any well-drained soil and will tolerate strong wind but dislikes coastal conditions and shade. It is a very easily grown plant, it succeeds in any moderately fertile well-drained but needs a moisture retentive soil in a sunny position.

Self-sows freely when growing in a suitable position. Seed is best sown early spring in a greenhouse and only just cover the seed. Germination should take place within three weeks. Prick out the seedlings into individual pots once they are large enough to handle and plant them out in early summer. If you have sufficient seed, it can also be sown in situ in late spring. Plants can be divided in spring. Larger divisions can be planted out direct into their permanent positions. Smaller divisions can be grown on in a greenhouse and planted out in the summer or the following spring. Basal cuttings can be made in early summer - harvest the shoots with plenty of underground stem when they are about 8cm above the ground. Pot them up into individual pots and keep them in light shade in a coldframe or greenhouse until they are rooting well.

## Vetch

Latin: Vicia (genus)
Irish: Peasair. Welsh: Gwŷg. Breton: Unknown.
Native to Europe, common in Britain and Ireland. PERENNIAL

Hated by farmers due to its tough roots, it can be eaten but has a bitter taste, although the young roots taste of liquorice. It was used as fodder for livestock and by the Scots to stave off thirst and hunger and also in advance of a drinking bout to reduce drunkenness. Medicinally it was used to heal wounds, for stomach ache, staunching blood loss and for back ache. The seed can be cooked, they are boiled or roasted. Leaves and young stems can also be cooked. It is used as a potherb and the leaves make a reasonable tea substitute.

### *Cultivation*

Vicia cracca is a perennial climbing plant growing to 1.8m. It is hardy and not frost tender. It is in flower from May to August, and the seeds ripen from July to September. The species is hermaphrodite (has both male and female organs) and is pollinated by insects and it is self-fertile. It prefers a well-drained soil but can grow in most soils and tolerate a wide pH range, semi-shade or full sun. Vetch has a symbiotic relationship with certain soil bacteria, these bacteria form nodules on the roots and fix atmospheric nitrogen. Some of this nitrogen is utilized by the growing plant but some can also be used by other plants growing nearby. Vetch can be used as a green manure. It is a dynamic accumulator gathering minerals or nutrients from the soil and storing them in a more bio-available form hence it can be used as fertilizer or to improve mulches. To grow from seed - pre-soak the seed for a full day in warm water and then sow in situ in spring or autumn.

# Violet

Latin: Viola (genus)

Irish: Sailchuach. Welsh: Fioled. Breton: Melion.

Native to Europe, common in Britain and Ireland. PERENNIAL

In folk belief they are linked to sadness and death, it was considered bad luck, omen of sickness or an omen of death to see them flowering in autumn and it was bad luck to bring a single common dog violet into the home. Conversely, perhaps due to the sweet fragrance, they are associated with love and also are a symbol of modesty. In Irish myth it appears as a symbol of beauty and to the Gauls a symbol of virginity, meanwhile the Greeks linked the violet with Aphrodite. Violet was used in perfumes and ancient cosmetics.

Medicinally the scent was used to revive someone who had fainted, for boils, headaches and also to cure cancerous tumours. Young leaves and flower buds are edible raw or cooked. An essential oil from the flowers and leaves is used in perfumery. A pigment extracted from the flowers is used as a litmus to test for acids and alkalis. The dried root has been used as an incense.

## *Cultivation*

Viola odorata is an evergreen perennial growing to 0.1m by 0.5m at a fast rate. It is hardy to zone and is not frost tender. It is in leaf all year, in flower from February to April, and the seeds ripen from April to June. This species is hermaphrodite (has both male and female organs) and is pollinated by insects and leistogomy (self-pollinating without flowers ever opening). This plant is self-fertile. It prefers sun and will grow well in any soil that is not water-logged. Viola canina (Dog Violet) is a perennial growing to 0.4m with similar characteristics, only larger.

Viola epipsila is also a growing to 0.1m and is hardy. The species is hermaphrodite (has both male and female organs) and is pollinated by insects. This violet prefers moist soil and will grow in bogs hence the common name Marsh Violet.

Seed is best sown in the autumn in a coldframe. Sow stored seed in early spring in a coldframe, it may require cold stratification first. Prick out the seedlings into individual pots when they are large enough to handle and plant them out in the summer. Plants can be divided in the autumn or just after flowering. Larger divisions can be planted out direct into their permanent positions, smaller ones can be grown on in pots in a coldframe or greenhouse. Plant them out in the summer or the following spring.

## Watercress

Latin: Nasturtium officinale
Irish: Biolar. Welsh: Berwr Y Dw^r. Breton: Beler.
Native to Europe, common in Britain and Ireland. PERENNIAL

A valuable food that grows in abundance it also has medicinal benefits. In Scotland and Ireland, it was believed it could be used magically to 'steal the goodness from milk' of other people's cows. In general, though it was thought to be beneficial to health and mental well-being. Magically it was thought to protect children from depression and improve intelligence if eaten. It was a valued food and a magical aid and is mentioned as such in Celtic myth. It was considered good for scurvy and as a blood purifier, being eaten raw, cooked or in soup for its health-giving properties. Medicinally it was used for colds, coughs, rheumatism, women's problems, skin problems, swellings, heart disease and labour pains. Leaves are edible raw or cooked, best grown rather than foraged. Watercress is mainly used as a garnish or as an addition to salads, the flavour is strong and hot. The leaves are exceptionally rich in vitamins and minerals, especially iron. Seeds can be sprouted and eaten in salads. The seed can be used to make a form of mustard.

*Note: Any plants growing in water that drains from fields where animals, particularly sheep, graze should not be used raw. This is due to the risk of it being infested with the liver fluke parasite.*

## Cultivation

Nasturtium officinale is a perennial growing to 0.5m by 1m at a fast rate. It is hardy and is not frost tender. It is in flower from May to October, and the seeds ripen from July to October. The species is hermaphrodite (has both male and female organs) and is pollinated by insects and is self-fertile. It is noted for attracting wildlife. A dynamic accumulator gathering minerals or nutrients from the soil and storing them in a more bio-available form - used as fertilizer or to improve mulches. It grows in moist soils and commonly will grow in water. It prefers full sun and will not grow in shade. This plant is very sensitive to pollution so clean water must be used, especially if you intend to eat it.

To grow from seed, sow in spring in a pot immersed to half its depth in water. Germination should take place within a couple of weeks. Prick out seedlings into individual pots whilst they are still small and increase the depth of water gradually until they are submerged. Plant out into a pond edge in the summer or a shallow pool. Cuttings can be taken at any time in the growing season. Virtually any part of the plant, including a single leaf, will form roots if detached from the parent plant, so cuttings are very simple to do. Just put it in a container of water until the roots are well formed and then plant out in soil, shallow water.

# Water Lily

Latin: Nymphaeaceae (family)

Irish: Bacán. Welsh: Alaw, Lili'r Dw^r. Breton: Loa-Zour.

Native to Europe, common in Britain, introduced into Ireland.

PERENNIAL

Considered somewhat dangerous, especially in Scotland, as it was thought it could cause children to become 'fairy struck' and also could nullify sexual desire in adults. It is linked with the Celtic water goddess Coventina of Britain, Iberia and Gaul who was depicted holding a water lily. In Scotland, the root was used to produce a black dye for wool and in England to deter cockroaches and crickets. Medicinally the root was used to calm sexual frustration or out of control libido, it was also used for reducing boils and to staunch wounds. The root is edible when cooked, it contains up to 40% starch and 6% protein. Some caution is advised as this plant contains the toxic alkaloids nupharine and nymphaeine, these substances have an effect on the nervous system. The roasted seed is a coffee substitute. Seeds can be eaten cooked; they contain about 47% starch.

## *Cultivation*

Nymphaea alba is a perennial growing in water. It is hardy and can survive freezing weather. It is in flower from July to August, and the seeds ripen from August to October. The species is hermaphrodite (has both male and female organs) and is pollinated by insects and is self-fertile. It grows in any soul type (in a pond) and tolerates a wide pH range. It needs full sun to grow, and usually grows in water.

To grow from seed - sow as soon as it is ripe in a greenhouse in pots submerged under 25mm of water. Prick out into individual pots as soon as the first true leaf appears and grow them on in water in a greenhouse for at least two years before planting them out in late spring. The seed is best collected by wrapping the developing seed head in a muslin bag to avoid the seed being lost in the water. Harvest it 10 days after the seed head sinks below the water surface or as soon as it reappears (floats up). Plants can be divided around May/June. Each portion must have at least one eye to be viable. Submerge in pots in shallow water until established and then plant out, preferably in late spring.

## Water Pimpernel/Brooklime/Speedwell

Latin: Veronica beccabunga
Irish: Lochall. Welsh: Llysiau Taliesin. Breton: Unknown.
Native to Europe, common in Britain and Ireland. PERENNIAL

Sometimes confused with Brookweed (Pliny's Samolus) it is possible that this is the plant referred to but this cannot be verified. It is common in the British Isles and France. It can be used to prevent scurvy, as a poultice for itching, burns and wounds. The juice also acts as a blood tonic, diuretic and treatment for kidney stones. Its Welsh name is linked to the legendary Bard and poet Taliesin. Magically it was used to increase psychic and visionary abilities. Leaves are edible raw or cooked. They can be added to salads, mixed with water cress or cooked with other strongly flavoured greens.

*Note: Any plants growing in water that drains from fields where animals, particularly sheep, graze should not be used raw. This is due to the risk of it being infested with the liver fluke parasite.*

### *Cultivation*

Veronica beccabunga is a perennial growing to 0.6m, on a wet bank or in water. It is hardy and is not frost tender. It is in flower from May to September, and the seeds ripen from July to September. The species is hermaphrodite (has both male and female organs) and is pollinated by insects and this plant is self-fertile. It is noted for attracting wildlife, especially bees. It will grow in most soils and tolerates a wide pH range. It will grow in semi-shade but prefers full sun for at least part of the day. It needs very damp soil or to grow in water. It is easily grown in a moderately fertile wet soil, growing best in water up to 15cm deep. Seed is best sown in autumn in a coldframe. When they are large enough to handle, prick the seedlings out into individual pots and plant them out in the summer. If you have sufficient, the seed can be sown in situ in the spring or the autumn. Plants can be divided at almost any time in the growing season with ease. Even a small part of the plant will root if put in water.

## Wild Carrot

Latin: Daucus carota
Irish: Mealbhacán. Welsh: Moron Gwyllt. Breton: Karotez gwez.
Native to Europe, common in Britain and Ireland. BIENNIAL

Associated with the autumnal equinox and the Feast of St. Michael, in Scotland they were collected by women, it being thought they brought fertility. They were valued in Ireland and Scotland as an autumn food that could be stored into winter. Medicinally it was used as a diuretic and in a poultice for treating sores and wounds. The whole plant is anthelmintic, carminative, deobstruent, diuretic, galactogogue, ophthalmic, stimulant. An infusion is used in the treatment of various complaints including digestive disorders, kidney and bladder diseases and in the treatment of dropsy. The flower clusters can be french-fried to produce a carrot-flavoured dish. The aromatic seed is used as a flavouring in stews etc. The dried roasted roots are ground into a powder and are used for making coffee. Roots can be eaten in the same manner as the modern domesticated carrot.

### *Cultivation*

Daucus carota is a biennial growing to 0.6m by 0.3m at a medium rate. It is hardy and is not frost tender. It is in flower from June to August, and the seeds ripen from August to September. The species is hermaphrodite (has both male and female organs) and is pollinated by insects. This plant is self-fertile and it is noted for attracting wildlife. Does poorly in clay or very damp soil and requires soil that is not too stony. The plant can tolerate maritime exposure. Prefers a sunny position and a well-drained neutral to alkaline soil. Seed should be sown August/September or April in situ. The seed germinates better if it is given a period of cold stratification first.

## Woad

Latin: Isatis tinctoria
Irish: Glaisín. Welsh: Llysiau Lliw. Breton: Unknown.
Native to Europe, common in Britain and Ireland. BIENNIAL/ PERENNIAL

An important plant to the British and Irish due to its blue dye, although it is now extinct in Ireland. It is referred to by both Pliny and Julius Caesar in reference to British people painting themselves with woad, especially warriors; it is likely that it was used for tattoos. It was probably used for the same purpose in Ireland as suggested by an 8th century poem referring to Amergin's blue tattoos. It appears that it was not used medicinally. The leaves are edible but they require long soaking in order to remove the bitterness, and even then, they are still bitter. The seeds contain 12-34% protein and 12-38% fat but were not commonly eaten, although not poisonous or harmful to ingest. It has been grown commercially on a small scale in Germany, since the 1990s, as a natural wood preservative.

### Cultivation
Woad is biennial or perennial growing to 1m by 0.5m. It is hardy to -15°C and is not frost tender. It is in flower from June to August, and the seeds ripen from August to September. The

species is hermaphrodite (has both male and female organs) and is pollinated by insects. It will grow in most soils but prefers a well-drained but reasonably moist soil. It will tolerate a wide pH range, including highly alkaline soil. It can grow in semi-shade or full sun. It is easy to grow but tends to deplete the soil if planted continuously in the same spot (two years or more). Plants self-sow freely when they are grown in a suitable position. Seed is best sown in spring in situ. Fresh seed can also be sown in situ in late summer, it will take at least a year and a half to flower, grown from seed.

## Wood Avens

Latin: Geum Urbanum
Irish: Machall Coille. Welsh: Mapgoll. Breton: Beneat.
Native to Europe, common in Britain and Ireland. PERENNIAL

Believed across Europe to protect against evil spirits, demons and wild animals, it was not widely used though in Ireland or Britain. It was used to flavour ales, as fly repellent and to protect clothes from moths. Medicinally it was used to prevent plague, for diarrhoea, stomach ache and sore throats. The young leaves are edible, as is the root - cooked. It was used as a spice in soups, stews etc., and also as a flavouring in ale. It is a substitute for cloves. The root is also boiled to make a hot beverage. The freshly dug root has a clove-like fragrance, which when dried was used in the linen cupboard to deter moths.

### *Cultivation*

Geum urbanum is a perennial growing to 0.5m by 0.5m. It is hardy and is not frost tender. It is in flower from June to August. The species is hermaphrodite (has both male and female organs) and is pollinated by insects. This plant is self-fertile. It prefers a well-drained soil but can grow in most soil types, over a wide pH range. It can grow in semi-shade or full sun. Easily grown in any moderately good garden soil that is well-drained and a soil rich in organic matter.

Seed should be sown in spring or autumn in a coldframe. When they are large enough to handle, prick the seedlings out into individual pots and plant them out in the summer. Plants can be divided in spring or autumn. This should be done every 3-4 years in order to maintain the vigour of the mature plant. Very easily divided, larger clumps can be replanted direct into their permanent positions, though it is best to pot up smaller clumps and grow them on pots. Plant them out in the spring.

## Yarrow

Latin: Achillea millefolium
Irish: Athair Thalún. Welsh: Milddail. Breton: Unknown.
Native to Europe, common in Britain and Ireland. PERENNIAL

A popular plant for love divination in Scotland and Ireland by women, it was also used as protection from evil and diseases. In Scotland it was also thought it had the power to increase feminine beauty or make a man fall in love with the wearer. It was also believed to restore the goodness of milk that had been magically stolen. It is also one of the seven sacred herbs immune to natural/supernatural influence. Yarrow was called 'herb of seven cures 'because of its healing properties. Medicinally it was used to staunch wounds and cuts by the Celts, Greeks and the Romans. It was used to stop nosebleeds and also to cause them — as a means of relieving headaches. It was also used for toothache, coughs, colds, fevers, rheumatism and boils.

The leaves can be eaten raw or cooked, although it has a rather bitter flavour, they make an addition to mixed salads and are best picked when young. The leaves are also used as a hop-substitute for flavouring and as a preservative for beer. Although in general yarrow is a very nutritious and beneficial plant to add to the diet, some caution is advised. An aromatic tea is made from the flowers and leaves. An essential oil from the flowering heads is used as a flavouring for soft drinks. The growing plant repels beetles, ants and flies, but attracts bees when in flower. The plant has been burnt in order to ward off mosquitoes, usually dried. A liquid plant feed can be made from the leaves that is high in nutrients. *Note: extended use of this plant, either medicinally or in the diet, can cause allergic skin rashes or lead to photosensitivity in some people.*

## Cultivation

Yarrow is a perennial growing to 0.6m by 0.6m at a fast rate. It is hardy to zone and is not frost tender. It is in flower from June to August, and the seeds ripen from July to September. The species is hermaphrodite (has both male and female organs) and is pollinated by insects. It is noted for attracting wildlife, particularly bees. It will grow in any soil, including poor soil so long as it is not waterlogged. It can tolerate a wide pH range and can grow in coastal conditions. Cultivated varieties are used in gardens in several colours. Seed should be sown in spring or early autumn in a coldframe. The seed usually germinates in 1-3 months. When large enough to handle, prick the seedlings out into individual pots and plant them out in the summer. Plants can be divided in spring or autumn with ease. The divided sections can be planted directly into their permanent positions. Basal cuttings can be made from new shoots in spring with ease. Simply collect the shoots when they are about 10cm tall, potting them up individually in pots and keeping them in a warm but lightly shaded position. They should root within three weeks or so and should be ready to plant out in the summer.

## Chapter 10

# Sacred Food: Fruit & Vegetables

*"You are what you eat." – common folk wisdom, derived from: "Dis-moi ce que tu manges, je te dirai ce que tu es." (Tell me what you eat and I will tell you what you are)*
Physiologie du Gout, ou Meditations de Gastronomie Transcendante, 1826

Up until relatively recently (after World War II), it was very common for all people of the world to grow food to eat. In the western world this practice has gone into serious decline due to the continued rise of capitalism and the wide availability of cheap fruit and vegetables. While this is a good thing, in many ways, the quality of the mass-produced plant produce, that is available in shops and supermarkets, is often of a doubtful nature.

In recent decades much of the food (at least in Europe) is imported from all over the world, with vastly different standards regarding fertilizers, pesticides and general quality control being applied. The rise of the organic movement, mostly due to careless use of pesticides, has meant that organic certified fruit and vegetables are now easily available. However, organic produce is 2–3 times more expensive that regular, intensively farmed produce. As a result of the price difference, organic fruit and vegetables are just not a viable option for a great many people - they are really a luxury item for the middle class and wealthy, or for those poorer people who are prepared to make cutbacks in other areas of life.

For many people, they feel that they are just too busy making a living to consider going to the effort of growing food. While this is understandable, the reality of growing does not have to be a nightmare of hard slog, if you go about it in the right way.

There are huge benefits to growing your own food. The most obvious benefit is the huge savings in cost – cheaper than even the cheapest mass-produced fruit and vegetables. Another considerable benefit is the knowledge of how the food has been grown – you are in control and can choose to go entirely organic, Biodynamic or permaculture in your methods. This generally means that your food will be healthier and totally lacking in nasty toxins that lace most supermarket fruit and vegetables. The other, less obvious, benefit is that your produce can be eaten fresh – within hours or even minutes of being collected. Much of the shop produce is weeks old and due to age has a declining level of vitamins and minerals. Also, some shop bought food may have been waxed, stored in formaldehyde or even irradiated!

The final benefit is also a health-related benefit – working in the garden gets you into the fresh air and away from the couch and the television! Gardening offers a form of moderate exercise that even very unfit of people can usually undertake. In addition to the physical benefits, growing food can offer mental and spiritual benefits. Growing food feels good and makes one appreciate where the food comes from and the effort that both man and nature puts into growing it. From a spiritual perspective, growing food reconnects you with the sacred earth and the simple fact that the produce of the earth is what sustains our existence. Without the soil to grow food for both us and animals we would all starve to death! In the past it was more common for people to give thanks for their food, (often to God/ Gods or the Earth itself), returning to growing your food revives that sense of gratitude and may help in renewing a spiritual connection in your life.

Personally, I like to say a blessing before I eat:

*"I give thanks for the blessings of this food, the life of this (animal/ fish) and the fruits of the earth."*

There are a great many prayers and blessings already in existence from all spiritual traditions which one could use or you can write you own, as I have done.

Modern fruit and vegetables are very different from those grown in the time of the Druids. Generally, varieties are larger and more productive in terms of quantity, however some of them are more vulnerable to disease than their wild counterparts. Even in the Middle Ages, there were far more varieties of fruit and vegetables than are commonly available now. A lot of plants that are no-longer considered food were commonly eaten in Druidic times and even up until the 20th century. Commercial concerns have greatly reduced the number of types of vegetables and fruits that we now regularly consume and for many people the knowledge of which plants are edible or good eat is completely lost. Necessity meant that ordinary people knew where they could find food in times of scarcity. With the luxury of consumerism, people no longer need to have an understanding of plants, that knowledge now remains only in the hands of herbalists and gardeners. If times of scarcity ever return to the 'civilized' world, this knowledge may prove vital to surviving a harsh winter or a period of war or famine.

Many of the old varieties of fruit and vegetables still exist, kept by organisations such as Seedsavers and historical or special interest groups. If you have sufficient space, you might consider growing some ancient varieties or vegetables that you have never tried before. The human diet has changed a lot (in the modernised world) in the last few centuries, but many interesting recipes for forgotten foods still exist. This section of this book is merely an introduction to the basics, to get you started in the right direction. If you are serious about growing your own food, I suggest that you invest in some good books, such as 'Gardening With The Moon & Stars' by Elen Sentier, 'Vegetables – For the Polytunnel and Greenhouse' by Klaus Laitenberger, 'Secrets and Tips From Yesterday's Gardeners' or any books produced by the Royal Horticultural Society (RHS).

## Getting Down to it!

If you have never done it before, starting a vegetable garden can seem daunting, but it's like many things in life – the fear of doing it is much worse than actually doing the job. Having taught an 8-week evening gardening course on this subject, for six years, it is clear to me that even the total novice can become fully competent within quite a short time. The first thing to do is to plan where your vegetable and fruit garden will be, as this is a vitally important decision. I have seen people try to grow vegetables in a damp and shady, north facing area, which is a recipe for total disaster, before you even get started!

### *Directions*

The first thing to do is orientation – if you have a compass you can find south. Failing that, if you go outside at exactly midday wherever the sun is at that time is south. As a general rule it is best to site your vegetable garden facing south. Of course, this is not always possible, but it should be as close to south facing as possible; east or west facing is at least better than north facing. This is the fundamental decision that you cannot afford to mess up – north facing gardens get very little light, as heat and light is what you need, this should be avoided at all costs.

## Conditions

The next step is to check out the conditions in your garden. If you only have a balcony then you can control the soil yourself and maybe offer some wind protection with a see-through screen. In the garden, you can test the soil for pH, nutrition content and texture yourself with cheap kits and doing a soil texture test (described in Chapter 3). If your soil is terrible (boggy clay, sand and rubble, or a thin layer on top of refuse) then you will probably want to consider raised beds instead. With a raised bed you can mix the soil yourself to suit what you are growing – for instance a manure rich bed for asparagus and brassicas or a fairly sandy one for carrots and parsnips.

Next you need to think about location. Are you high up in a windy spot? Are you next to the sea? Is there insufficient water or too much in the soil? Are there problems with wild animals or pets invading your garden? All of these problems can be overcome with a little thought. For instance - putting a series of bamboo rods in your raised beds (like a pin cushion) deters cats, dogs and other animals climbing into it and wrecking your hard work! Once you have made modifications to your garden to deal with anticipated problems then you are ready to get going for real. If you live at altitude you may have to start later due to colder temperatures, a way around this is to make use of coldframes, greenhouses, polytunnels or sunrooms. If you are really stuck for a solution you can make a coldframe out of two shower doors or buy a cheap propagator box from garden centres or some supermarkets.

It is important to prepare the soil in advance if possible, if it is needed. If you are lucky, you will have good soil that is loamy and does not need to be modified in some way – e.g. if it is too acidic/alkaline, too sandy, too heavy, low in nutrient, too stony, full of rubbish. If you have opted for raised beds you will need to get good top-soil and some manure, possibly some sand (not from a beach) and some mulch to go on top (to suppress weeds and retain moisture). If you are going for conventional plots then you have to decide whether or not to dig it over or go for the 'no-dig' method. Many problems in soil can be fixed - boggy soil can be aerated (to some extent) sandy soil can have nutrient added, acidic peat can be added to alkaline soil, lime can be added to acidic soil, compost can be added to depleted soil and so on.

It is a good idea to think about locating the vegetable garden not far from your house – you want water via a hose, rainwater tanks etc. to be within practical reach. You also want to be able to harvest the food without too much difficulty – e.g. herb beds are traditionally near the house for easy access. Fruit trees can be further away, but again they need to be in a sunny location that is preferably not too windy. Too much wind can mean flowers are blown off, hence no fruits, if it is not sunny there will be few or very small fruits.

As a general rule, it is far better to get things right at the beginning in the planning stages, rather than have to try and fix a bodged job later on – moving trees and raised beds to a better location is annoying and time consuming and best avoided, by choosing the right locations to start with!

### *Crop rotation*

Crop rotation has been around for a long time. Experience has proven that growing the same things in the same place continuously leads to problems – pests and diseases and depletion of the soil. For obvious reasons one should have at least three sections to your plot or at least three raised beds.

If you are going for permaculture with different zones, then companion plants are key here, and zones can be periodically changed and regenerated.

Beds or plots should be rotated every year – with different groups being planted each year. You can do this with three plots or if you have sufficient space, you can have four and one of the beds/plots is left fallow (empty). By doing this you reduce the likelihood of soil depletion and a buildup of diseases in the soil and attracting large numbers of pests that eat your produce.

The main groupings for vegetables are as follows. Of course, some companion planting (synergistic plants that help one another) can also occur if you want to try that out, but the general groupings should be adhered to for good results.

BRASSICAS – broccoli, cabbage, cauliflower, romanesca, brussels sprouts etc. Needs nitrogen (N) and potassium (K) especially.

LEGUMES – Peas, beans, mange tout etc. Needs potassium especially (K) but fixes nitrogen (N) in the soil which is especially helpful to other groups.

ROOT CROPS - Carrots, parsnip, beetroots, potato etc. Needs phosphorus especially (P) as well as nitrogen (N).

ALLIUMS - Onions, leeks, garlic etc. Needs phosphorus especially (P) as well as nitrogen (N).

LEAF - Lettuce, spinach, kale. Needs nitrogen (N).

FRUITS - Tomato, soft fruits (e.g. strawberry). Needs potassium (K).

PERMANENT CROPS – perennials that are best left in situ, such as asparagus, artichokes, Rhubarb. Need compost to refresh nutrients.

*Rotation Plan*

|        | Year 1         | Year 2         | Year 3         |
|--------|----------------|----------------|----------------|
| Bed 1  | Brassica/Leaf  | Root           | Legume/Allium  |
| Bed 2  | Root           | Legume/Allium  | Brassica/Leaf  |
| Bed 3  | Legume/Allium  | Brassica/Leaf  | Root           |

If you have the space, it is better to have an extra fallow bed/plot.

|        | Year 1         | Year 2         | Year 3         | Year 4            |
|--------|----------------|----------------|----------------|-------------------|
| Bed 1  | Brassica/Leaf  | Root           | Legume/Allium  | Fallow            |
| Bed 2  | Fallow         | Brassica/Leaf  | Root           | Legume/Allium     |
| Bed 3  | Legume/Allium  | Fallow         | Brassica/Leaf  | Root              |
| Bed 4  | Root           | Legume/Allium  | Fallow         | Brassica/Leaf     |

You should probably have separate beds/plots again for tomato, soft fruits and permanent crops. Strawberry and cane fruits beds are usually permanent fixtures.

## Growing in confined spaces

If you are not lucky enough to have a decent sized garden that does not mean that you have to give up! Amazing results can be achieved with window boxes and hanging baskets. For instance – some varieties of tomato are perfect for hanging baskets and will do very well so long as they get regular liquid feed and plenty of sun. Most crops do fine in pots or window boxes if they are kept an eye on and given sufficient water and nutrients.

A useful tip for potatoes is to use a collapsible barrel or old tyres, located in a sunny spot. The potatoes (2 or 3 max) must be planted in the bottom, covered over with 5cm of good soil and with 10cm underneath. Good drainage is essential! Potatoes can be 'chitted' first – left out in the light to develop 'eyes', the start of roots and shoots before planting.

Once the plants have a good bit of foliage, extra soil is added and banked up around the plant to leave just four or five leaves exposed above the soil. Wait until the plant grows leafy again and repeat – adding tyres or raising the height of the barrel. You can keep going at this for weeks and then just leave the plants to grow on to maturity. Of course, you will have to consider liquid feeds if the soil you used is not particularly nutrient rich. When the plants have flowered and begin to die off you should have a tower of tyres or barrel full up with potatoes! This method minimizes space and maximizes tubers (potatoes) for you to harvest and enjoy.

One important point with beds and plots is access. With plots you need to ensure access routes so that you do not trample your crops! With raised beds they should not be wider than twice the length of your arm – so that you can reach the centre for weeding and attending to or removing your crops.

### Herbs

Many popular herbs are from the Mediterranean region and do better in light soil that is not too wet. A rockery or special bed for these types of herbs is advisable if you live in a wet region (Ireland!) or certain areas of many countries. Also, some herbs such as mint or oregano can be very invasive so you might wish to contain them in some way so that they don't take over the entire herb garden. If possible, it is a good idea to site it near the house so that fresh herbs can be easily collected and used immediately for cooking.

Herb gardens can be informal, no organized appearance or more formal – having clearly defined sections. Below are two possible formats for a herb garden, but any design could be used so long as it is located to maximize sunlight and is reasonably sheltered from strong winds.

### Fruit Trees

These are a long-term investment, so it is worth putting in the effort to do it right! You need to allow enough room for trees to grow, which generally means a gap of at least 2-3 metres, even with trees grown on a rootstock. Most fruit trees (not grown from seed) are grown on a restrictive rootstock such as crab apple or a slow growing fruit tree variety. Bear in mind the fact that the trees should still be there in 20-30 years and will no longer be stick like objects, they will be fairly mature by then.

Most fruit trees (often referred to as top fruit) require full sun to produce good fruit. Certainly, in temperate countries of northern and western Europe they need to get as much sun as is possible. Even in a sunny position, certain fruit trees will struggle in Ireland and to some extent in Britain, Scandinavia and north western coastal countries. Apples, pears, cherries and plums can do reasonably in colder climates with moderate sun, however cherries do badly in very damp conditions. Also, fruits such as peach, nectarine and apricot really struggle in damp countries, such as Ireland, and need a decent amount of warmth, sunlight and relatively dry conditions. For them to succeed in the Irish (or similar) environment they should be grown in a greenhouse or sunroom. The same issues generally apply to citrus trees, and these also need special soil, that is not commonly found in places like Ireland.

When selecting trees, it is important, not only to select the right species for your conditions, but also to select varieties that are likely to succeed. A perfect example of this is apples – Cox's Orange Pippin is a popular variety that may do well in France, USA or south east England, but is likely to disastrously badly in Scotland or Ireland. I would suggest avoiding this variety, like the plague, if you live in a damp and cold location. The same principle applies to all varieties – it is best to pick a variety that is known to prosper in your locality e.g. native apple varieties from Ireland that have a proven viability and resistance to disease.

Another issue with certain fruit trees is pollination – some require other varieties to be pollinated (e.g. Bramley apple needs two others). It is handy to have a wild apple or crab apple tree, as these can cross-breed with virtually all domesticated apple varieties. More than one variety may also be required for certain pears, cherries, peaches etc. If you have a tiny garden you can get some columnar (narrow) self-fertile varieties that were created for this purpose and don't take up a lot of space or need another tree to produce fruit.

Fruiting uses a lot of energy, from the sun and nutrients from the soil. Many fruit trees may appear to go into decline after some years, but most likely this is due to neglect. Fruit trees need to be fed with manure and/or liquid feeds to maintain good crops, They also need to be pruned effectively every year or two, to remove dead, diseased or damaged branches and maintain a healthy tree.

Cherry trees can be problematic in damp climates, especially if they are not acclimatized, native varieties. Cherry trees are quite prone to bacterial canker and other diseases so they need special care in damper countries. In places like Ireland, Wales and Scotland, they can only be pruned in summer during dry weather, to avoid infection. Another point to note with cherries is that birds are very fond of the fruit – you will have to be quick off the mark to collect them or use a net to keep the birds off your trees close to ripening time.

## Soft fruit

There are a great many soft fruits that can be grown, both wild and cultivated. Strawberries come in many varieties, all descended from the wild strawberry, which is tiny but generally has a far superior flavour to any cultivated ones. Strawberries are one of the easiest of fruits to grow and can be easily propagated by 'runners' which can establish in the ground or by laying the 'runner' on a pot-full of soil.

Many enjoyable fruits grow on canes or bushes – raspberries, loganberries and blackberries grow on canes, the cultivated varieties are often thornless (blackberry) and produce larger fruit that their wild ancestors. Fruits such as gooseberries, currants (black, red, white), blueberries etc. will grow into small bushes and a single bush can provide large quantities of fruit if well looked after. As with the trees, they need to have a decent distance (1.5m-2m) between them and be located in a sunny position, again they might need to be protected from birds and other creatures that fancy a free, sweet tasting meal!

## Giving something back to nature

It might be tempting to keep every last berry and every last carrot for yourself and prevent other creatures from enjoying the fruits of your labour. This is understandable, given the hard work put in to growing. However, this is a very selfish and unholistic attitude, given that the food is created by nature and taken from nature for our survival. Other creatures have a right to eat and to survive, so it is better to leave a certain percentage to nature, for non-humans to enjoy. Not only is this generous, but it enables many other species, that are all part of the eco-system to survive.

It is not a great hardship to say overplant cabbages by 10% and allow caterpillars to enjoy that 10%. In many cases this can done with a bit of intelligence – e.g. transferring all of the caterpillars you find to the designated sacrificial cabbages. By acting in this way, you give something back to the garden and ensure that you are not acting like a genocidal maniac, in your efforts to grow food for yourself.

Another good option is to leave a wild area not too far away from your vegetable garden – this will hopefully be as attractive or more so to many of the creatures, that would otherwise be helping themselves to your food supply. An additional sacrificial option is to plant certain species (e.g. marigolds or salvias for slugs) that will act as a magnet for certain species and draw them away from your vegetables or fruit. This strategy is not costly if you grow these plants in quantity from seed and will usually have the desired effect.

### Greenhouses, polytunnels and sunrooms

In northern Europe (and other regions of the world) it is difficult to grow certain herbs, fruit and vegetables due to the cool temperatures, excessive rain and highly variable levels of sunlight. Although it is not possible to change the weather patterns, it is possible to compensate for this by using a protective environment in which to grow more vulnerable plants. If you have a sunroom or conservatory attached to your house, hopefully south facing, it can double as a greenhouse effectively, although it will not be quite as bright, unless you have a glass or plastic roof. If you don't have either of these then you will need to put up a greenhouse or a polytunnel. Greenhouses are generally far more expensive to buy but can be done very cheaply if you have reasonable wood-working skills and access to free or cheap windows. Often glazing companies will sell off rejects, seconds or surplus windows at huge discounts, which you may be able to use in a greenhouse. If you cannot make one yourself, you can buy DIY kits, or arrange for a supplier to come and erect one for you.

With a polytunnel, the structure is usually made from galvanized steel, consisting of semi-circular hoops and straight supports. This structure, when secured, is covered with UV resistant plastic, which has to be stretched taught over the frame in order to be resistant to the wind. Do not be tempted to cut corners by using very thin plastic or plastic that is not UV resistant – this may save money in the short term but will prove to be a short-sighted decision, when the plastic deteriorates at a rapid pace. Polytunnels can be bought as a DIY kit or you can often pay the supplier to put it up for you.

There are small DIY greenhouses and polytunnels available from garden centres, hardware shops and some supermarkets that are affordable. These can work quite well but are generally pretty flimsy and are not at all suitable for windy sites. Plastic coldframes are also available which, again are not suited to windy sites. I have experimented with small greenhouses, a cheap polytunnel and finally with a professional polytunnel. The earlier experiments taught me a lot, but ultimately, they were wrecked by bad weather as they could not endure storms. A cheap alternative to a small greenhouse, cloche or coldframe is to use old shower doors to create a triangular prism. This can be left open at each end, or you can make triangular wooden ends to close them off, although it is advisable to drill a few air holes for ventilation.

Growing in the greenhouse or polytunnel requires some modification of your techniques – there is no rain or wind. This is an artificial environment and hence problems can arise from this. Too much water will lead to very high humidity and with the higher heat levels will lead to mould and fungus, diseases such as botrytis and mildew. Too little water will mean that your plants will either die of be severely stunted. A method of reducing the humidity is to allow some air flow by opening doors or windows, especially during hot weather. Apart from reducing excess humidity, this allows insects into the greenhouse/ polytunnel to pollinate your plants when they flower.

If you can afford it, you can buy an irrigation or sprinkler system or create a home-made version by drilling tiny holes in a hosepipe at regular intervals, this will distribute water into the beds whenever you turn it on. You can also buy automatic ventilation systems, that measure temperature and humidity and open flaps/windows accordingly. However, these systems are expensive and more for the serious or professional grower.

I would recommend twice daily inspection of the greenhouse/polytunnel, both for watering and humidity levels. It is also an opportunity to check plants for diseases and pests and generally keep an eye on how they are doing. In a sunroom, or even using south facing windows, you will most likely have your plants in containers and hanging baskets, being in the house already it is easier to check on them frequently and easy to water them.

Inside the greenhouse/polytunnel you can plant directly in the soil (no-digging), dig it over into a plot or create enclosed beds using planks. Whichever way you choose, I would recommend creating some paths, possibly with cheap paving slabs, so that you can access all of the growing areas without stepping on the plants. As with outside, you can plant different areas and rotate them each year.

An approach to watering that can save, time, effort and reduce humidity problems is spot watering. This involves individually watering plants and keeping surrounding areas bone dry. This lowers the overall humidity of the tunnel, which means damping off and mould problems are less likely. It also means that weeds will have a very hard time getting established as they are starved for water – any that do grow are likely to be weak and easily dealt with. This also reduces problems with pests such as snails and slugs as they will be deterred by having to cross a barren desert in order to get to your tasty morsels! I have used this technique with great success and found it to be of great benefit, reduce work and still give excellent results.

Another interesting approach is to use hanging baskets, which is easiest if you have 'cropping bars', that offer more support to the greenhouse/polytunnel but are ideal for hanging things from. Although the growing space is confined, as is water retention, it uses space well and makes life hard for land-based pests that have great difficulty to climb up to your plants.

As a general rule, good garden hygiene is important, but this is even more important in your greenhouse/polytunnel to avoid pests and diseases that might decimate your growing area and destroy all your efforts!

1. Don't allow messy corners or dumping areas.
2. Remove any dead or diseased plants or cut off damaged/ diseased parts of plants.
3. Clean your glass/plastic once a year, usually in autumn when most of your crops are finished.
4. Keep any potting/propagation areas clean and keep tools clean.

## Plants for the polytunnel/greenhouse

Some people have been known to grow cabbage in the polytunnel, but this is totally unnecessary and a poor use of this warm and protected space. Small plants can be started off in the tunnel, especially in early spring. If they are to be planted outside, they may well need to be 'hardened off', which basically means gradually acclimatizing them to the outdoors. This can be done by putting them outside for the day (in ok weather) and back in the polytunnel/greenhouse at night. Once they are getting used to the colder conditions they can be planted out. Failure to harden up many vegetables will lead to them dying of shock or severe setbacks. Think of what it would be like to suddenly dump a person from northern or central Africa at the South Pole, with no coat etc.! They would be less than happy, to say the least, and the same problem applies to plants.

Plants that could or should remain in the polytunnel/ greenhouse permanently (in colder countries) are:

Aubergine, Bean (French, Runner) Calabrese, Celery, Chicory, Chilli Pepper, Claytonia, Coriander, Corn Salad, Courgette, Cucumber, Endive, Florence Fennel, Gherkin, Kohlrabi, Lemon Verbena, Lettuce, Melon, Occra, Oriental Mustard, Pak Choi, Pepino, Pepper, Pumpkin, Spinach, Squash, Stevia, Strawberry, Sweet Potato, Sweetcorn, Swiss Chard, Tomato, Yacon.

Some trees and shrubs will do better (in cold countries) in a polytunnel, greenhouse or sunroom:

Apricot, Citrus (Lemon, Orange etc.), Fig, Passion Fruit, Peach, Plum, some apples (e.g. Cox's Golden Pippin). This is also true of many ornamental plants that are native to hot countries.

## Propagation and succession planting

This is an area that many beginners struggle with. It is perfectly fine to buy seedlings from a garden centre if you are not confident at growing from seed, but it will save a lot of money in the long run and provide more produce if you get to grips with seeds. It can be handy to buy propagation trays, often with a clear plastic lid. An electric propagator (heated) can also be useful to help your seed germinate. Most seeds germinate in the dark and need heat primarily to get them started – this is why the airing cupboard was always a popular place to get seed germinated! Once germinated plants need light – immediately. If you have then outside or in a greenhouse/polytunnel they will not need turning. If you have them on a window sill, they will need to be turned at least daily in order to prevent uneven growth (plants bend towards the light).

Beginners tend to plant all of their seeds at the same time. Doing this means that you will have a glut of produce all in one go. Obviously, different plants take varying amounts of time to be ready to eat, but you might find that you are overwhelmed in summer with more food than you can possibly eat or store. In this scenario, gardeners often have to give away lots of their produce in order to prevent it being wasted. The solution to this problem is to do staggered or succession planting. In this method, small quantities of seed are planted at one time, followed by more planting each week or every second week. By doing this you will have a continual supply of each crop rather than one giant crop. The other advantage to this method is that if one batch is destroyed by disease or by pests, or an unexpected frost or storm, then you have more on the way and have not lost your entire crop. This approach to crops is more effort than a single batch, however, it makes a lot of sense and generally is worth the effort, particularly for crops that do not store well, such as tomatoes or lettuce.

## No magic bullet

I could lie to you and tell that growing food is really easy. It isn't. If you learn good techniques, make a good plan, start at the right time and continue to maintain your vegetable, herb and fruit plants then you should get, at least, reasonable results. Like anything, it takes hard work and practice to become good at anything. Virtuoso violinists do not become mind-blowingly good overnight – it takes years to reach a really impressive standard. The same applies to anything, from sport to science, art and gardening. The good news is that, in one growing season, you can learn a lot and become fairly competent. In following years, you will discover techniques that work better for you or things that should be avoided. Every garden is unique, so the growing methods will need to be specific to your garden in order to achieve the very best results. Certain things can be made easier through, short-cuts, knowledge and experience gained, but a modicum of work will always be required, come what may. It was always thus – the Druids didn't have any magical short cuts to eliminate weeds or to make apples grow to double size. Hard work was always a major part of the formula for success and there will also be years when there are disappointments due to bad weather, a plague of a particular predator or some other form of bad luck.

If you stick at it, gardening for food gets a lot easier as you become more experienced and hopefully you will also find it enjoyable. Personally, I find going and picking a leek (or whatever vegetable) that I have grown and nurtured myself and cooking and eating it a very rewarding process. I feel connected to my food, to the journey from soil to plate, connected to nature through the work I put in and also grateful for the life given up to sustain my own existence.

# Chapter 11

# Gardening with the Four Elements

*"While all bodies are composed of the four elements, that is, of heat, moisture, the earthy, and air, yet there are mixtures according to natural temperament which make up the natures of all the different animals of the world, each after its kind."*
Marcus Vitruvius Pollio (1st century BCE)

In the modern Druidic tradition, the four elements are a key component of Druidic training and a constant part of Druidic life and practice. The fundamental reason for this is that the four elements represent creation, the natural world and all life on this planet. The neo-Platonic four elements, found in western esotericism come to us from the ancient Greeks, although they appear to be used by the Egyptians and Sumerians before them.

The four elements were certainly known to the Druids in Gaul, due to the Greek colony of Massalia (modern Marseille). Druids in Gaul, Britain and Ireland were known to speak ancient Greek so one could fairly safely assume that they were familiar with Greek ideas and culture. Sometime around 330 BCE, Pytheas, a Greek merchant, from Massalia, embarked on an astonishing voyage around the far reaches of Europe, leaving the relative safety of the Mediterranean via the Pillars of Hercules (Gibraltar Straight).

Renowned as a skilled navigator, astronomer, and mariner, Pytheas sailed around Britain, possibly Ireland and up the northern coast of Europe before returning to Massalia. His account of this journey was called On the Ocean (Peri tou Okeanou), published around 325 BCE, but sadly lost to us. It was well known in ancient times and fragments survive in the works of other, later classical writers. His work was discussed by Timaeus, Eratosthenes, Pliny the Elder, Diodorus Siculus, Strabo, and Polybius, not all of whom regarded his work as entirely factual.

It is quite clear that the Druids had contact with Ancient Greek culture and probably were familiar with the concept of the four elements, although this is denied by some reconstructionist Druids. They insist that the four elements are foreign to Druidry and that the ninefold system (consisting of nine elements and three realms) that survived is the only legitimate Druidic cosmology. I would be inclined to dispute this claim as I believe that Druids were familiar with both systems and may well have integrated the two, as a multi-dimensional view of creation.

Regardless of the complexities of Druid philosophy and cosmology, the four elements have survived into mainstream modern culture and the Irish/Welsh/Gaulish nine elements have not, remaining obscure and largely forgotten. The four elements continued to be employed after the demise of Druidic, Greek and Roman cultures, retained to a large extent by the Christian monastic communities. In France, a unique survival of the earlier knowledge of the Gauls, Greeks and Romans, still exists, this is the *Jardin De Simples* or The Garden of Essential Plants, which incorporates the four elements and four directions.

## *Jardin De Simples*

This type of medieval garden is clearly derived from Greco-Roman culture, possibly with some native input from the Gauls and later arrivals to France, such as the Lombards, Franks and Normans.

It is said that the *Jardin De Simples* was inspired by two biblical texts, its design being derived from a description of the Garden of Eden. Another source of inspiration is thought to be the Song of Songs, a biblical poem from Genesis. Christianity has claimed it for itself, but the knowledge and inspiration behind this type of garden clearly reaches back into the Pagan period. The layout of these gardens is clearly defined, nothing is left to chance. These gardens, that survive, are enclosed by walls, within ancient abbeys and monasteries in France. The four sections are clearly delimited and separated by 'plessis' or woven fences, hedges, trellises and stone walls. Within each of the four areas, further divisions are achieved through raised bed made of interwoven wood or stonework. These gardens are usually square or rectangular in shape. Access to the areas of the garden (footpaths) are in the shape of an equal armed cross – a symbol that is overtly Christian but, in truth, a much older spiritual symbol, known to and used by the Druids. At the centre of the cross shaped paths is often a fountain or well. The various beds are separated by fence, timbers, hoops, trellis, low hedges or wooden boxes filled with earth and plants.

As well as being a spiritual place of peace and serenity, these gardens were highly practical and contained a wealth of food, medicinal and magical plants, as well as ornamental plants. The structure was clearly defined and strictly adhered to, with minor variations.

EAST – The Vegetable Garden, *"Hortus"*
In the place of air and the rising sun is the vegetable garden – containing vegetables, fruits and herbs for sustenance of the monastic community. In this section were root crops, vegetables for stews and soups – spinach, leeks, cabbage, peas, lentils, garlic etc. There were also herbs and spices such as horseradish, lovage, mustard, fennel and aromatic plants such as basil, chives, mint rosemary or lavender.

SOUTH – The Orchard, *"Le Verger"*
In the place of fire and the power of the midday sun is the orchard. The French word for orchard, *verger* derives from the word *'verge'*, or stick used to knock fruit down from the trees. This section contained fruit trees grown against palisades – espaliers, cordons or fans to save space. Apples, pears, apricots and plums were commonly grown. A vine would almost certainly have been there to supply grapes and smaller fruit such as strawberries would also have been present.

WEST – Essential herbs, *"Herbularius"*
In the place of water and of wisdom is the herb garden. Every monastery, castle or large domain would have had something similar, if not grown in such a formal and structured way. Before pharmaceuticals, humanity was entirely reliant upon medicinal plants to treat most illnesses. The herbs grown here would have been essential for treating wounds, fevers, disease and for maintaining good health. Among the plants found here would be marigold (Calendula officinalis), thyme, chamomile, verbena, sage, thistle and vervain. For all known common illnesses there was its respective plant or plants, that one would expect to find here. There would be plants for exclusively female health problems, especially in convents – such as lemonbalm. In addition, one could expect to find some poisonous plants that had magical uses, such as Belladonna, foxglove or hemlock.

In the west you might also find useful plants such as flax and hemp, dye plants and crocus (for saffron).

NORTH – Garden Of Mary, "*Bouquetier*"

In the place of earth, of the land and heavenly connection is the ornamental garden. This is essentially a flower garden, dedicated (in Christian times) to Mary. Here you would expect to find roses, lilies and specific herbs. seven sacred plants are found here – St. John's Wort, Sagebrush, Ivy, Plantain, Verbena, Fern and Elder(berry). These seven all have medicinal uses, with elderberry also being a useful food. These were traditionally picked on the morning of 24th June (St. John's Day) which falls just after the summer solstice. The sacred picking of such plants at the summer solstice can be traced back to the Druids and this practice survived into the modern era in Ireland and Scotland. Later in the year, chrysanthemums flowered, along with the roses as well as gladioli and blueberries.

This type of garden is a clever and efficient use of a relatively small space, that provides a wealth of both food and useful and medicinal plants. Obviously, this has long been a Christian tradition in France, but there are clear links to a Roman pre-Christian and Celtic Pagan past. Such a garden can be recreated and adapted as a universal spiritual garden, or for any specific religious or spiritual path.

From a Druidic point of view, one might prefer to create a circular garden, in four sections that are oriented to the four directions, following the general principles of the *Jardin De Simples*. This might incorporate a sacred well or a standing stone at its centre, and even an altar to the gods and goddesses or Great Spirit. Today there are a huge variety of plants that could be picked from, but it would make most sense to use plants that are native to whichever country you live in.

**Jardin De Simples**

Another interesting idea is the labyrinth. This is generally not a functional part of the garden; it is intended for spiritual contemplation. Examples of this can be found throughout Europe and in Ireland I can think of three – one in Dingle at *An Díseart*, a former monastic community, which is hundreds of years old; one at Three Castles in Co. Kilkenny, used by Druids; and one at Derrynagittah, Co. Clare. The final one (created by spiritual practitioner, herbalist and writer, Carole Guyett) is unusual in that it is also functional. The labyrinth is comprised of a continuous stone raised bed, in which plants are grown. This serves as a spiritual tool in itself, as well as a source of plants for her medicinal and spiritual practice.

Other possible sacred spaces in the garden are a standing stone, a stone circle or tree circle. I constructed a simple stone circle in my garden in Co. Wexford. The circle was nine feet in radius (2.74m) and has a central stone, surrounded by four stones on the circumference, one for each cardinal direction (N, E, S &

W). This was surprisingly easy to do – I used two sticks, string and a compass to mark out the positions. The most difficult part of the job was to roll the stones, end to end, down the garden to their respective holes.

A more complex stone circle could be constructed, with alignments to cosmic events such as the solstices or equinoxes. This is slightly more complex than my own design, but is by no means difficult to achieve – either by experience or through researching the appropriate positions in books or online.

A grove of trees is another, interesting and pleasant idea. I have seen several *ogham* gardens, including one created by Liam McGrath, in the Ring Gaeltacht of Co. Waterford. I was also able to design and create a grove of Irish (sessile) oak in Co. Carlow, with the help of other members of Druid Clan of Dana. The grove, in honour of the founders of the Fellowship Of Isis (FOI) and Druid Clan of Dana was created to mark the 40th anniversary of FOI and consists of nine oak trees, equidistant, surrounding a central oak tree, 9m from the edge of the circle. Circles or groves of trees are not hard to create and will provide a sacred space that may endure long after our own lifetimes.

These are just a few examples of a sacred space that can be created within a garden, the possibilities are only limited by the extent of your available space, manpower, budget and imagination!

## Chapter 12

# Dealing with Pests & Diseases

*"Nature is the source of all true knowledge. She has her own logic, her own laws, she has no effect without cause nor invention without necessity."*
Leonardo da Vinci

This is an issue that has become of increasing importance in the last few decades. The issue of pesticides has become more and more prominent since the publication of Rachel Carson's 'Silent Spring', which proceeded the banning of DDT and other hazardous pesticides. Pesticides are still with us, and this issue continues to be a cause for concern, not least because it has become enmeshed with genetically modified organisms (GMO) in agriculture. Pests have always plagued the gardener, but this situation has been greatly exacerbated by international travel and the accidental transfer of all kinds of species from one area of the world to another. This all sounds rather grim, but faced with greater challenges, we are now finding more creative, intelligent and humane ways to deal with the problems of pests and diseases.

## Pests – weeds

A weed is defined as 'a plant growing where it is not wanted'. This is a fairly comprehensive definition, what is of interest here is how we deal with this problem. If we are willing to accept weeds in our gardens, then may cease to be defined as a problem. Some people are willing to accept this despite the detrimental effect that they have on efforts to grow plants of our choosing.

Most people, myself included, are not willing to give weeds free reign and allow them to conquer the garden. The reaction to weeds can cover a wide spectrum – all-out war and zero tolerance to complete toleration in some areas and partial toleration in others. Personally, I am of the opinion that weeds also have a right to live and should be left unrestricted in designated wild areas (that all gardens should have). In the productive areas I tend to have low tolerance for weeds as they compete with the plants that we have intentionally planted and wish to nurture. One major area that I will tolerate weeds is lawns.

The conventional method today is to zap the weeds with weedkiller, glyphosate being the most popular solution. This does not fit with any sense of connection with the Earth or Organic, Biodynamic or Permaculture techniques. Recent research indicates that glyphosate is linked with cancers in both animals and humans, although it has yet to be banned. There are a very select few weedkillers that are defined as Organic. There is one that I use myself (from Germany) called 'Finalsan', which is basically an acid combined with a growth inhibitor. This is very effective, if applied in dry weather, even in winter and does no harm to bees and other insects, it also biodegrades quickly and harmlessly.

An alternative is to use a big bag of salt (on driveways, patios, paths etc.). This is also effective if there is no rain for at least 8 hours after application, but this method cannot be used on beds as it will salinate the soil for some times. Salt is essential for plants, but it is lethal for plants and damages other organisms if applied in any large amount. Another alternative is to use a burner – this is basically a mini flame-thrower, that utilizes a small gas canister attached to a tubular burner, which is used to burn away weeds.

The obvious other solution is to get down in the dirt and manually remove the weeds. Some of these weeds might be plants that you might consider keeping (in a different location) such as tree seedlings. The rest of the weeds, that you wish to destroy, can be burned, put into the compost heap or into a separate weed heap. Some weeds can also be fed to animals e.g. a pet rabbit will be delighted to eat up your dandelions, others can be used to make fertiliser. Many weeds carry diseases and also if gone to seed will cause problems in the compost heap – this is why many gardeners do not put weeds in their heaps. Some weeds are edible (see chapter 9) and can be used to spice up salads (e.g. hairy bittercress, or chickweed), others can be cooked in a stew or other dishes.

There is no real easy way to do manual weeding, it is hard work. However, you can make it a little easier if you use knee pads or a foam pad and if you use a trowel to take them out of the soil.

Another way of controlling weeds is to use mulches. Plastic sheeting (such as Mypex) is popular as a barrier for weeds, but it is expensive and looks unsightly. A good natural alternative to this is to use gravel or bark mulch. Personally, I like to use fine bark mulch, as this usually clumps together to form a mat and so does not blow away, like the larger bark mulch. Mulch has the additional benefit of helping to reduce water loss through evaporation, and it looks nice too.

A combination of techniques can reduce the amount of weeding required to quite a small level, a fancy term for this is Integrated Pest Management (IPM). IPM is a sensible approach but the worst thing to do is to leave it until summer, by then the ephemeral weeds will have had several generations and many of the perennial weeds will also have gone to seed. An early start, in winter or early spring will help you to keep on top of the weeds and other pests, and keep them at bay.

Some weeds are useful in many ways (see Chapter 9) but are too much to tolerate if they are invasive (e.g. ground elder) or carry disease (e.g. groundsel carries rust). Some weeds are really troublesome, such as hedge bindweed or Japanese knotweed, and really do need to be dealt with. There are so many weeds that it is beyond the scope of this book to describe them all, however I will mention some of the most problematic:

**Hairy bittercress** – spreads like mad due to its brief lifecycle, it is edible and quite tasty in salads. It is best to pick these before they go to seed!

**Bindweed** (hedge/field/black) – these grow fast, strangle your plants and often carry diseases. They can produce a lot of seed and so should be pulled out by the roots, or at least to ground level.

**Thistle** (spear/creeping/common/dwarf) – these are hungry and steal nutrients and they spread easily. They can be dug up, but often part of the tap root is left and regenerates. They can be useful to insects, particularly butterflies, so it is a good idea to remove them only when the flowers are dying off, but before seeding.

**Groundsel** – with small yellow flowers, it is like a mini dandelion, but it also carries rust and can produce seed all year round.

**Ragwort** – it is poisonous to mammals and spreads easily. It can be easily pulled up but makes sure to wear gloves!

**Rhododendron** – an introduced ornamental plant that has become invasive. The wild variety is particularly problematic as each flower cluster can produce thousands of seeds. The roots can also regenerate easily so it has to be dug up completely or poisoned.

**Buttercup** – spreads through rhizomes (root), under the soil and small bits of root can regenerate. Very annoying once it gets established as it can take over entire bed quite quickly.

**Japanese knotweed** – An invader that is hard to kill and which can destroy foundations and grow through tarmac! This also can spread through rhizomes and small fragments will regenerate. It is usually poisoned but you can kill them by covering them repeatedly with heavy dark plastic.

**Cleavers** – also known as stickybacks, these produce seed that sticks to clothes and other objects and easily gets spread around the garden. It also has a tendency to strangle plants that it climbs on.

**Horsetail** – very hard to control and spreads easily. It is edible and also useful for making an anti-fungal spray.

**Nightshade** – this is poisonous and the berries can kill children. Remove if you have young children using your garden!

**Couch grass** – this has clumps that can be removed but regenerates from small pieces, this pernicious grass can drive gardeners half mad!

## *Pests – slugs and snails*

These molluscs are the bane of many a gardeners' life. They are good at hiding and also have nasty habit of leaving their eggs under plant pots, or in gaps in fences or polytunnel folds. There are many ways to deal with this problem, and most of them are detailed in Sarah Ford's rather fun book *50 Ways to Kill a Slug*. Egg shells, straw and the spot watering methods can be quite effective deterrents, as can serrated copper strips on raised beds. Slug pellets are unpleasant and usually are bad for the soil, unless they are Organic slug pellets. This is expensive and also the pellets are mostly useless after a period of heavy rain. An interesting alternative poison is alcohol – slugs seem to love beer and will often drown in it. You can buy covered slug traps that you can partially fill with very cheap beer. The slugs (but not the beer) can be put in an aerobic compost bin.

Ducks and chickens are good for eating slugs, the trouble with them is that they are usually more destructive to the garden than the actual slugs! However, it is not a bad idea to collect up slugs and snails in a container and then throw them into the poultry coup. Another, rather higher risk, strategy is to plant their favourite foods somewhere far away from the food you don't want them to eat (e.g. marigolds). While this may work in the short-term, it does nothing to reduce their numbers.

### Pests – cats, dogs and other annoying mammals

Keeping cats, dogs, rabbits and even small children off of your precious plants can sometimes be a challenge. The most obvious answer to this problem is to enclose your growing areas in a fence or wall but this does not always work, especially with cats. I have found that putting short bamboo canes into a bed, like a pin-cushion, is very effective at deterring all kinds of animals. Another strategy is to draw the unwanted pests away with something that they like – with cats this can be quite easy – Catnip Nepeta Cataria) drives most cats into a frenzy of addiction as will tend to keep them well away from other areas if you plant it in your garden. Dogs are not so easy – you may have to tie them up or take them for frequent walks, otherwise just don't let them out except on a lead. Rodents can also be a problem; this can be dealt with by poison or traps. These days there are humane traps that don't harm them, the trapped rat or mouse can be taken to some other location (such as a field) and released, in the hope that it won't return to your garden.

## Pests – insects

These can be a major problem in the garden. A particular pain can be aphids, which infest and multiply in a few days. There are many types, not just greenfly, and they are all very destructive. You can poison aphids but it is also possible to kill them with a strong solution of washing-up liquid (preferably an eco-friendly brand) as the soap blocks the breathing pores on their backs and they suffocate. Another method is to introduce as many ladybirds onto your afflicted plants as possible – they will eat the aphids.

Another major pest is the vine weevil, that comes from North America, but has been resident in Europe for decades. The adults bite chunks out of the edges of leaves, giving them the nick name 'ticket-collector'. The larvae are actually more destructive as they eat the roots and can often lead to the death of plants that look healthy above ground. The little terrors love grape vines and honeysuckle but they will attack a huge number of plants. The adults are active mostly at night and can be shaken off onto paper or cardboard and the squashed. A wash can be bought that poisons the larvae, meaning that there will be no further generations to bother your plants.

Various grubs and worms do damage underground and above ground caterpillars and beetles do a lot of damage. These can be physically removed (above ground) if seen and above or below ground they can be poisoned. Another approach is to introduce a predator (such as certain wasps) or to companion plant, for instance cabbages with lavender, which can deter pests.

## Disorders

Just like other creatures, plants can suffer from deficiencies, physical problems or disorders that are not related to disease or pests.

**Chlorosis** is a common example is – where chlorophyll is insufficient in the plant. This is highly visible as yellowing and is generally caused by deficiency in iron, manganese or magnesium. This problem is solved by providing these nutrients, it is often found in potted plants, as the supply of nutrients is constrained by space limitations.

**Frost damage** is another common problem that causes dieback. This can be prevented by keeping plants inside during frost, planting later or by using horticultural fleece.

**Drought** will do huge amounts of damage. If the plant goes past its 'permanent wilting point' it will not recover, no matter how much water you give it. The trick here is so to spot wilting quickly and give the plant water before it is too late.

**Nutrient depletion** – similar to chlorosis, but more general. Plants will be slow to grow, stunted, may bolt (run to seed fast), look straggly or produce no or poor fruit. They will also be more vulnerable to disease and pests such as aphids. The solution is to make sure that the soil has sufficient nitrogen, phosphorus, and potassium (N, P, K) and other trace elements.

## Diseases

Disease can be a major problem for plants, just like it is for humans and animals. In western fringes Europe the wetter and warmer weather has caused an increase in fungal infections and these can be quite serious. Viruses and bacterial infections can damage or kill plants, just as they do in humans. Here are some of the main, well-known problems:

**Bacterial canker** – affects many fruit trees, especially cherries, gum oozes from legion in the bark. Infected parts should be removed and burned if possible and the tree sprayed with a copper compound such as Bordeaux Mix.

**Grey mould** – also called botrytis is a fungal disease brought on by excessive dampness, overwatering, poor drainage and poor airflow. Diseased parts should be cut out and the dampness remedied.

**Powdery mildew** – a white coating, a bit like chalk is caused by overcrowding and lack of moisture in the roots. Myclobutanol spray is effective at treating this.

**Damping off** – seedlings become black and withered at the base, oversowing can cause this or using already infected soil/compost. Remove affected plants and don't sow too closely together, don't use old or formerly infected soil or compost.

**Rust** – orangey splotches on the leacves that weaken the plant, treat with Myclobutanol spray.

**Viruses** – these cause splotches, patches or a variegation pattern on leaves. These cannot be cured but infected parts can be removed. Keeping your plants fed, watered and well will increase resistance.

**Black spot** – commonly affects roses most of all. Yellow patches and black spots appear before the leaves die off. Bad weather and poor airflow make this more of a problem. Myclobutanol spray is effective if used early enough.

**Fireblight** – this infection is incurable, it affects lots of shrubs and trees, including roses. Infected plants should be dug up and burned to avoid it spreading around your garden.

**Honey fungus** – this affects many plants, causing death. Infected stems are discoloured at the base and white fungus appears below the bark, roots turn black. In autumn toadstools appear in ground near stems. Remove the infected stems and roots, or the whole plant if severe, and burn.

NEVER PUT INFECTED PLANTS IN THE COMPOST HEAP!
BURN THEM.

**Equistum tea** (Biodynamic preparation 508) can be effective in treating fungal problems, especially if used early. It is made from horsetails and can be bought dried from the Biodynamic Association or prepared yourself (with care not to spread them). 20g of dried horsetail is boiled in 1L of water for 1 hour. The mixture is added to 5-10L of water and used as a spray on plants affected by fungus – this should be done three days consecutively at least. It can also help with mildew and blackspot

There are a massive number of diseases that affect plants, which is beyond the scope of this book. However, here are some common problems that can be dealt with by using chemicals or by more natural methods:

**Brassica club root** – this fungal disease can be treated with Equistum tea, raising the pH with acidic water, crop rotation helps. Severely diseased plants should be removed and destroyed.

**Cabbage moth** – These leave holes and destroy the cabbage heart and also affect swedes and turnips. Bacterial spray (Bacillus thuringiensis) or insecticide is effective or you can manually check for moth eggs and destroy them.

**Cabbage rootfly** – maggots eat the root. Collars of carboard on the cabbage base trick the fly, which lays the eggs on them. These can be removed and burned. Nettle tea fertilizers helps with resistance as does crop rotation.

**Cabbage white butterfly** – also affects cauliflower, brussels sprout and broccoli. Remove the caterpillars and the eggs or use bacterial spray (Bacillus thuringiensis) or Derris dust.

**Leaf spot** – this affects potato, carrot and chickory. This brown fungus can be treated with Mancozeb spray or Equistum tea.

Remove infected leaves and stems. Companion planting with horseradish may prevent this.

**Beet leaf miner** – affects beetroot and spinach plants. The larvae can be squashed after affected leaves are removed. Insecticide also works.

**Carrot fly** – also affects parsnip, chickory and celeriac. There are some resistant varieties you can use or you can sow after the breeding period, in summer.

**Eel worm** – affects potato, onion and tomato. Sowing with French or African marigolds helps, crop rotation also helps.

**Leaf mosaic virus** – affects tomato, cucumber, courgette, marrow. Prune the affected parts before it spreads.

**Peach leaf curl** – affects many fruit trees, including peaches. Use a copper fungicide such as Bordeaux Mix. Equistum tea may also help. Remove infected leaves in the early stages.

## *Observation and rapid response*

There are limits to what you can do, but paying attention can help with pests and diseases. A good doctor in a hospital checks on his/her patients and does not sit around reading the paper all day! In effect, you are the doctor for your plants and it is your job to check that they are ok and do something quickly if they are sick. If you come to regard the plants of your garden as friends or family then you will take better care of them. They have so much to offer us humans, it is only right that we try to take care of them in return. Nature will kill a percentage or your plants, this is just the normal cycle of life and death, as with all creatures, but you have the power to intervene and prevent unnecessary casualties.

Quick action can often deal with a small problem and stop it from becoming a major one. Regular checking of plants is a good routine to get into – 90% is down to observation. When you are watering, sowing, collecting produce or doing various other jobs in the garden, make it your normal procedure to look for pests and diseases. Invest in a visual guide to pests and diseases, this will help enormously, save time and enable you to make the right decisions when they are needed. Quick intervention will hopefully ensure that all your troubles are small ones!

There is no easy solution to the problems of pests and diseases – natural methods are harder work than use of chemicals. Use of chemicals has had devastating effects on the environment over the last hundred years or more. Chemicals should be used sparingly and in a targeted manner, with careful selection of pesticides that will do minimal environmental damage. The modern approach of IPM is a good path to take, if you choose not to go for entirely natural methods. Certainly, the days of a genocidal chemical warfare approach should be a thing of the past – this is a total disaster. This approach damages the land and wildlife, puts farmers in a dependent and vulnerable position and poisons our food. The only benefits to this system are for the huge corporations, who continue to try to convince us that chemical warfare on the natural world is a good idea.

# Afterword

One could read a hundred or even a thousand books on horticulture and gardening, but it isn't until you get your hands dirty that you really begin to understand what it is all about. Many things in life are like this – descriptions, explanations and analyses only get you so far, you have to experience it yourself to know what it is.

This book is my attempt to impart knowledge that will help unite two disciplines that may appear to have little overlap – Druidry/Druidism and Gardening. In my mind they, are complementary and certainly, from a Druid standpoint, part of the same body of knowledge. One does not need to be a Druid to appreciate Gardening, or indeed to be a Gardener to gain an interest and understanding in Druidry. However, I hope that I have managed to bring these two worlds closer together for you, the reader, in a way that is practical and useful.

As I sit here writing these final words, the world is in lockdown. A terrible pandemic, emerged from nature seemingly, has gripped the human world in fear and panic and thrown our fragile political and economic systems into chaos.

I cannot help but feel that we are on the verge of something new – a new era of technocracy and totalitarian oppression or a new age of tolerance, wisdom and re-engagement with the natural world. As I write, it is not yet clear what will transpire, and there is much that is yet to be decided. Perhaps it will be possible for humanity to retain the best of our technological marvels, for the good of all beings and this wonderful planet? If you have got this far in this book, you are probably of the view that a holistic, rather than a purely technological, vision of the future would be a better and more benign option.

One can only hope that all of us that care about this Earth and all existences upon, it can use what skills, time and energy we possess to bring about the most favourable outcome. The future is in our hands, it is being written now and in the coming months and years ahead, and we must all play our part.

Luke Eastwood, County Kerry, Ireland – March 2020.

# Index of plant common names

* Given as one of the 7 Druidic herbs

Vegetables and fruits have their own
    chapter.

# Bibliography

Bonwick, James – Irish Druids and Old Irish Religions (Sovereign Press)

Brickell, Christopher (Ed.) – The Royal Horticultural Society Encylopedia of Gardening (Dorling Kindersley)

Brickell, Christopher (Ed.) – The Royal Horticultural Society New Encylopedia of Plants and Flowers (Dorking Kindersley)

Candin, Alison (Ed.) – Secrets and Tips from Yesterday's Gardeners (Readers Digest)

Culpepper, Nicholas – Culpepper's Complete Herbal (W. Foulsham & Co.)

Deane, Thomas – Scots Pine is Irish Through and Through (Article, Trinity College, Dublin)

Ebury Press – Encylopedia Botanica (Ebury Press)

Eastwood, Luke – The Druid's Primer (Moon Books)

Evert Hopman, Ellen – A Druid's Herbal (Destiny Books)

Florin, Jean-Michel – Our Earth, A Global Garden? (Article, Star & Furrow)

Ford, Sarah – Fifty Ways to Kill A Slug (Hamyln)

Forest, Danu – Celtic Tree Magic (Llewellyn Publications)

Gurudas – The Spiritual Properties of Herbs (Cassandra Press)

Guyett, Carole – Sacred Plant Initiations (Bear & Co.)

Gwynn, Edward (Tr.) – The Metrical Dindshenchus (Dublin Institute for Advanced Studies)

Hessayon, Dr. D. G. – The Pest & Weed Expert (Expert Books)

Kelly, Fergus – Early Irish Farming (Dublin Institute for Advanced Studies)

Kelly, Fergus – Trees in Early Ireland (Article, Irish Forestry)

Laitenberger, Klaus – Vegetables, For the Polytunnel and Greenhouse (Milkwood Farm Publishing)

Lovel, Hugh – Quantum Agriculture, Biodynamics & Beyond (Quantum Agriculture Publishers)

Jones, Francis Avery – Herbs: Useful Plants (Journal of The Royal Society of Medicine, Vol. 89)

MacAlister, Robert Alexander (Tr.) – Lebor Gabála Érenn: The Book Of The Taking Of Ireland (Irish Texts Society)

MacCoitir, Niall – Irish Plants, Myths, Legends & Folklore (The Collins Press)

MacCoitir, Niall – Irish Trees, Myths, Legends & Folklore (The Collins Press)

McGrath, Liam – The Olive Tree Medicine Mystery (Self-published)

Moloney, Michael F – Irish Ethnobotany and the Evolution of Medicine in Ireland (M. H. Gill & Son)

Moriarty, Colm – Sacred Trees in Early Ireland (Article, Irish Archaeology)

Mulcahy, Risteard – For the Love of Trees (Environmental Publications)

Murphy, Margaret (Ed.) – Agriculture and Settlement in Ireland (Four Courts Press)

Nelson, Charles – Wild Plants of The Burren and the Aran Islands (The Collins Press)

O'Grady, Standish H. (Ed. & Tr.) – Silva Gadelica, Vol. 2 (Williams and Norgate)

Pollan, Michael – Second Nature (Grove Press)

Pollan, Michael – The Intelligent Plant (Article, The New Yorker)

Sentier, Ellen – Gardening with The Moon & Stars (Earth Books)

Stokes, Whitley (Tr.) – The Second Battle of Moytura (Revue Celtique, volume 12)

Thun, Maria – Gardening for Life: The Biodynamic Way (Hawthorn Press)

Tompkins, Peter & Bird, Christopher – The Secret Life of Plants (Harper & Row)

**MOON
BOOKS**

## PAGANISM & SHAMANISM

What is Paganism? A religion, a spirituality, an alternative belief
system, nature worship? You can find support for all these defini-
tions (and many more) in dictionaries, encyclopaedias, and text
books of religion, but subscribe to any one and the truth will evade
you. Above all Paganism is a creative pursuit, an encounter with
reality, an exploration of meaning and an expression of the soul.
Druids, Heathens, Wiccans and others, all contribute their insights
and literary riches to the Pagan tradition. Moon Books invites you
to begin or to deepen your own encounter, right here, right now.
If you have enjoyed this book, why not tell other readers by
posting a review on your preferred book site.

## Recent bestsellers from Moon Books are:

### Journey to the Dark Goddess
How to Return to Your Soul
Jane Meredith
Discover the powerful secrets of the Dark Goddess and
transform your depression, grief and pain into healing
and integration.
Paperback: 978-1-84694-677-6 ebook: 978-1-78099-223-5

### Shamanic Reiki
Expanded Ways of Working with Universal Life Force Energy
Llyn Roberts, Robert Levy
Shamanism and Reiki are each powerful ways of healing; together,
their power multiplies. *Shamanic Reiki* introduces techniques to
help healers and Reiki practitioners tap ancient healing wisdom.
Paperback: 978-1-84694-037-8 ebook: 978-1-84694-650-9

### Pagan Portals – The Awen Alone
Walking the Path of the Solitary Druid
Joanna van der Hoeven
An introductory guide for the solitary Druid, *The Awen Alone* will
accompany you as you explore, and seek out your own place
within the natural world.
Paperback: 978-1-78279-547-6 ebook: 978-1-78279-546-9

### A Kitchen Witch's World of Magical Herbs & Plants
Rachel Patterson
A journey into the magical world of herbs and plants, filled with
magical uses, folklore, history and practical magic. By popular
writer, blogger and kitchen witch, Tansy Firedragon.
Paperback: 978-1-78279-621-3 ebook: 978-1-78279-620-6

## Medicine for the Soul
The Complete Book of Shamanic Healing
Ross Heaven
All you will ever need to know about shamanic healing and how to
become your own shaman...
Paperback: 978-1-78099-419-2 ebook: 978-1-78099-420-8

## Shaman Pathways – The Druid Shaman
Exploring the Celtic Otherworld
Danu Forest
A practical guide to Celtic shamanism with exercises and
techniques as well as traditional lore for exploring the Celtic
Otherworld.
Paperback: 978-1-78099-615-8 ebook: 978-1-78099-616-5

## Traditional Witchcraft for the Woods and Forests
A Witch's Guide to the Woodland with Guided Meditations and
Pathworking
Mélusine Draco
A Witch's guide to walking alone in the woods, with guided
meditations and pathworking.
Paperback: 978-1-84694-803-9 ebook: 978-1-84694-804-6

## Naming the Goddess
Trevor Greenfield
*Naming the Goddess* is written by over eighty adherents and
scholars of Goddess and Goddess Spirituality.
Paperback: 978-1-78279-476-9 ebook: 978-1-78279-475-2

**Shapeshifting into Higher Consciousness**
Heal and Transform Yourself and Our World with Ancient
Shamanic and Modern Methods
Llyn Roberts
Ancient and modern methods that you can use every day to
transform yourself and make a positive difference in the world.
Paperback: 978-1-84694-843-5 ebook: 978-1-84694-844-2

Readers of ebooks can buy or view any of these bestsellers by
clicking on the live link in the title. Most titles are published in
paperback and as an ebook. Paperbacks are available in traditional
bookshops. Both print and ebook formats are available online.

Find more titles and sign up to our readers' newsletter at
http://www.johnhuntpublishing.com/paganism
Follow us on Facebook at https://www.facebook.com/MoonBooks
and Twitter at https://twitter.com/MoonBooksJHP

## Other Moon Books by Luke Eastwood...

### The Druid's Primer

*A comprehensive guide to genuine druidic knowledge and practice*
*based on ancient texts and surviving Celtic lore and customs*

978-1-84694-764-3 (Paperback)
978-1-84694-765-0 (ebook)

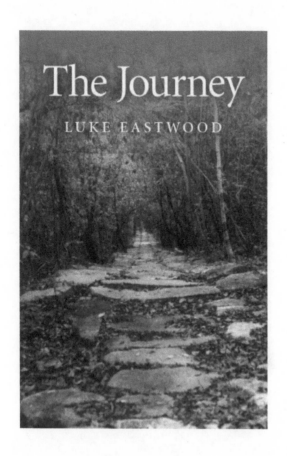

**The Journey**
*Exploring the spiritual truth at the heart of the world's religions*
978-1-84694-014-9 (Paperback)
978-1-84694-012-5 (ebook)